Rereading George Eliot

Changing Responses to Her Experiments in Life

Bernard J. Paris

State University of New York Press

Published by
State University of New York Press, Albany

For information, address State University of New York Press,
90 State Street, Suite 700, Albany, NY 12207

Production by Marilyn P. Semerad
Marketing by Anne M. Valentine

Library of Congress Cataloging-in-Publication Data

Paris, Bernard J.
    Rereading George Eliot: changing responses to her experiments in life /
Bernard J. Paris.
        p. cm. — (SUNY series in psychoanalysis and culture)
    Includes bibliographical references (p.) and index.
    ISBN 0-7914-5833-4 (alk. paper) — ISBN 0-7914-5834-2 (pbk : alk. paper)
    1. Eliot, George, 1819–1880—Knowledge—Psychology. 2. Psychoanalysis and
literature—England—History—19th century. 3. Psychological fiction, English—
History and criticism. 4. Eliot, George, 1819–1880. Daniel Deronda. 5. Eliot, George,
1819–1880. Middlemarch. 6. Eliot, George, 1819–1880—Characters. 7. Psychology in
literature. I. Title. II. Series.

PR4692.P74 P37 2003
823'.8—dc21   2002036483

10 9 8 7 6 5 4 3 2 1

Rereading
George Eliot

SUNY series in Psychoanalysis and Culture

Henry Sussman, editor

For Hinda

Contents

Preface

One of the functions of criticism is to illuminate literary works by approaching them from a variety of perspectives. These perspectives are influenced by a multitude of factors, too numerous to specify here. Among them are the conventions of reading that critics employ; their sensitivities to particular facets of literature; their political, social, moral, and religious philosophies; their cultural conditioning; and their individual psychologies. Because the factors are so numerous and people are so different, no two perspectives are quite the same; and no one is entirely satisfied with someone else's point of view. Perspectives keep changing, moreover, so that the spotlight keeps falling on different aspects of literature, and the process of interpretation never ends. Each age must reinterpret classic works for itself, and the rate of cultural change is such that an age now seems to be measured in decades or less.

The process I have been describing occurs in the critical community as a whole and also in individual critics as they interact with new currents of thought and as their personalities and approaches evolve over a period of time. I have observed the process in myself, most strikingly in my changing responses to George Eliot. As an undergraduate, I wrote a paper on *The Mill on the Floss* that eventually became my first publication (Paris 1956). I then wrote a doctoral dissertation on George Eliot that turned into my first book, *Experiments in Life: George Eliot's Quest for Values* (1965). This book has had a considerable impact on George Eliot studies, I continue to receive appreciative comments, and it remains, I think, a valuable work of its kind. But after I completed my dissertation, my critical perspective began to change; and I included a chapter on *The Mill on the Floss* in my second book, *A Psychological Approach to Fiction* (1974), that took issue with my earlier readings. I still largely agree with what I said in that chapter, although I would write it differently now. The present book continues my rereading of George Eliot, focusing on *Middlemarch* and *Daniel Deronda*. The critical approach taken here has evolved over many years of teaching, reading, writing, and personal growth and is very different from the one I employed in *Experiments in Life*.

Our critical approach determines which aspects of a literary work we will focus on and which we will ignore. That is one reason we have much to learn from those who may be sensitive to things we have overlooked. *Experiments in Life* reflects my training at Johns Hopkins in thematic analysis and the history of ideas. It examines George Eliot's ideas in relation to her intellectual background, and her novels in relation to her ideas. It also reflects my personal search for a secular ethic and, as I came later to understand, my need for the defenses against frustration and failure that George Eliot celebrates. In discussing the novels, I pay close attention to George Eliot's themes and to the ways in which her characters embody them. George Eliot saw her novels as "experiments in life" in which she tested her beliefs by clothing them in human figures and individual experience, and I accepted her epistemological claims. Like her, I saw her novels as confirming the results of her quest for values in a godless universe.

I was a true believer in George Eliot's Religion of Humanity when I wrote my dissertation, but by the time it was published as a book, I had lost my enthusiasm for her ideas. I analyze this crucial episode in my personal and intellectual history in the opening chapter, for it bears strongly on one of the topics of this book: namely, the way in which our responses to literature are influenced by our character structures and emotional needs, and how we become different interpreters as we undergo psychological change.

I came to understand my shifting attitude toward George Eliot partly through my fortuitous reading of Karen Horney, who had been recommended to me by a colleague, and partly through my experience in psychotherapy. As a result of these two influences, I began to look at literature in a very different way and to develop a psychological approach, the implications of which I have explored in a series of books (Paris 1974, 1978, 1986b, 1991a, 1991b, 1997). The present book is in a way part of that series, further extending it into the area of reader response (see also Paris 1976, 1994b). It differs from the others, however, in its less explicit use of psychological theory. I talk about Horney in chapter 1 because she helped me to understand why I had become such a different interpreter, and my perceptions continue to be influenced by her ideas, but I have tried to formulate my discussions of the novels in a broadly accessible way.

One of the results of my having become a very different interpreter is that I am now often critical of George Eliot's interpretations and judgments, whereas before I relied on them as guides to the understanding of her characters and, indeed, to the meaning of life. Another result, of a more positive kind, is that I now appreciate her psychological intuitions, which are embodied not in her commentary

Ps notional & characteristics of impartiality

but in her mimetic portrayals of characters and relationships. After my initial disenchantment, I have come back to seeing George Eliot as a very great novelist, but for entirely different reasons than I did before. Like most other critics, in *Experiments in Life* I did not register George Eliot's mimetic achievement because I was employing an approach that paid no attention to it. Also, I was blinded by the power of her rhetoric, which obscures the characters she has actually created and replaces them with simplified and often inaccurate versions of who they are.

A colleague who has read some drafts of my chapters observed that I certainly make George Eliot's characters "pop out." That comment pleased me very much. One of my objectives is to provide close readings of the mimetic portraits of the major figures in *Middlemarch* and *Daniel Deronda*, which, along with *The Mill on the Floss*, are George Eliot's greatest psychological novels. These mimetic portraits are largely responsible for the enduring interest of these novels, and readers have silently appreciated them, but they usually have been ignored in literary criticism. It is part of my mission to make them "pop out." In the process of studying them closely, I have often been amazed at how much more lifelike and complex George Eliot's imagined human beings are than her sometimes cloying rhetoric suggests. Even Daniel Deronda has turned out to be a fascinating character. The novels seem very different to me now than they did when I wrote *Experiments in Life*. By focusing on their mimetic component, my current approach has made them new for me. I hope it will do the same for others.

In discussing *Middlemarch* and *Daniel Deronda*, I shall be doing a number of things. I shall be focusing on the concrete, detailed portrayal of the major characters in an effort to recover George Eliot's psychological intuitions and appreciate her mimetic achievement. I shall be comparing the characters George Eliot has actually created (as I see them, of course), with the version of them that we find in her rhetoric. There is often a great disparity between the two. In most cases her rhetoric is consistent with itself, but her treatment of Gwendolen Harleth is quite bewildering. There are almost always tensions between theme, form, and mimesis, as the characters come alive and, in E. M. Forster's phrase, "kick the book to pieces" (1927, 64). George Eliot thought that clothing her ideas in human form and individual experience would provide a kind of experimental confirmation; but instead, as I shall show, her success in creating imagined human beings frequently subverted the ideas she was trying to verify. Although she was not aware of it, her experiments usually failed to support her beliefs.

In addition to examining George Eliot's great character creations and their subversive effect, I shall be comparing my present readings with my earlier ones, as part of my exploration of the dynamics of reader response. I shall do this more frequently in my chapters on *Middlemarch*, a novel on which I have been brooding for many years as I have taught it again and again, than in my chapters on *Daniel Deronda*, which I did not reread closely until I began preparing this book. And I shall, of course, compare my readings with those of others from time to time in order to place my interpretations in the context of the critical discourse about George Eliot and to suggest their originality. To date, no one has analyzed Dorothea Brooke, Tertius Lydgate, Mary Garth, Fred Vincy, Gwendolen Harleth, or Daniel Deronda as closely as I do; and no one has critiqued the rhetoric surrounding these characters in the same way.

This book began as a chapter on *Middlemarch*, dealing primarily with Dorothea, that was originally part of *Imagined Human Beings: A Psychological Approach to Character and Conflict in Literature* (Paris 1997), which I wrote for the series on Literature and Psychoanalysis edited by Jeffrey Berman for the New York University Press. I am grateful to Jeffrey for the invitation to contribute a book to his series and for his careful comments on the manuscript. When the press asked me to reduce the length, I removed the chapter on *Middlemarch* with the vague idea that I would have a future use for it. I published a version of the chapter (Paris 1999) when Douglas Ingram, then editor of *The American Journal of Psychoanalysis* (AJP), proposed that I guest edit an issue on psychoanalytic approaches to George Eliot. Material from my *AJP* essay has been utilized here with the permission of the journal. Through the kind offices of my colleague Norman Holland, in his capacity as editor of an electronic journal, the entire *AJP* issue has been made available in volume 4 (2000) of *PsyArt: An Online Journal for the Psychological Study of the Arts* (*www.clas.ufl.edu/ipsa/journal/*).

I taught *Middlemarch* almost every year for three decades, and I am indebted to my students at Michigan State University and the University of Florida for their stimulating questions and challenging ideas. When she was my research assistant in the mid-1980s, Catherine Lewis transcribed the tapes of a seminar I had devoted to *Middlemarch*, and I have drawn frequently on these excellent transcripts in my subsequent teaching and writing about the novel. More recently, Khonguk Wongkittiroch has assisted my research. I have benefited greatly from the feedback of colleagues and friends who have commented on the *Middlemarch* portions of the present study. These include Jeffrey Berman,

Phyllis Grosskurth, Hillis Miller, Margret Schaefer, and Marcia Westkott. I owe large debts of gratitude to Anna Bernet, Mary Ellen Doyle, Norman Holland, and Douglas Ingram, all of whom read most of the manuscript, including chapters on *Daniel Deronda*, and with all of whom I have had ongoing conversations about George Eliot over a period of years. In his current post as editor of the *Journal of the American Academy of Psychoanalysis*, Douglas Ingram invited me to submit an essay on *Daniel Deronda* (Paris 2002), which is a version of chapter 7 below. Material from this essay is republished here with the permission of the journal. I presented a version of chapter 1 to the Group for the Application of Psychology (GAP) at the University of Florida and learned much from lively discussion that ensued. I have been fortunate to have had many people engaged with my work in ways that have made it better, I think, in both substance and style. In addition to those already mentioned, these include Rosemarie Bodenheimer and Gordon Hirsh, readers of this study for SUNY Press, whose comments have been astute and helpful, and Susan Abel, my manuscript editor, whose sharp eye and sensitive ear have improved my prose and saved me from many a mistake. My first reader, as always, has been my wife, Shirley, who has given me not only incisive observations but also unwavering love and support. It is she, above all, for whom I write.

This book is dedicated to my sister, Hinda Cohen, who in recent years has endured a series of major surgeries with extraordinary fortitude. Her gallantry and courage have been an inspiration to all who know and love her.

1

No Longer the Same Interpreter

READING GEORGE ELIOT THEN AND NOW

Toward the end of *Adam Bede*, after Dinah has confessed her love and returned home to wait for the "guiding voice from within," Adam becomes impatient and decides to visit her, traveling the route he followed when he went to Snowfield in search of the missing Hetty. As he retraces his earlier journey, the road seems "to be telling him afresh the story of that painful past which he knew so well by heart" (ch. 54). But George Eliot says that the road has different meanings for him now, because "no story is the same to us after a lapse of time; or rather, we who read it are no longer the same interpreters."

The truth of this observation has struck me many times as I have reread George Eliot over the years. I have been reading, teaching, and writing about her novels for half a century, and I have come to see them quite differently from the way I did at first. Whereas I initially regarded George Eliot not only as a great novelist but also as a sage whose Religion of Humanity solved the problem of values in a universe without God, I now find that I cannot subscribe to many of her beliefs.

My attitude toward George Eliot's novels as instruments of knowledge has also changed a great deal. In my early work, I adopted the view of her fiction she had set forth in a letter of January 1876 to Dr. Joseph Frank Payne. "My writing," she said, "is simply a set of experiments in life—an endeavor to see what our thought and emotion may be capable of. . . . I become more and more timid—with less daring to adopt any formula which does not get itself clothed for me in some human figure and individual experience, and perhaps that is a sign that if I help others to see at all it must be through that medium of art (Haight 1954, vol. 6, 216–17). George Eliot saw her novels as a means of discovering the enduring truths contained in our inheritance from the past, of exploring human possibilities, and of validating and communicating her Religion of Humanity. Because her novels deal with human figures and individual experience, they can arrive at something "more sure than shifting theory" and flash conviction on the world.

I now believe that her experiments in life are flawed in both method and result and that George Eliot was fooling herself. Influenced by her own psychological needs, her experiments are often rigged in such a way as to confirm her own predispositions. They hardly have the objectivity or safeguards we associate with the term *experiments,* and what George Eliot is capable of imagining is profoundly affected by her own personality and experience. As I currently see them, her novels arrive not at "a better after which we may strive" but at a philosophy of living for others, the destructiveness of which is usually obscured by plot and rhetoric.

And yet because they deal with human figures and individual experience, the novels *do* arrive at truths more sure than shifting theory—that is, at mimetic truths which are embodied in the concrete portrayal of social and psychological reality. Whatever we may think of George Eliot's values and beliefs, her characters are convincing and continue to live. While plot and rhetoric work in favor of her preferred defensive strategies, her realistic portrayal of human figures allows us to see the inadequacies of the solutions she celebrates.

The problem is that the truths she discovers through her mimesis often do not register on George Eliot. She misinterprets the results of her experiments, thus making it difficult for her readers to see and judge for themselves. Whereas in my early work I attended primarily to the thematic component of Eliot's fiction, I shall now focus on her depiction of psychological realities, which I previously failed to appreciate, and compare it with the interpretations and judgments conveyed by her rhetoric, with which I now often disagree.

George Eliot's novels have such different meanings for me than they used to because I am no longer the same interpreter. It has become a critical commonplace that interpretations are psychologically motivated, that the ways in which we respond to texts are affected by our own personalities. It is possible to investigate this phenomenon by analyzing the responses of different readers, as Norman Holland has done, for instance, in *Five Readers Reading*; but another valid approach consists in analyzing different reactions of the same reader over time, as I shall do here, using myself as an illustration. One of my objectives is to explore the role of individual psychology in reader response by comparing my current reactions to George Eliot's novels with my earlier ones and trying to understand why I responded as I did then and why my responses have changed. It is to be understood, of course, that my explanations of my changing responses are psychologically motivated also and are subject to the psychologically motivated interpretation of others.

I first studied George Eliot at Johns Hopkins in 1951, in an undergraduate course on the English novel taught by Earl Wasserman. What especially fascinated me was her search for a secular ethic, for I, too, was an agnostic, and her questions were my questions also. In my dissertation, I showed how her protagonists arrive, through a varied course of experience, at some version of the Religion of Humanity, in which living for others, for something beyond the self, gives meaning and value to their lives.

While I was writing my dissertation, I subscribed to George Eliot's beliefs. I was convinced that she had answered the agnostic's need for a humanistic value system that could replace those which were supernatually based. When my director, Hillis Miller, posed questions about why George Eliot thought as she did, I felt it was silly of him to ask why someone believed the truth. But a strange thing happened after I completed my dissertation. When I was given the chance to teach George Eliot in a graduate course, I found that my enthusiasm for her ideas had disappeared. I remained convinced that I had understood her correctly, but I was no longer sure of my own attitude toward her philosophy, and my loss of fervor bewildered me.

I began to understand what was happening when, at the suggestion of Theodore Millon, a colleague in psychology, I read Karen Horney's *Our Inner Conflicts* and *Neurosis and Human Growth*. According to Horney, people defend themselves against feeling unsafe, unloved, and unvalued by developing both interpersonal and intrapsychic strategies of defense. The interpersonal strategies involve moving toward, against, or away from other people and adopting a self-effacing, expansive, or resigned solution, respectively. Each of these solutions entails a constellation of personality traits, behaviors, and beliefs about human nature, the human condition, and human values. Each also involves a bargain with fate in which obedience to the dictates of that solution is supposed to be rewarded (see Paris 1991a). Self-effacing people try to achieve their objectives predominantly through dependency, humility, and self-sacrificing "goodness"; expansive people through the pursuit of mastery and triumph; and resigned people by not wanting much, expecting little, and striving for self-sufficiency.

People are likely to employ all these defensive strategies at one time or another, and to the degree that they do, they suffer from inner conflicts. In order to avoid being paralyzed or torn apart, they make that strategy predominant which most accords with their culture, temperament, and circumstances; but the repressed tendencies persist, generating inconsistencies and rising to the surface if the predominant strategy fails.

When I read Horney after completing my dissertation, her description of how our belief systems are often a function of our defensive strategies seemed directly applicable to me and, by extension, to George Eliot. Miller's questions began to make sense. I came to see that my response to George Eliot had been profoundly influenced by a shaky performance on my doctoral oral that had hurt my pride, undermined my confidence, and made me regard my dissertation as the means by which I would vindicate myself. Because the dissertation had to be magnificent, it became almost impossible to write; and there were long periods during which I despaired of ever completing it. With my dreams of a glorious academic career in ruins, I needed to discover a new meaning for my life.

While I was in this state of mind, I found George Eliot's philosophy of living for others to be absolutely convincing. Even if I did not become a great scholar and critic, I could be a wonderful husband, father, and friend; and I persuaded myself that I was. The stories of Maggie Tulliver and Dorothea Brooke appealed to me as celebrations of gifted young people, much like myself, who attained a kind of moral grandeur even though they failed to achieve an epic life. In short, my difficulty in writing my dissertation led me to abandon my expansive dreams of glory, which I now saw no way of fulfilling, and to embrace the self-effacing solution I found so powerfully set forth by George Eliot.

The successful completion of my dissertation and its warm reception changed everything. Finishing the work in which I had articulated my defense against failure did away with my need for that defense. Since my ambitious goals once again seemed within reach, I no longer needed to live for others in order to feel that my life was worthwhile—hence my lack of enthusiasm when I had the chance to teach George Eliot. I had been looking forward to preaching her Religion of Humanity, but I found myself strangely indifferent to her ideas.

Looking back on my experience, it seems to me that my personal identification with George Eliot produced a combination of blindness and insight. It enabled me to understand her ideas from within and to give them a full and sympathetic exposition. I still believe I saw her characters as she meant them to be seen and that I gave their experience the meaning she intended it to have. I was highly responsive to her rhetoric.

That very responsiveness blinded me, however, to a number of things that I think I now see more clearly. Because I was so intent on understanding George Eliot's characters as illustrations of her ideas, I failed to see them as imagined human beings who are fascinating in their own right and who are not always in harmony with their formal and thematic roles. I paid no attention to George Eliot's mimetic achievement and had very little sense of the brilliance of her psychological insights. I did not see the need to distinguish between her *representation* of character, which is usually accurate, complex, and enduring, and her *interpretation*, which is often misleading, overly simple, and confused.

I also had little sense of the unrealistic elements in George Eliot's fiction. Because of my need to believe in her consistency and the viability of her solutions, I could not see that she frequently celebrated a magic bargain in which one achieves glory by being humble, good, and loving, by sacrificing for others, and, above all, by submitting oneself to a larger power outside oneself that will provide protection and justice. To make this bargain work, she often created a universe close to that of her earlier Christian beliefs, a universe in which aggressive qualities are punished and self-effacing ones are rewarded. In *Experiments in Life*, I argued that George Eliot's fictions were governed by the laws of nature as described by the science of her day. I now see that they are not.

My most striking blindness, I think, was to the destructiveness of the solutions George Eliot celebrates. She shared with most nineteenth-century novelists the illusion that suffering and frustration can make one into a noble person. She vividly depicts the conditions that thwart her protagonists' development, but she does not see that their frustrations have damaged them psychologically. She *shows* us the destructiveness of the self-effacing solution her characters employ in response to deprivation; but since she shares this solution herself, her rhetoric glorifies it as a sign of moral nobility. Since I had adopted this solution when I was writing my dissertation, I presented it with a proselytizing zeal that annoyed the members of my committee. In revising the work for publication, I strove for a more dispassionate tone.

As I see it now, one of the most serious deficiencies of George Eliot's philosophy is her emphasis on living for others as the means by which we give value to our lives. If we believe that our life has the meaning that other people give it, we may be driven to try to live up to their values or to satisfy their needs at all costs. George Eliot fails to discriminate between the legitimate needs of others and their unreasonable claims. Her characters can rarely defend themselves when other people make irrational demands, and she tends to glorify their compulsively self-sacrificial behavior.

There are some striking examples of this in George Eliot's last two novels, on which I shall concentrate here. In *Middlemarch*, Dorothea and Lydgate are presented as contrasting characters, with Dorothea's problems being caused by the deficiencies of her society and Lydgate's by his personal flaws; but the two are much more alike than the author suggests. Lydgate is destroyed by his compulsive submission to Rosamond, and Dorothea would have been destroyed by her compulsive submission to Casaubon had she not been saved by his death—a good example of a rigged experiment. The story of Mary Garth is also one in which the protagonist is in danger of ruining her life because of her psychological vulnerabilities. George Eliot places Dorothea, Lydgate, and Mary in situations in which they are coerced by the needs of others. All lack the capacity to extricate themselves from these situations, but George Eliot treats their weaknesses very differently and gives them quite different fates.

In *Daniel Deronda*, it is Deronda whose compulsively self-sacrificial behavior is glorified. Daniel sacrifices himself for Hans Myerick when they are students together at Cambridge, and he would be ready to devote his entire life to meeting Gwendolen's needs if he were not otherwise engaged. His mentoring of Gwendolen, which is usually seen as therapeutic, consists of leading her not toward autonomy or self-fulfillment but toward a self-effacing solution similar to his own.

A PSYCHOLOGICAL PERSPECTIVE

I should observe that the radical change in my response to George Eliot was not produced simply by the successful completion of my dissertation. This led to my loss of enthusiasm for her ideas, but it did not turn me into the critic of them that I have since become. That was largely the result of my experience in psychotherapy.

I entered psychotherapy because of the difficulties I had had with writing. I was able to finish my dissertation because I received an ultimatum from my department chairman, who threatened not to renew my contract; and the anxiety of survival overcame the anxiety of perfection. With the Ph.D. in hand, I was able to get a better job, but I knew I would have to publish in order to keep it. I sought help because I was afraid that writing would always be an ordeal, but I soon discovered that this was far from being the only problem on which I needed to work.

In therapy I came to a deeper understanding of what I had learned from reading Horney, and I gained many other insights as well. I had grown up under great pressure, coming largely from my mother, to "reach the top," to "be number one," an aspiration I embraced not only to please her but also to compensate for feelings of physical inferiority and social isolation (Paris 1994b). I tried to deal with my frustrations and anxieties by developing an expansive solution and also the intrapsychic strategies of defense that Horney describes.

To compensate for feelings of weakness, inadequacy, and low self-esteem, we develop, says Horney (1950), an "idealized image" of ourselves that we seek to actualize by embarking on a "search for glory." The idealized image generates a "pride system," which consists of "neurotic pride," "neurotic claims," and "tyrannical shoulds" or "inner dictates." We take pride in the imaginary attributes of our idealized selves, we demand that the world treat us in accordance with our grandiose conception of ourselves, and we drive ourselves to live up to the dictates of our solution. The pride system tends to intensify the self-hatred against which it is supposed to be a defense, for any failure to live up to our shoulds or of the world to honor our claims leads us to feel like our despised rather than our idealized selves.

Because I was a good student, my search for glory took the form of academic achievement; and, with the encouragement of an influential teacher, I decided to pursue a Ph.D. in English. The atmosphere at Johns Hopkins when I was in graduate school (1952–1956) exactly suited my neurosis. The English Department admitted many more Ph.D. candidates than it expected to graduate, and at the end of the first year most were not invited back. Don Cameron Allen was chair when I entered the program, and he told the eighteen new students assembled at our orientation meeting that the department produced an average of two Ph.D.'s per year. He asked us to look at the person on our right and then at the person on our left, predicted that one or both would not be here next year, and said that it was up to us to make sure that they weren't. Journal Club meetings gave us splendid opportunities to attack the work of our fellow students and to display our superior knowledge and insight. Those of us who survived the winnowing process regarded ourselves as the chosen few. I felt at once abysmally inferior to my professors and vastly superior to all the poor souls who were not graduate students at Johns Hopkins. I did not know how they could endure their pointless lives.

Although my need for love (another side of my personality) had led me to marry while still in my teens, I was under such internal and external pressure that I became obsessed with my studies and had no time for my wife and later for my child. I had no qualms about accepting financial help, first from my parents and then from my wife when she began to teach. I had little to give in return but felt that I was providing my family with the opportunity to do something meaningful by enabling me to pursue my important studies. It was my wife's complaint of neglect four days before my doctoral orals that led me to go blank during the examination. I was furious with her; but, as I discovered in therapy, I unconsciously turned my destructive impulses against myself in order to show her what she had done to me.

My poor performance on the orals shattered my idealized image and crushed my pride. Flooded with the feelings of worthlessness against which I had been defending myself, I tried to restore my pride by producing a magnificent dissertation; but the demands I made on myself were so great that nothing seemed good enough; and I became demoralized, unable to write. This led me to switch defensive strategies. My self-effacing side now came to the fore, and I embraced George Eliot's philosophy of living for others. Having become highly critical of my expansive self, I condemned the competitiveness at Hopkins, my earlier arrogance, and my callous behavior toward my family.

Although completing the dissertation enabled me to resume my ambitious course, I now dreaded writing and felt intellectually at sea. During the period of my identification with George Eliot, I knew what I thought about everything; but when my enthusiasm for her ideas disappeared, I had nothing to put in their place. My experience in therapy added to my bewilderment, for I was undergoing constant change, and things looked different to me every day. I decided to revise my dissertation by simply cutting and polishing, without rereading George Eliot or rethinking anything I had said. This turned out to be wise, because what I had written had its own value, and my beliefs did not begin to stabilize until after the revision was complete.

When I started to reread George Eliot, I had been in therapy for close to four years, had studied a great deal of psychoanalytic theory, and had begun to develop the psychological approach to fiction that I presented in my second book (Paris 1974). The first novel I reread was *The Mill on the Floss*, to which I did not respond at all as I had done before. Going back to the copy I had marked while working on my dissertation, I found that I had underlined passages of rhetorical and thematic significance and had left unmarked the pages that depicted the inner life of Maggie Tulliver and her interactions with other people. Now the novel's portrayal of Maggie's character and conflicts seemed remarkably perceptive to me. I began to admire George Eliot and to be excited by her work in an entirely new way. I wanted to recover her psychological intuitions and do justice to her genius in mimetic characterization. Although I gained new respect for her as a great psychological novelist, I was resistant to her rhetoric and found myself arguing with her interpretations and judgments. I was no longer simply less interested in her ideas: I had become actively opposed to some of them.

There were psychological reasons for my revised view of George Eliot, of course, just as there had been for my earlier one. In criticizing George Eliot, I was trying to exorcize my self-effacing trends and to prove that I was not susceptible to them any more. I *was* susceptible, of course, or I would not have reacted against her rhetoric as intensely as I did. The expansive side of me was embarrassed, no doubt, by my earlier enthusiasm for self-effacing values; and my detached side took pleasure in seeing through all kinds of defenses—I had great pride in my psychological insight. For these and probably for other reasons as well, it gave me considerable satisfaction to expose the weaknesses in George Eliot's philosophy; and I wrote an essay on *The Mill on the Floss* (Paris 1969) that became a chapter in *A Psychological Approach to Fiction* (1974).

But there was more, I think, than a rearrangement of defensive strategies behind my altered response. When I first read Horney, I recognized myself in almost everything she said and was amazed at how well she knew me. One thing to which I did not respond, however, was her concept of the "real self." I realized that this concept was fundamental to her thinking, for she taught that health consists in the actualization of the real self, and neurosis in alienation from it. Yet her idea of a real self seemed vague, mystical, and elusive, something I could not grasp. It did not make sense until I made contact with what I felt to be my real self after a number of years of therapy. When I then reread Horney, I realized that she had anticipated this sequence of events. The real self will seem like "a phantom," she wrote, unless we are "acquainted with the later stages of analysis" (1950, 175). It is a "possible self," what we would have been if we had developed in a nurturing environment, or what we can become if we are "freed of the crippling shackles of neurosis" (158).

For Horney, the real self is not a fixed entity but a set of "intrinsic potentialities" (1950, 17)—including temperament, talents, capacities, and predispositions—that are part of our genetic makeup and require a favorable environment in which to unfold. It is a self-in-the-world that may evolve differently in different surroundings. Horney paid considerable attention to culture, but she regarded the family as the most important influence on the child's development. When their own psychological problems prevent parents from loving the child or even conceiving "of him as the particular individual he is," the child develops a feeling of basic anxiety that prevents him "from relating himself to others with the spontaneity of his real feelings, and forces him to find ways to cope with them" (18). The child's emotions and behaviors, no longer expressions of his or her genuine self, are dictated by defensive strategies.

According to Horney, a poor fit between child and environment sets in motion a process of self-alienated development in which an idealized image replaces the real self as the primary source of motivation. We now have two selves in Horney's theory: the real self, which requires a great deal of nurturing in a healthy family and culture, and the idealized self, which is impossible to actualize because it transcends human possibilities and is full of contradictions. Self-idealization gives rise to yet a third self, the "despised self," which is what we feel ourselves to be when we fail to live up to our inner dictates or when the world does not honor our claims. Horney also posits an "actual self," which is who we really are at any given time. The actual self is a mixture of the strengths and weakness, defensive strategies and strivings for health, that has been produced by the interaction between our given nature and our environment. When the fit is good, little disparity will exist between the real and actual selves, and we will have a clear sense of who we are. When the fit has been poor, the disparity will be great, and we will be confused about our identity.

All this felt right to me after I had reached a certain point in therapy, even though I realized that I still had a long way to go. My understanding of the real self and the process of healthy growth was further influenced by the writings of Abraham Maslow and other Third Force (or humanistic) psychologists, whose theories are complementary to Horney's (see Paris 1986a, 1994a). Like Horney, Maslow argued that we have an intrinsic nature which it is our object in life to fulfill. In addition to conditioning and the desire to reduce tension, a third force motivates us: an inherent striving for growth that impels us to realize our given potentialities.

I found Maslow's hierarchy of basic needs to be a particularly useful concept. According to Maslow, all people have needs for physiological satisfaction, for safety, for love and belonging, for esteem, and for self-actualization. The needs are arranged hierarchically in order of their strength. Our motivational system tends to be organized at any given time around the lowest unmet need. We are motivated by higher needs as the lower ones are met, until, ideally, we are free to pursue self-actualization, the intrinsically satisfying use of our inherent potentialities. Maslow also posited basic needs for the enjoyment of beauty and for knowledge and understanding that he did not incorporate into his hierarchy.

Frustration of the basic needs produces pathology. It arrests our development, alienates us from our real selves, and leads us to devise strategies for making up for our deficiencies. The basic needs are inherently healthy and are capable of being gratified, but they turn into insatiable neurotic needs when they are insufficiently fulfilled. Reading Horney from a Maslovian perspective, I could see that she was concerned mainly with the strategies we develop to deal with the frustration of our *neurotic* needs for safety, love and belonging, and esteem.

I found in Horney, Maslow, and other Third Force psychologists a humanistic value system that, after my experience in therapy, I much preferred to George Eliot's. Values are generated by human needs, with undistorted basic needs generating healthy values and neurotic needs unhealthy ones. What was missing in George Eliot was the ability to distinguish between healthy and unhealthy needs and values. (For a fuller discussion of the ideas summarized here, see Horney 1945 and 1950, Maslow 1970, and Paris 1986a and 1994a.)

Through a combination of reading and psychotherapy, I was able to arrive at a sense of meaning, purpose, and value such as I had once found in George Eliot. Horney described the real self as "the alive, unique, personal center of ourselves" (1950, 155), the actualization of which is the meaning of life, and alienation from which is a psychic death (1945, 183). She quoted John Macmurray to the effect that life has no other significance "than to be ourselves fully and completely" (1945, 183). For Horney, the wish to develop oneself "belongs among those strivings that defy further analysis" (23). The real self is her first cause, her prime mover, a source of intrinsically satisfying activity that requires nothing else to justify or explain it. I felt comfortable with this.

Alienation from the real self leaves us without a clear sense of purpose, and we are governed instead by the conflicting demands of our defensive strategies. Although we make one of our strategies predominant, the others continue to be components of our idealized image, which reflects the "basic conflict" (Horney 1945) between our tendencies to move toward, against, or away from others. Each of these moves generates its own set of beliefs, values, behaviors, and inner dictates; and we are often caught, Horney says, in a "crossfire of conflicting shoulds" that leads us to oscillate back and forth between our solutions, much as Raskolnikov does in *Crime and Punishment* (see Paris 1991c, 1994b). Since obeying one set of inner dictates leads us to violate others, we are bound to hate ourselves whatever we do and to try to find ways to escape that self-hatred.

Rereading George Eliot from my new perspective, I recognized the characters she celebrates as frustrated, self-alienated individuals, beset by inner conflicts. Their living for others is often a defense against despair, as mine had been when I was having so much difficulty writing my dissertation. I now felt that the highest good was not living for others but self-actualization. This was a better after which we can strive that George Eliot was unable to envision and hence could not discover through her experiments in life.

Although I have been discussing the shift in my response to George Eliot that occurred in the years between the completion of my dissertation and the writing of *A Psychological Approach to Fiction*, much of what I have been saying applies to my current readings of her novels as well. I have begun work on this book several times over the past twenty-five years but have put it aside because I found dwelling on my state of mind when I was writing my dissertation to be too painful. The book is different now, of course, than it would have been had I written it at any of those earlier times; for my understanding has continued to evolve as I have pondered George Eliot's novels, engaged with my students' reactions, and read the work of other critics. Although certain of my core beliefs have remained the same, I am no longer quite the same interpreter that I was even a few years ago. For one thing, although my readings are still informed by my knowledge of Horney, I use her theories much less systematically here than I have done in my previous work, although I continue to benefit from her insights.

In discussing George Eliot's novels, I shall have occasion to juxtapose my present responses with those in *Experiments in Life*. As I do so, the role of personal psychology in reader response will be evident; for I have already provided some explanation of why I am now so troubled by precisely those aspects of George Eliot to which I was most attracted before. Because my earlier study was more sympathetic to George Eliot, it offers a better account of her perspective; but I think that my current stance allows me to see many things I missed before. As George Eliot observes of Dorothea's faith in Casaubon, "What believer sees a disturbing omission or infelicity?" (ch. 5). No longer a believer, I now see much that disturbs me. But, as I have indicated, I still admire George Eliot greatly, although for different reasons; and one of my major objectives will be to do justice to her genius in mimetic characterization, which I had previously failed to recognize. George Eliot's greatest psychological novels are *The Mill on the Floss*, *Middlemarch*, and *Daniel Deronda*. Because I still agree with most of what I said about *The Mill on the Floss* in *A Psychological Approach to Fiction*, I shall concentrate on the last two novels here.

RHETORIC VERSUS MIMESIS

I have so far discussed some of the reasons for the change in my response to George Eliot: the successful completion of my dissertation, which did away with my need of the living-for-others defense, and my experience in psychotherapy, which made me aware of the destructiveness of the solutions George Eliot celebrates. Accompanying these developments, was a change in the way I approached fiction.

The theories of Karen Horney had helped me to understand my loss of enthusiasm for George Eliot's Religion of Humanity and my subsequent resistance to her philosophy, but I did not employ them in the study of literature until one day in 1964 when I was explaining the thematic contradictions of *Vanity Fair* to a graduate class. It suddenly occurred to me that the novel's inconsistencies made sense if I viewed them as part of a structure of inner conflicts such as Horney describes; and my next realization was that the major characters of the novel— Becky, Dobbin, and Amelia—are portrayed in such rich psychological detail that they can be understood in motivational terms, independently of Thackeray's commentary, which is often unreliable and confused (see Paris 1974).

It soon became clear that the other novels I was teaching in my Victorian and comparative fiction courses also contained highly developed characters whose behavior was inwardly intelligible. I had been taught to view literary characters almost exclusively in terms of their formal and thematic functions; but in the great realistic novels, numerous details have been called forth by the author's desire to make the protagonists lifelike, complex, and inwardly intelligible; and these will go unnoticed if we interpret the characters only in functional terms. Although round, or mimetic, characters are part of the fictional world in which they exist, they are also autonomous beings with an inner logic of their own. In E. M. Forster's phrase, they are "creations inside a creation" (1927, 64) who tend to go their own way as the author becomes absorbed in imagining human beings, motivating their behavior, and supplying their reactions to the situations in which they have been placed. Since mimetic characters have a life independent of their creator's conscious intentions, we cannot identify an author's conceptions of such characters with the characters that have actually been created.

When I began looking at the great realistic characters as creations inside a creation, I came to see that they almost always subvert their formal and thematic functions (see Paris 1991b for a full discussion of character as a subversive force). As Forster observes, round characters "arrive when evoked, but full of the spirit of mutiny. For they have these numerous parallels with people like ourselves, they try to live their own lives and are consequently often engaged in treason against the main scheme of the book" (1927, 64). That seems exactly right to me. As wholes in themselves, mimetic characters can be understood in motivational terms; and when they are so understood, they often appear to be out of harmony with the larger whole of which they are a part. They are frequently in conflict with their aesthetic and illustrative roles.

When I first became aware of the incongruities between form and theme on the one hand and mimesis on the other, I felt that they were failures of art; however, I have since found them to be almost inescapable in realistic literature and have come to regard them as a concomitant of great characterization. As Forster observes, realistic writers face a dilemma. If their characters "are given complete freedom, they kick the book to pieces, and if they are kept too sternly in check, they revenge themselves by dying and destroy it by intestinal decay" (1927, 64). The artists' character-creating impulses work against their efforts to shape and interpret experience; and they must either allow the characters to come alive and disrupt the book or subordinate them to the main scheme of the work, which damages it in a different, more serious way. In the great realists, fidelity to their psychological intuitions triumphs over the demands of theme and form, usually without the author's conscious knowledge.

Mimetic characters are almost bound to subvert a work's formal structure, because literary form and realistic characterization involve canons of decorum and universes of discourse that are incompatible. Realistic characterization aims at verisimilitude; it follows the logic of motivation, of probability, of cause and effect. But, as Northrop Frye has observed, when judged by the canons of probability, "every inherited convention of plot in literature is more or less mad" (1963, 36). Form and mimesis arouse different sets of expectations in the reader. Mimetic characters create an appetite for a consistently realistic world. We want their behavior to make sense and their fates to be commensurate with the laws of probability. Realism does not round out a shape, however, and mimetic characters are often put into manipulated plots that have rather arbitrary conclusions. One of our cravings, either for realism or closure, tends to be frustrated at the end.

In many realistic works, the formal pattern is closed, despite the improbabilities that creates, and the characters, in remaining true to life, subvert that closure. In Jane Austen's novels, for example, the happy endings demanded by the comic structure seem much less satisfactory when we become aware of her protagonists' unresolved psychological problems and the deficiencies in their relationships (see Paris 1978). One of the most common formal patterns in fiction is the education plot, based on the archetype of the fortunate fall, in which protagonists err because of their flaws, suffer because of their errors, and achieve wisdom and maturity because of their suffering. Another frequent plot involves a pattern of vindication, based on the Cinderella archetype, in which a virtuous but scorned or persecuted protagonist finally achieves the status and approval he or she deserves. Both these patterns are undermined by the mimesis, which shows the "educated" characters to have switched from one destructive solution to another and the vindicated characters to be less deserving of approval than the author would have us believe. When we become sensitive to the mimetic portrayal of character, the resolutions of such plots seem out of keeping with the characterization. In the novels I shall be discussing, the most striking examples of these patterns are the vindication of Dorothea Brooke in *Middlemarch* and the education of Gwendolen Harleth in *Daniel Deronda*.

It is important to distinguish between the mimetic portrait of a character and the rhetoric surrounding the character. By *rhetoric*, I mean what we normally think of as theme, and a good deal more besides. Rhetoric consists of all the devices an author employs to influence readers' moral and intellectual responses to a character, their sympathy and antipathy, their emotional closeness or distance. It may involve not only authorial commentary but titles, chapter headings, epigraphs, characters' observations about one another, the use of foils and juxtapositions, and a wide variety of stylistic and tonal devices (for good discussions of fictional rhetoric, see Booth 1961 and Doyle 1981). Mimetic portraits of character consist of detailed, often dramatized renderings of thoughts, feelings, speeches, actions, and interactions. To use the language of creative writing courses, to some extent the distinction is that between telling and showing; and, as D. H. Lawrence put it, we should believe not the teller but the tale.

It should be kept in mind that although the distinction between representation and interpretation often seems clear, in some passages the two strands are hard to disentangle. The distinction can be difficult to make, and readers will disagree. Rhetoric is sometimes presented as though it were mimesis and may, indeed, contain useful information, while mimesis sometimes seems intended to serve a rhetorical purpose. What constitutes authorial interpretation is itself open to interpretation. I shall be presenting my own readings, of course.

When I try to understand mimetic characters as imagined human beings, I usually find myself responding in ways that are different from those which, as I perceive it, the rhetoric seeks to induce; and I often take issue with the author's interpretations and judgments. Great psychological realists like George Eliot have the capacity to see far more than they can conceptualize. Their grasp of inner dynamics and of interpersonal relations is so subtle and profound that concrete representation is the only mode of discourse than can do it justice. When they comment on what they have represented or assign their characters illustrative roles, they are limited by the inadequacy of abstractions generally and of the conceptual systems available to them. They are also limited by their own psychological needs and blind spots. Writers tend to validate characters whose defensive strategies are similar to their own and to satirize those who employ solutions they have repressed. As a result of these factors, their interpretations of their characters are often wrong and almost always too simple, in contrast to their intuitive grasp of the characters' psychology, which can be remarkably profound.

The more we recover authors' intuitions and do justice to their mimetic achievement, the more disparities we perceive between their representation of human behavior and their interpretation of it. Insofar as characters are mimetically portrayed, we are given an opportunity to understand them on our own terms and to form our own judgments. When we arrive at interpretations and judgments that are different from those of the author, the spell of the rhetoric is broken and the characters are seen to rebel against the main scheme of the book. In *Experiments in Life*, I tried to show how George Eliot's most fully developed characters illustrate—indeed, validate—her Religion of Humanity. Here I shall be examining the ways in which they subvert the formal and thematic structures they inhabit.

CRITICAL CONTROVERSIES

I have been contrasting my current approach to George Eliot, and indeed to fiction in general, with the one I employed in *Experiments in Life*. It may help to clarify my past and present positions if I place them in the context of a recurring controversy in George Eliot criticism. From the beginning, there has been a division between critics who have been disturbed by the moral, philosophical, and analytical components of George Eliot's work and those who have welcomed them. In her own time, George Eliot was regarded as a sage. Edward Dowden reflected a strong current in the Victorian response when he spoke of her as "our great imaginative teacher" (Haight 1965, 115), a description that accords with George Eliot's own sense of her role as a novelist and with my view of her in *Experiments in Life*. Many readers complained, however, about her moral and intellectual preoccupations, which were often felt to be intrusive and inartistic. Her contemporaries often preferred the early, less cerebral novels.

Perhaps the best known and most sophisticated contemporary response to George Eliot was that of Henry James. In his review of Cross's *Life*, James identified as George Eliot's chief fault an "excess of reflection," which he attributed to her irregular union with George Henry Lewes. Her "compensatory earnestness," "her refined conscience, her exalted sense of responsibility, were colored by her peculiar position" (Carroll 1971, 495). Especially in her later novels, she lacked spontaneity, an ability to take pleasure "in the fact of representation for itself" (499). In the early works "perception and reflection . . . divided George Eliot's great talent between them"; but as time went on, "the latter develop[ed] itself at the expense of the former" (498). The novel for her was "not primarily a picture of life, capable of deriving high value from its form, but a moralized fable, the last word of a philosophy endeavoring to teach by example" (497). Her "figures and situations are evolved from her moral consciousness"; "the philosophic door is always open, on her stage, and we are aware that the somewhat cooling draught of ethical purpose draws across it" (498).

Despite his reservations, James greatly admired George Eliot, finding hers to be "one of the noblest, most beautiful minds of our time" (503)—"vigorous, luminous, and eminently sane" (501). Many reacted negatively, however, to the publication of Cross's *Life*, which had a devastating effect on George Eliot's popularity. Its emphasis on her serious, sagelike, pontifical side reinforced the feeling, already widespread, that she was more a moralist and philosopher than a novelist. In 1919, Virginia Woolf praised George Eliot's "tolerant and wholesome understanding" (Haight 1965, 186) and described *Middlemarch* as "the magnificent book which with all its imperfections is one of the few English novels written for grown-up people" (186-87). This praise had little effect.

In 1935, Lord David Cecil observed that George Eliot's "reputation has sustained a more catastrophic slump than that of any of her contemporaries. It is not just that she is not read, that her books stand on the shelves unopened. If people do read her they do not enjoy her. It certainly is odd" (Haight 1965, 205). Much like Henry James, Cecil felt that George Eliot sacrificed spontaneity and the representation of life for its own sake to her moral and intellectual concerns: she "could not let her imagination have its head. Her intellect was always at its side, tugging at the reins, diverting it from its course, weighing it down with a great load of analytic comment" (209). Nonetheless, she was a great writer: "a massive caryatid, heavy of countenance, uneasy of attitude; but noble, monumental, profoundly impressive" (210).

As rapidly as it had fallen, George Eliot's reputation began to ascend with the publication of F. R. Leavis's *The Great Tradition* in 1948 and Gordon Haight's edition of *The George Eliot Letters* in the mid-1950s. By the time I published *Experiments in Life* in 1965, Leavis's study had been followed by a number of others, most notably those of Barbara Hardy and W. J. Harvey; and I was able to write that the case had been made for George Eliot's greatness, that the time had come "when she no longer needs to be defended as an important artist" but "can be studied as an acknowledged master" (ix). Over the past thirty-five years, an explosion in scholarship and criticism devoted to George Eliot has taken place; she is taken more seriously today than ever. It is her late novels rather than her early ones that are now held in highest esteem, *Middlemarch* being regarded as not only her best work but perhaps the finest novel in English.

Although George Eliot's "intellectual weight and moral earnestness" had struck "some critics as her handicap," for F. R. Leavis they were her strengths (1948, 9). The "charm" of her early works is overrated when it is preferred to "the supremely mature mind of *Middlemarch*" (39), in which her "great intellectual powers" play a "necessary part" (61). George Eliot's weaknesses lay not in her moral earnestness and propensity toward reflection but in her emotional intrusions into her work, particularly in her treatment of protagonists like Maggie Tulliver, Dorothea Brooke, and Daniel Deronda.

I quarreled with Leavis in *Experiments in Life*, especially about George Eliot's weaknesses, which I was reluctant to recognize; but in retrospect I realize that George Eliot appealed to me for much the same reason she impressed him. We both applauded her high seriousness, her concern with the big questions—with human nature, the human condition, the meaning of life. I used to teach courses in the novel that focused on how each writer addressed the question of Ecclesiastes: "What is it good for the sons of men that they should do under the heaven all the days of their life?" My great tradition consisted of writers whose answers I liked.

Between the 1960s and today, new issues have arisen in George Eliot criticism, as her novels have been approached from a variety of perspectives—archetypal, psychoanalytical, Marxist, structuralist, feminist, deconstructive, cultural, and biographical—that have generated important insights and from which I have learned much. Notwithstanding the changes in the critical approach to George Eliot, interest in her moral and intellectual qualities has persisted, and critics still argue about the aesthetic effects of her reflectiveness, her intrusiveness, and her ethical preoccupations. The discomfort with George Eliot's moral and intellectual seriousness, so pronounced in some earlier critical assessments, seems largely, though not entirely, to have disappeared, and Leavis's point of view has won out.

Harold Bloom offers a notable treatment of such issues in *The Western Canon*, in which George Eliot is one of the highly select group of twenty-six writers he identifies as being "authoritative in our culture" (1994, 1). Like Leavis, Bloom is wholly appreciative of George Eliot's moral and intellectual seriousness. "If there is an exemplary fusion of aesthetic and moral power in the canonical novel," he writes, "then George Eliot is its best representative, and *Middlemarch* is her subtlest analysis of the moral imagination, possibly the subtlest ever achieved in prose fiction" (320). Bloom says that he rarely agrees with George Eliot's "frequent interventions" in *Middlemarch*, but he finds them "as welcome as everything else in the book" (324). He can think of "no other major novelist, before or since, whose overt moralizings constitute an aesthetic virtue rather than a disaster" (324).

When I was writing *Experiments in Life*, I would have agreed with Bloom, but I do not do so now. I regarded George Eliot's overt moralizings as an aesthetic virtue partly because, unlike Bloom, I usually assented to what she had to say. I did not object to her frequent interventions or feel that she was too reflective or that her novels were weighed down with analytical comment. I welcomed her comments as guides to the understanding and judgment of her characters, to the way one should live, to the meaning of life. Bloom says that "a canonical novel is not supposed to be wisdom literature" but that perhaps *Middlemarch*, and "only *Middlemarch*," is (324). Given that I embraced George Eliot's beliefs, her novels were certainly wisdom literature to me. Like Leavis, I felt that her intellectual weight and moral earnestness were her great strengths, and, like Bloom, I felt that she had succeeded in "harmonizing . . . morals and aesthetics." I did not agree with James that she proceeded "from the abstract to the concrete," that "her figures and situations" had evolved "from her moral consciousness" (Carroll 1971, 498). I saw her novels not as moralized fables seeking to teach by example, but as experiments in life in which she was putting ideas to the test of experience. She was able to harmonize moral concerns and aesthetics because her ideas were not separate from her art but embodied in and verified by it.

As I have indicated, I no longer feel that George Eliot's ideas are embodied in and verified by her novels. If we regard mimetic characterization as an aesthetic feature, the aesthetic and moral dimensions of her novels are not fused, as Bloom contends, but are often in conflict with each other. It is not that reflection develops at the expense of perception, as Henry James suggests. With the possible exception of *The Mill on the Floss*, the later novels are actually richer in perception, mimetically conveyed, than the earlier ones; and this perception often subverts the narrator's reflections by making us aware of her mistakes, misjudgments, and insufficiencies. We have seen that Lord David Cecil felt that George Eliot sacrificed the representation of life for its own sake to her moral and intellectual concerns, that she "could not let her imagination have its head." She does let her imagination have its head in her portrayal of characters and relationships, though, and this is one of the main reasons her attempts to order life into "tidy little compartments of right and wrong" leave us dissatisfied (Haight 1965, 205).

From the beginning, two George Eliots, in effect, the moralist and the realist, exist side by side and are in conflict with each other (the subtitle of my dissertation was "George Eliot's Reconciliation of Realism and Moralism"). The later novels are both more moralistic and more realistic than the earlier ones, and hence in them the conflict is intensified. Cecil recognized George Eliot's "grip on psychological essentials" (202) but felt her characters to be "envisaged exclusively in their moral aspect" and therefore lacking the fullness and complexity that give life to the great figures of fiction (200–201). It is my contention that her greatest characters do have such fullness and complexity and that this is why they tend to kick her books to pieces.

George Eliot conceived of her novels as experiments in life in which she would test her ideas by clothing them in human figures and individual experience. She hoped to arrive in this way at something more sure than shifting theory, something that would not only satisfy her own need for greater certainty but would, through its truth to life, flash conviction on the world. Her experiments were flawed, in that they were full of contradictions between what she thought she was showing us and her concrete portrayals of social and psychological realities. Insofar as she offered us enduring mimetic truths, her experiments were successful; but these truths are obscured by her rhetoric, which, from my point of view, is full of faulty interpretations and judgments. George Eliot did not recognize that clothing her ideas in human figures and individual experience did not validate them but called them into question. In *Experiments in Life*, I did not see that either.

It is in the nature of mimetic truths that each age and individual will interpret them differently. Although the great literary characters certainly reflect their societies and although certain aspects of their experience may be unrecoverable, they have a well-nigh universal appeal: readers from a wide variety of periods and cultures find them recognizably human. While the vitality of the characters is unaffected by changes of mores, values, and explanatory systems, interpretations are local, culture-bound, and profoundly affected by the psychology of readers and the conventions of reading they employ. My quarrel with George Eliot is not, as a rule, about her characters, whom I feel to be wonderful creations. It is about how we are to interpret them, about the meaning of their experience and the results of her experiments. Finding that George Eliot's flawed interpretations create problems in her novels, I feel that mine do more justice to the mimetic truths it is her genius to portray but which she herself fails to understand. Of course, my interpretations are just as local, culture-bound, and psychologically conditioned as hers; and other readers will no doubt disagree with them, just as I do now with those set forth in *Experiments in Life*. Should I undergo another psychological transformation and become yet a different interpreter, I might disagree with them myself.

2

"An Angel Beguiled": Dorothea Brooke

CALVIN BEDIENT ON *MIDDLEMARCH*

We have seen how highly *Middlemarch* has been praised. It is this work more than any other that has led critics to speak of George Eliot's eminent sanity (James), her "wholesome understanding" (Woolf), her "supremely mature mind" (Leavis). Harold Bloom feels that *Middlemarch* may be the "subtlest analysis of the moral imagination . . . ever achieved in prose fiction." Those familiar with George Eliot criticism will be aware of how easily I could multiply such encomiums.

I have found the praise of Calvin Bedient to be particularly interesting, in view the fact that he is one of George Eliot's severest critics and that his complaints touch on many of my own concerns. Bedient exempts *Middlemarch* from his strictures and proclaims it to be "not merely a fine novel but a great one, indeed possibly the greatest in the language" (1972, 69). He contends that, with the exception of *Middlemarch*, George Eliot's characteristic as a novelist is to use her plots and characters primarily as a means of "sowing counsel," that the typical George Eliot critic "seems to welcome the counsel," and that the "resurrection" of her reputation has been accomplished mainly by "moralists" who are "of George Eliot's own persuasion" (40). I was certainly one of those moralists in *Experiments in Life*.

Bedient is of a different persuasion; and for reasons with which I now frequently sympathize, he does not like George Eliot's counsel. His strongest objections are to her celebration of Duty, her translation into secular terms of the "ancient and powerful religious ideal of selflessness" (11), and her belief that "a man's value increases in proportion to his

23

self-denial" (13). He contrasts this with the ideal of self-realization that
he finds, in differing forms, in Lawrence, Forster, and Joyce. Lawrence
turns, he says, "from adhering to the doctrine of living for others . . . to
the doctrine of living out all the 'promptings' of the self" (28). George
Eliot lived out many of her promptings—in her relationship with
George Henry Lewes, for example, and her rebellion against traditional religious belief—and it was for this very reason that she so
strenuously advocated Duty and self-abnegation: "She wrote not only
out of a pious memory but out of . . . unexamined guilt" (38). The
novels "exist primarily to salve the author's sense of her wrongful
independence" by portraying "repeatedly, and as a supposedly edify-
ing spectacle, the surrender of personal freedom" (81).

I think that Bedient's discussion of George Eliot's Religion of
Humanity is often very astute. Having "succumbed, with her age, to
the fiction of a species somehow greater than the sum of its members"
(13), George Eliot transferred "the concept of the significant life" from
the individual to the community: "the social self" was the only thing
"that could give the individual a sense of value—not of his own value,
to be sure, but the value of the 'whole' of which he was a 'part' " (52).
"To die to oneself and live for others; to be governed always by the
'reliance others have in us' " was the central article of George Eliot's
faith (83). Her protagonists, "finding themselves not only problemati-
cal but 'insignificant,' invariably live for others. And yet it never occurs to them that, if they are indeed insignificant, the 'others'—so
frankly presented as their inferiors—must be insignificant, too" (83). It
is the suffering of others, not possibilities they have for happiness or
self-fulfillment, that creates an opportunity for both George Eliot and
her protagonists to lead a significant life. Being a salvation is at once
"the aim" and "the subject" of George Eliot's novels (50). The need "to
be the rallying point for others and to thrive in their gratitude, con-
sumes the fiction": "To such egotism of altruism did the justification
of life by charity lead both the author and her characters" (50–51).

Bedient feels that *Middlemarch* is different from George Eliot's other
fictions in that it celebrates the individual rather than the collective,
which is shown to be dreadfully obtrusive here. In this novel, her
sympathies are with the Romantic self and its frustrations, not with
society, which is no longer a guide but is "in need of guidance" itself
(85). The "superior few" are "sucked into the orbit of the plebeian,"
and "it is the sorrow of their fall that gives the novel its realistic
poetry—its disillusioned poignancy and impact" (85). *Middlemarch*, says
Bedient, is "a prolonged protest of the dissatisfied ego" (86). It is a
critique of the philosophy of self-abnegation in the name of the greater
whole, for it shows the rewards of self-abnegation to be an illusion

and the greater whole to be "not a sacred cause but a menace," an oppressive "accumulation of . . . petty self-interest" (84).

It is important to recognize that while Bedient occasionally describes the Romantic self in terms of wholeness, integration, and self-realization (24), it is more often the idealized self about which he is speaking. I think that the novel's disillusioned poignancy is evoked not by the thwarting of the characters' healthy self-expansion, as Bedient sometimes seems to suggest, but by the frustration of insatiable hungers that are compensatory in nature. George Eliot is mournful because the search for glory of her protagonists, and especially of Dorothea, cannot succeed; and it is this mournfulness that Bedient celebrates as her realistic poetry. What he responds to most favorably in *Middlemarch* is its "lamentation on the darkness of life without fame" (86). I find this lamentation to be just as disturbing as George Eliot's celebration of living for others.

Bedient feels that *Middlemarch* is different from the rest of George Eliot's novels not only in its sympathy with individual aspirations, but also in its freedom from the sowing of counsel: "Reading *Middlemarch*, we need not discount the author and her noble, her compulsive illusions. Here, as it were, she stands off to the side of her work, having performed creatively that self-abdication that her novels themselves always urge upon the reader. With magnificent restraint, she lets her sanctities fare as they can—which is very poorly indeed" (82). I fail to see George Eliot's restraint. Her sanctities do fare poorly in the novel, but mainly because her characters are imagined human beings who subvert her interpretations and judgments. Her counsels or interventions are present in abundance.

According to Bedient, *Middlemarch* is a book that "is all vehicle, all medium, all transparency: dead to itself" (96). I cannot agree with this. Indeed, I think that far from being a work that has "merely passed through the novelist" and has "written itself" (94), this is a novel in which the author's hand is heavily felt. Bedient grants this to be the case in the Prelude and Finale but feels that in the rest of the novel George Eliot "does not impose a scheme, she reveals a condition" (82). I think that George Eliot does impose a scheme and that she also reveals a condition. The revelations are contained in the mimetic component of the work. It is there we find the "detachment," the "impersonality," the "freedom and hardness of observation" that make *Middlemarch* the "creative miracle" Bedient claims it to be (82).

George Eliot did not stand off to the side in this novel any more than she did in the others. She tried to test and communicate some of her most cherished ideas by clothing them in human figures and individual experience. In the process, she revealed their inadequacies, but she did not know she had done so. Nor did I know she had done so when I wrote my dissertation, for I was under the spell of her rhetoric.

Harold Bloom feels that the greatness of *Middlemarch* lies in George Eliot's cognitive power, which has not been sufficiently appreciated. Including my work in *Experiments in Life* and to some extent stimulated by it, there has been much study of George Eliot's thought and of her extraordinarily sophisticated mind, so I was surprised by Bloom's remark about insufficient appreciation. Yet he may be right. We have been appreciating George Eliot's conscious awareness and understanding, her moral subtlety and the complexity of her ideas; but the different kind of cognitive power that is expressed through her concrete portrayal of life has received much less attention. Here I shall try to recover Eliot's psychological intuitions, as mimetically conveyed, and to explore the tensions between them and the rhetoric by which they often have been obscured.

RHETORICAL TREATMENT OF DOROTHEA

With regard to plot and rhetoric, Dorothea's story is a good example of what I have described as the pattern of vindication. Dorothea is presented as a superior being who is at first disapproved by the people around her but who receives many tributes as the novel progresses, including some from those who have previously failed to appreciate her. She is championed from the beginning by the narrator, who employs a powerful rhetoric in her behalf. I think that few readers have realized just how extravagant this rhetoric is; I certainly did not in *Experiments in Life*, where I not only assented to its celebration of Dorothea but based my picture of her personality almost entirely upon it. When I began to look at Dorothea as a mimetic character, I came to feel that the rhetoric and mimesis present quite different stories and that the rhetoric blinds us to George Eliot's brilliant portrayal of Dorothea's psychology. I think that George Eliot's rhetoric is a fairly reliable guide to characters of whom she is critical—such as Rosamond, Casaubon, and Bulstrode—but that it tells us much more about the author than it does about characters like Dorothea Brooke and Mary Garth, with whom she closely identified.

George Eliot's effort to shape our view of Dorothea begins with the Prelude, where she distinguishes between the way Dorothea will appear to "common eyes" and the proper view of her as a "later-born" and less fortunate Saint Theresa who is deserving of sympathy and admiration. George Eliot knows that Dorothea is not the kind of woman of whom her readers are predisposed to approve and that they might regard her behavior as foolish when she marries Casaubon. She therefore glorifies her by comparing her to Saint Theresa and exculpates her in advance by putting what might be seen as her mistakes and flaws of character in a favorable light. Readers will be guilty of sharing vulgar prejudices if they agree with Dorothea's detractors, but they can take pride in their enlightenment if they adopt the narrator's perspective.

The Prelude prepares us to approve of Dorothea's search for glory. Saint Theresa had a "passionate, ideal nature" that demanded "an epic life." Chivalric romances and "the social conquests of a brilliant girl" meant nothing to her: "Her flame quickly burned up that light fuel; and, fed from within, soared after some illimitable satisfaction, some object which would never justify weariness, which would reconcile self-despair with the rapturous consciousness of life beyond self." This description of Theresa is meant to sanctify Dorothea, who also demands an epic life and is indifferent to things that interest ordinary girls, such as fashions, jewelry, and suitors like Sir James. The craving for some "illimitable satisfaction" is presented as a sign of nobility, the mark of a "passionate, ideal nature," rather than of insatiable claims. The mention of "self-despair" suggests a dim awareness on George Eliot's part of the compensatory nature of the need for an epic life, but it is not intended to reflect on the mental health of either Saint Theresa or Dorothea. I think that *Middlemarch* appealed to me so profoundly while I was working on my dissertation because it promised to help me find a way to achieve glory despite my despair over not being able to write.

Saint Theresa's search for glory was successful. She "found her epos in the reform of a religious order." Dorothea's search for glory does not succeed, but that is not her fault. She tries to shape her "thought and deed in noble agreement"; but because she is "helped by no coherent social faith and order" that can "perform the function of knowledge for the ardently willing soul," her struggles seem "mere inconsistency and formlessness" to "common eyes." Although her aspirations are as lofty as Saint Theresa's, she lives in an age in which the medium for heroic deeds no longer exists, especially for women. As a result, she leads "a life of mistakes, the offspring of a certain spiritual grandeur ill-matched with the meanness of opportunity." This formula not only excuses Dorothea's mistakes but makes them the sign of her noble, ardent nature.

The Prelude prepares us for Dorothea's marriages to Casaubon and Ladislaw and for the criticism of them by other characters. Unable to find an epic life in an unheroic age, Dorothea "alternate[s] between a vague ideal and the common yearning of womanhood; so that the one was disapproved as an extravagance, and the other condemned as a lapse." George Eliot does not deny that Dorothea makes mistakes or that the outcome of her life is disappointing (I think we are *meant* to feel dissatisfied with the marriage to Ladislaw), but the author implies that any shortfall is occasioned by external obstacles. Dorothea is "a Saint Theresa, foundress of nothing, whose loving heart-beats and sobs after an unattained goodness tremble off and are dispersed among hindrances."

It is the usual fate of such women to "sink unwept into oblivion" with no "sacred poet" to memorialize them, but George Eliot will be Dorothea's sacred poet, and *Middlemarch* will celebrate her spiritual grandeur. It will be an epic poem in prose about a heroine who cannot find a grand life because of the meanness of opportunity. Dorothea's frustrations become the basis for George Eliot's social satire.

The Prelude is almost entirely rhetoric. It gives us little information about Dorothea but much about how George Eliot wishes us to see her. When the story begins and we have an opportunity to learn about Dorothea for ourselves, the large admixture of rhetoric tends to obscure the mimetic portrait of her character. In the first paragraph of the first chapter, the glorification of Dorothea continues: "Her hand and wrist were so finely formed that she could wear sleeves not less bare of style than those in which the Blessed Virgin appeared to Italian painters." Dorothea is linked to the Virgin and other religious figures throughout the novel. She is presented as being in a different class from most other people, much as an epic hero far outshines ordinary warriors. Alongside provincial fashions, her plain garments give her "the impressiveness of a fine quotation from the Bible,—or from one of our elder poets,—in a paragraph of to-day's newspaper" (ch. 1).

The claims for Dorothea's superiority recur again and again, often accompanied by a condescending or satiric attitude toward ordinary mortals. After she begins to develop a rapport with Will Ladislaw, Dorothea is compared to a "princess in the days of enchantment" who has encountered a "human gaze" in one of the "four-footed creatures" that "live in herds" and who looks for that gaze again as "the herds" pass her by (ch. 54). In this analogy, Will is a human being who has been turned into an animal but has retained his human gaze, while just about everyone else in Dorothea's world is regarded as a subhuman creature. What I now see as George Eliot's exaggerated claims for Dorothea and her condescending attitude toward the mass of humankind did not register on me when I was writing *Experiments in Life*, probably because they corresponded to my own condescension and my claims for myself.

George Eliot defines Dorothea's problems in such a way that they increase rather than diminish her stature and are an indictment of the people around her. What is a noble, ardent, gifted woman to do in nineteenth century England, with its demeaning attitudes toward women, its refusal to give them a real education, and its exclusion of them from socially important work? Dorothea can do little except marry, but marriage is bound to be a problem for such an unusual female. Her desire for "intensity and greatness" and her "theoretic" mind tend to "interfere with her lot, and hinder it from being decided according to custom, by good looks, vanity, and merely canine affection" (ch. 1)—as is the lot of women who are part of the common herd. From the conventional male point of view, an enthusiast like Dorothea is a dangerous choice, for she "might awaken you some fine morning with a new scheme for the application of her income which would interfere with political economy and the keeping of saddle horses." From Dorothea's point of view, ordinary suitors like Sir James are unappealing, since they cannot offer her an epic life. The only possibly suitable man in Middlemarch is Lydgate, but he has conventional attitudes in everything but medicine, and Dorothea is not his style of woman.

When Dorothea chooses the highly unsuitable Casaubon, George Eliot goes to great lengths to defend her. Dorothea is incorrect in her inference that Casaubon is "a man who could understand the higher inward life," but life could not have gone on without "this liberal allowance of conclusions, which has facilitated marriage under the difficulties of civilization. Has anyone ever pinched into its pilulous smallness the cobweb of pre-matrimonial acquaintanceship?" (ch. 11). Dorothea is a victim of the conditions of civilized courtship, which do not allow the parties to gain much knowledge of each other. She is also a victim of semiotic problems, for "signs are small measurable things, but interpretations are illimitable" (ch. 3). These problems are compounded by her "sweet, ardent nature," which leads her "to conjure up wonder, hope, belief, vast as a sky" out of every sign. George Eliot is quick to observe that Dorothea's haste in bestowing trust does not necessarily mean that it was misplaced—after all, discovering the truth is often a matter of luck. Later the author will point out that the believing disposition which contributed to Dorothea's mistake about Casuabon leads her to have a redeeming faith in Farebrother, Lydgate, and Ladislaw.

Dorothea is attracted to Casaubon because he seems to offer her the opportunity "to make her life greatly effective," but the people around her cannot understand her feelings (ch. 3). They "would have thought her an interesting object if they had referred the glow in her eyes and cheeks to the newly-awakened ordinary images of young love," such as "Miss Pippin adoring young Pumpkin and dreaming along endless vistas of unwearying companionship"; but no one would have "a sympathetic understanding for the dreams of a girl whose notions about marriage took their colour entirely from an exalted enthusiasm about the ends of life."

> If she had had some endowment of stupidity and conceit, she might have thought that a Christian young lady of fortune should find her ideal of life in village charities, patronage of the humbler clergy, the perusal of 'Female Scripture Characters,' unfolding the private experience of Sara under the Old Dispensation, and Dorcas under the New, and the care of her soul over her embroidery in her own boudoir—with a background of prospective marriage to a man who, if less strict than herself, as being involved in affairs religiously inexplicable, might be prayed for and seasonably exhorted. From such contentment, poor Dorothea was shut out. (ch. 3)

In defense of Dorothea, George Eliot paints a satirical picture of the conventional ideal of young love and a Christian young lady of fortune. Dorothea is perceived to be odd, perhaps even a little mad, by ordinary folk, for "sane people did what their neighbors did, so that if any lunatics were at large, one might know and avoid them" (ch. 1). To counterbalance this perspective, George Eliot mocks ordinary people and the social norm.

Dorothea is an anomaly, but the rhetoric turns her oddness into a mark of her superiority rather a sign that there may be something wrong with her. She is shut out from the contentment available to Christian young ladies of fortune by her lack of stupidity and conceit. She does not care about "the niceties of the *trousseau*, the pattern of plate, nor even the honours and sweet joys of the blooming matron" (ch. 3) because of her exalted enthusiasm about the ends of life. She chooses a Casaubon rather than a young Pumpkin because of her "ardent, theoretic, and intellectually consequent" nature. She wants a union that will satisfy her "intensely religious disposition," that will "deliver her from her girlish subjection to her own ignorance, and give her . . . a guide who would take her along the grandest path." She thinks that Casaubon is the man for whom she has been looking, because "the radiance of her transfigured girlhood" falls "on the first object that [comes] within its level" (ch. 5).

From the perspective of the rhetoric, Dorothea's error about Casaubon is the product of her spiritual grandeur, ill matched with the meanness of opportunity. A lesser woman, like Celia, would never make such a mistake. Dorothea is carried away by her feelings, but George Eliot observes that "to have in general but little feeling, seems to be the only security against feeling too much on any particular occasion" (ch. 7). Dorothea's "passionate faults," which "lay along the easily-counted open channels of her ardent character" (ch. 77), are difficult to distinguish from her virtues. The epigraph to chapter 55 says it best:

> Hath she her faults? I would you had them too.
> They are the fruity must of soundest wine;
> Or say, they are regenerating fire
> Such as hath turned the dense black element
> Into a crystal pathway for the sun.

The reference here is to Dorothea's ardent faith in people like Will Ladislaw, which, though it has little foundation, turns out to be well placed and has a regenerating effect. Her idealism leads to one big mistake, but more often its effects are benign, and we cannot wish Dorothea to have been different so that she would have avoided her error about Casaubon.

DOROTHEA AS A MIMETIC CHARACTER

George Eliot seems to offer us two ways of looking at Dorothea: from the perspective of "common eyes," which she satirizes, or from that of the narrator, who is Dorothea's "sacred poet." She appears to be afraid that most readers will share the attitudes of Dorothea's detractors and will have to be convinced of her spiritual grandeur. But Dorothea does not exist simply in the opinions of the narrator and other characters. A brilliantly rendered mimetic portrait, she can be seen independently both of George Eliot's favorable rhetoric and of the chorus of disapproval by which she is initially surrounded. As an imagined human being, she becomes a "creation inside a creation" that is intelligible in motivational terms.

When I look at Dorothea as a mimetic character, she seems different from the person described by the rhetoric. Her desire for intensity and greatness and need for an epic life are not manifestations of spiritual grandeur but of a compulsive search for glory. Her craving for "illimitable satisfaction" is an expression of insatiable compensatory needs, and her "self-despair" results from hopelessness about actualizing her idealized image of herself as a person of world-historical importance. She misperceives Casaubon not because of the "pilulous smallness . . . of pre-matrimonial acquaintanceship" and the difficulty of interpreting signs, or because the "radiance of her transfigured girlhood" falls on the first object that comes within its level, but because her need for glory leads her to idealize him.

After learning of the proposed marriage to Casaubon, Mrs. Cadwallader concludes that Dorothea's "Methodistical whims, that air of being more religious than the rector and curate together," come "from a deeper and more constitutional disease than she had been willing to believe" (ch. 6). Although Mrs. Cadwallader's is one of the "common" views of Dorothea that are objects of satire, George Eliot may sense at some level that she is not far from the truth. Dorothea's disease is not constitutional in the sense of being inherent, but it is deeply ingrained in her character. It is the result of her experience as a sensitive, intelligent young woman living in an environment that frustrates her psychological needs.

We know nothing about Dorothea's childhood before she loses her parents at the age of twelve. Attempting to "remedy the disadvantages of her orphaned condition," her uncle has her educated, along with her sister, "on plans at once narrow and promiscuous" (ch. 1), first in an English and then in a Swiss family; but he provides neither emotional support nor an appreciation of her aspirations and abilities. Dorothea wants to be taken seriously and to do something significant with her life, but she feels that she is ignorant and is uncertain about her ideas. Her sense of inadequacy is exacerbated by the dismissive attitudes toward women in her culture. These are conveyed to her in many ways, most directly perhaps by Mr. Brooke, who comments on the "flightiness" of young ladies (ch. 2), the "lightness of the feminine mind" (ch. 7), women's inability to think (ch. 6), and their incapacity to understand such subjects as political economy (ch. 2).

Dorothea's craving for a life filled with intensity and greatness must not be confused with a healthy desire for self-realization, for the adverse conditions in her environment have not allowed that desire to survive. Having been underestimated because of her gender, she embarks on a search for glory, in an attempt to actualize an idealized image of herself as an extraordinary person who will make a great difference to the world. This project is bound to fail, not only because of the meanness of opportunity but also because of the grandiosity of Dorothea's objectives. In *Experiments in Life*, I did not see that George Eliot bases her criticism of society on its frustration of Dorothea's compensatory needs. She feels that there is a tragic quality to Dorothea's story because, as a woman, Dorothea is unable to lead an epic life. As I see it now, the saddest aspect of Dorothea's story is that she is forced into a self-alienated development because of the frustration of her basic needs for love, esteem, knowledge and understanding, and a fulfilling vocation. Many of these frustrations are gender-related, of course. Instead of lamenting the damage done to Dorothea, George Eliot glorifies the resulting defensive strategies and criticizes society for not providing her with the opportunity to actualize her grandiose conception of herself.

In her search for a life filled with intensity and greatness, Dorothea turns to religion, not the kind practiced by Christian young ladies of fortune, but that found in the pages of Jeremy Taylor and Pascal. She devotes herself to higher, spiritual matters and, immersed in her own inner drama, often behaves "as if she thought herself living in the time of the Apostles" (ch. 1). Her neighbors find her religion "too unusual and striking"; and she, like the author, looks down on their trivial concerns: "to her the destinies of mankind, seen by the light of Christianity, made the solicitudes of feminine fashion appear an occupation for Bedlam. She could not reconcile the anxieties of a spiritual life involving eternal consequences, with a keen interest in guimp and artificial protrusions of drapery." It is difficult to differentiate between rhetoric and mimesis here, to separate George Eliot's satire from Dorothea's contempt for other women. Mild satire is directed at Dorothea as well, as it frequently is in the early chapters, but we are not to forget that her quirks are the product of her frustrated lofty soul.

Dorothea's sense of spiritual superiority is especially evident in her relationship with her sister. Celia encourages Dorothea to take some of their mother's jewels, so that Celia can feel more comfortable about wearing them herself. Dorothea insists that Celia accept a fine amethyst necklace and wants her to have a cross to wear with her dark dresses. "O Dodo," says Celia, "you must keep the cross yourself." "Not for the world, not for the world," Dorothea replies. "A cross is the last thing I would wear as a trinket" (ch. 1). When Celia is afraid that Dorothea will think it wicked in her to wear it, Dorothea reassures her: " 'No, dear, no,' said Dorothea, stroking her sister's cheek. 'Souls have complexions too: what will suit one will not suit another.' " Celia feels hurt by the "strong assumption of superiority in this Puritanic toleration." In good spirits when Celia tells her that Sir James has agreed to her plans for building cottages, Dorothea thinks her sister "fit hereafter to be an eternal cherub, and if it were not doctrinally wrong to say so, hardly more in need of salvation than a squirrel" (ch. 4). This is enormously condescending, giving Celia the status of one of the four-footed creatures without a soul.

Dorothea longs to be nobly Christian but has great trouble finding something nobly Christian to do. Planning cottages for the poor is her only practical outlet, but she feels she must give this up when she learns that Sir James is in love with her. Her dream of glory has chiefly taken the form of fantasies about marrying a very different kind of man: "She felt sure that she would have accepted the judicious Hooker, if she had been born in time to save him from that wretched mistake he made in matrimony; or John Milton when his blindness had come on; or any of the other great men whose odd habits it would have been glorious piety to endure" (ch. 1). In charactering these ideas about marriage as "childlike," George Eliot makes them seem a matter of inexperience or immaturity; but they clearly reflect Dorothea's compensatory needs. Because she is a woman, Dorothea cannot dream of doing splendid deeds herself but must live vicariously through a man. "It always seemed to me," she later tells Will, "that the use I should like to make of my life would be to help some one who did great works" (ch. 37). She longs to marry a great man, not only to participate in his glory but to facilitate his achievements and thus do something of world-historical importance herself. She needs him to need her help. The idea of Sir James as a suitor seems "a ridiculous irrelevance" (ch. 1) to Dorothea because it has nothing to do with her dream of glory. Although marriage to him would be a brilliant social triumph, it would mark her as an ordinary woman and prevent her from ever leading an epic life.

Casaubon, however, seems to be exactly the man for whom she is looking, especially since she perceives him in the light of her fantasies. She has wanted a husband who would be "a sort of father" and "teach [her] even Hebrew" if she wished (ch. 1), and the forty-five-year-old Casaubon qualifies on both counts. She has constantly doubted her conclusions because of her feeling of ignorance, but here is a man "whose learning almost amounted to a proof of whatever he believed!" (ch. 2). Dorothea looks to him as a kind of "Protestant pope" who will provide the certitude and authority for which she hungers. No one has sympathized with "the intensity of her religious disposition" (ch. 3), but she thinks that Casaubon has a great soul and can "understand the higher inward life" (ch. 2). He has weak eyesight and requires help with his work, a requirement that serves her need to be needed.

What makes the marriage to Casaubon so disgusting to other people—the age difference and his lack of "red-blooded manhood" (ch. 8)—is part of his appeal to Dorothea. Having an idealized image of herself as an ascetic who scorns worldly pleasures, she feels threatened by the "amiable handsome" Sir James (ch. 1), with his dimpled hands. Marriage to him would be too much like riding, which she intends to give up because she feels she enjoys it "in a pagan sensuous way." Mrs. Cadwallader says that marrying Casaubon will be "as good as going to a nunnery" (ch. 6), and perhaps that is what Dorothea wants. She will be able to achieve a glorious piety through sacrifice and self-mortification.

Casaubon appeals to Dorothea above all because he is reputed "to be engaged on a great work" (ch. 1). She looks forward to meeting him with a "venerating expectation"; and, captivated by the wide embrace of "The Key to All Mythologies," she sees him as a "living Bossuet," a Pascal, a "modern Augustine who united the glories of doctor and saint" (ch. 3). If he wanted her as his wife, "it would be almost as if a winged messenger had suddenly stood beside her path and held out his hand towards her!" It would be like stepping into her dream, much as Pip does in *Great Expectations* when he learns that he is to become a gentleman (see Paris 1997). Such a marriage would enable Dorothea to rise above the trivial routines of her social world and "to lead a grand life, here—now—in England." Casaubon "would take her along the grandest path"; she would "learn everything" in order to "help him the better in his great works."

Many feel that George Eliot sees Dorothea pretty clearly early in the novel but loses her critical distance later, when she identifies too closely with her heroine. George Eliot does have more distance in the beginning, for she wants us to be aware of Dorothea's mistakes, which she treats with gentle mockery, and she presents her as a slightly ludicrous figure. She compares her to Don Quixote in the epigraph to chapter 2 and keeps us aware of the difference between Dorothea's illusions about Casaubon and the reality. As Celia says, Dorothea sees "what nobody else sees" but "never see[s] what is quite plain" (ch. 4). When Celia exclaims that Casaubon is "very ugly," Dorothea pronounces him "one of the most distinguished-looking men" she has ever seen:

> "He is remarkably like the portrait of Locke. He has the same deep eye-sockets."
> "Had Locke those two white moles with hairs on them?"
> "Oh, I daresay! When people of a certain sort looked at him." (ch. 2)

In this case, common eyes have the clearer perception.

Yet while George Eliot makes fun of Dorothea's excesses and misperceptions, which are similar to those of her own Evangelical girlhood, she does not understand their source in Dorothea's compensatory needs but persists in rationalizing them. She idealizes Dorothea much as Dorothea idealizes Casaubon. Her language calls attention to the coerciveness of Dorothea's religious disposition, to her obsessive need for greatness, but these traits receive sympathetic treatment. From the author's point of view, Dorothea's problem is that she cannot find a grand life, not that she is driven into delusional and self-destructive behavior by her compulsive need for glory.

Although the rhetoric is misleading and may generate resistance, George Eliot's mimetic portrait of Dorothea allows us to understand her motivations and to respond to her empathetically. George Eliot explains Dorothea's reaction to Casaubon's incredibly pompous proposal in terms of the "radiance of her transfigured girlhood" and her struggle "towards an ideal life" (ch. 5). "How could it occur to her," the narrator asks, "to examine the letter, to look at it critically as a profession of love?" It does not occur to Dorothea to examine the letter in this way because she is looking not for love but for exactly what the letter has to offer. Casaubon writes that the "tenor" of his "life and purposes" is unsuited "to the commoner order of minds" but that he has discerned in her "an elevation of thought and a capability of devotedness" which he had "hitherto not conceived to be compatible" with such youth and beauty. The letter separates Dorothea from the commoner order of minds, recognizes her spiritual and intellectual qualities, and serves as an antidote to the depreciation to which she has been subjected all her life. It feeds her pride and confirms her idealized image of herself.

Not only does Casaubon see Dorothea as she wishes to be seen, but his praise counts, unlike that of Sir James, because he is a man whose judgment she venerates. She feels a sense of "proud delight" to have been "chosen by the man whom her admiration had chosen." Dorothea had earlier thought of possible marriage to Casaubon in winged messenger imagery suggestive of the Annunciation. She experiences his proposal as an election to greatness, a confirmation by the universe that she *is* an extraordinary person who will have a grand destiny.

DOROTHEA'S "EDUCATION": CASAUBON

Although George Eliot sometimes makes fun of Dorothea's quixotic misperceptions, her primary object is to vindicate her heroine by presenting her errors as the product of the customs of courtship, the difficulty of interpreting signs, and frustrated spiritual grandeur. Initially only the narrator properly appreciates Dorothea, but eventually many of the characters come to recognize her virtues. It is important to recognize, however, that Dorothea's story has an education as well as a vindication pattern. Even as she glorifies Dorothea, George Eliot also presents her as an immature young woman who must undergo a process of moral development. It is only after Dorothea is "educated"

by her suffering in marriage that George Eliot's treatment of her becomes unreservedly favorable. Whereas I agreed with the author's
view of Dorothea's development in my earlier study, I now have serious reservations. What George Eliot sees as moral growth, I see as
compulsive self-effacement.

Let me begin with George Eliot's perspective as I presented it in
Experiments in Life. In George Eliot's novels, there are three basic ways
in which individuals relate to the world. They may relate to the world
subjectively or egoistically, seeing themselves as the center of the world
and the world as an extension of the self. The encounter with harsh
realities may overwhelm them and lead them to see the world as alien
and themselves as insignificant. Or they may relate to the world objectively, by accepting its autonomous existence but feeling that they have
a place in the network of relations that make up the human order.

The three ways in which people relate to the world are also stages
of moral development through which George Eliot's characters go in
the course of maturation. The inevitable awakening to the disparity
between the inward and outward is frequently a source of moral
growth; it makes clear the real relations between things and is the
baptism of sorrow that renders individuals capable of sympathy. It
makes them sharers in the common lot, and if it does not drive them
back into illusion or an embittered egoism, it nurtures their capacity
for human fellowship. In the third stage of moral development, a
vision of their connection with their fellows and a sense that all human beings share a common nature and destiny moderates their painful sense of living in an alien universe. Their purpose becomes not
merely the pursuit of personal gratification but the achievement of
genuine significance by living for others. Their feeling of solidarity
with other human beings gives them a sense of religious orientation
in the cosmos.

George Eliot presents Dorothea's initial response to Casaubon as
egoistic. Instead of regarding him as a being with needs and desires
of his own, she sees him as a means to her ends. She is immensely
gratified by his desire to marry her but never dwells on his motives
and expectations, only on her hopes for an exalted existence. Casaubon's
way of relating to Dorothea is equally self-centered. He is given "to
think that others were providentially made for him, and especially
to consider them in the light of their fitness for the author of a 'Key
to all Mythologies' " (ch. 10).

Dorothea enters the second stage of moral development when her
illusions about Casaubon are shattered. The incomprehensibility of Rome
intensifies her feelings of disenchantment, and when she returns to England, her once familiar surroundings also seem strange. The reality into

which she awakens is so alien to her experience that it seems dream-like, whereas her self-reflecting dream world had seemed genuine.

Dorothea's disillusionment gradually leads her to the third stage of moral development in which she understands her husband as he is for himself. George Eliot proclaims that "we are all of us born in moral stupidity, taking the world as an udder to feed our supreme selves" (ch. 21). Dorothea had "early begun to emerge from that stupidity" as a result of her frustrations; and her education is completed when she realizes through the intimate experience of marriage that Casaubon has "an equivalent centre of self, whence the lights and shadows must always fall with a certain difference." As she becomes aware that he also is suffering, there are stirrings within her "of a pitying tenderness fed by the realities of his lot and not by her own dreams." She is now capable of sympathizing with her husband, despite her disappointment.

For George Eliot, a sympathetic feeling is one that is excited by the signs of feeling in another person, and mental vision is needed to read the signs. Vision and sympathy are both dependent on experience. Unless we have had an experience much like that which another person is undergoing, we cannot recognize and share the states of feeling reflected in his or her behavior. Thus, George Eliot felt that suffering humanizes. Our own suffering, if it does not simply embitter, leads us to understand and sympathize with the unhappiness of others and to try to lighten their misery.

Instead of rejecting her disappointing husband, as Rosamond does, Dorothea is moved to sympathy by her vision of his inner state, and she strives to resign her claims for herself and to comfort him. She is even ready to promise that she will try to complete his work in the event of his death, although she no longer believes in its value. She is "compelled" to this, says George Eliot, by neither law nor the world's opinion but, "only her husband's nature and her own compassion, only the ideal and not the real yoke of marriage" (ch. 48).

I still believe this to be an accurate account of George Eliot's view of Dorothea, but I can no longer assent to her interpretations and judgments. Dorothea does become more sympathetic toward Casaubon as she understands his problems, but she becomes even more alienated from herself as a result. Once she decides to give Casaubon the promise he wants, she feels that she is "going to say 'Yes' to her own doom." She is "too weak, too full of dread at the thought of inflicting a keen-edged blow on her husband, to do anything but submit completely" (ch. 48). George Eliot celebrates this as a manifestation of compassion and of loyalty to the ideal of marriage, but her language suggests an uneasiness with Dorothea's decision. Dorothea is compelled out of weakness and dread to act in a way that she knows to be self-destructive. She saw "clearly enough" the consequences of her submission, "yet she was fettered: she could not smite the stricken soul that entreated hers. If that were weakness, Dorothea was weak."

The object of George Eliot's rhetoric is to dismiss the idea that Dorothea is weak; but Dorothea *is* weak, and I suspect that George Eliot would not have raised the issue had she not had some sense that this was the case. She obscures the self-destructiveness of Dorothea's behavior by having her spouse die in a timely manner, a favor she does not extend to Lydgate, who ruins his life when he compulsively submits to the irrational demands of his wife. Dorothea's weakness would have had a similar result had Casaubon lived another half-hour, until he had secured her promise to complete his work. As I have said, this is a good example of a rigged experiment.

Why is Dorothea compelled to commit herself to a task she feels to be pointless? To answer this question, we must understand the psychological changes that have occurred as a result of her disappointments in marriage. When Dorothea realizes that she will not be able to do something of world-historical importance, she must redefine her idealized image and seek glory in a different way. To avoid despair, she tries to give her life a sense of purpose through devotion to duty. To be heroically self-sacrificial in the absence of high prizes has its own kind of grandeur for her. To actualize her new idealized image, she must regard the feelings of others as more important than her own and try to have "no desires merely for [herself]" (ch. 39).

Dorothea's disillusionment begins on her honeymoon. Frustrated by her exclusion from her husband's work, she urges him to make use of her help and begin to write the book that will make his "vast knowledge useful to the world" (ch. 20). Casaubon reacts defensively, asserting that only he knows the "times and seasons" for the "different stages" of his work and attacking the "facile conjectures of ignorant onlookers." Initially he had fed Dorothea's pride by praising her elevation of thought and regarding her as a fit helper in his scholarly endeavors, but now his dismissiveness reinforces the sense of uselessness and inferiority that she married him to escape. The marriage is equally disastrous for Casaubon, for he, too, was looking for someone who would assuage his insecurities and confirm his idealized image of himself. Instead, Dorothea is "a personification of that shallow world which surrounds the ill-appreciated or desponding author."

George Eliot has brilliantly portrayed the interaction between Dorothea and Casaubon, showing how they first bolster and then threaten each other's pride. The authorial commentary, however, tends to obscure the similarities between the two characters. Dorothea and Casaubon are both engaged in a search for glory, but hers is attributed to spiritual grandeur, whereas his is presented as egoistic. The rhetoric encourages us to sympathize with Dorothea's disappointment and to see Casaubon's reactions as unreasonable. It obscures the fact that Dorothea puts her husband under terrible pressure because of her need for him to be another Hooker, Milton, or Pascal. Dorothea is presented as noble because "however just her indignation might be, her ideal was not to claim justice, but to give tenderness" (ch. 20). Is her indignation just? She is indignant because Casaubon has failed to honor her magic bargain, which is that if she devotes herself to him, he will enable her to lead an epic life by helping him to write a great book.

Why is Casaubon's inability to be a great man any more culpable than Dorothea's unreasonable demand that he be one? He is a failure, to be sure, a blocked writer at work on a futile project; but consider the degree of success he would have to achieve to satisfy Dorothea. Given his needs and self-doubts, she is the worst possible wife he could have chosen. George Eliot rationalizes and excuses Dorothea's mistake in marriage, but from a psychological point of view, her mistake is not much different from Casaubon's. Both have irrational expectations, and both are bound to be disappointed.

George Eliot glorifies the way in which Dorothea eventually handles her frustrations. She initially reacts with "anger and despondency" but fights against this response and reaches "towards the fullest truth, the least partial good" (ch. 20). Shaken out of her "moral stupidity," she becomes aware that "there might be a sad consciousness in [her husband's] life which made as great a need on his side as on her own" (ch. 21). Looking steadily at Casaubon's "failure, still more at his possible consciousness of failure, she seem[s] to be looking along the one track where duty [becomes] tenderness" (ch. 37). The "educated" Dorothea relinquishes her illusions about her husband, and, becoming aware of his equivalent center of self, seeks to succor him in his pain. Casaubon's pride leads him to repel her sympathetic concern, even when he learns from Lydgate that his death may be imminent, and Dorothea has a fit of "rebellious anger" (ch. 42). But when she thinks of her husband's grief at the arrest of his work, the "noble habit of the soul reasserts itself," and she achieves a "resolved submission."

There is something wrong with all this that I was unable to see when I was writing *Experiments in Life*. Dorothea is *not* reaching "towards the fullest truth, the least partial good." In George Eliot, the least partial good does not involve a balancing of the legitimate needs and desires of all concerned. It is other people's good, as they define it, and it leaves out what is good for oneself. After Dorothea arrives at a resolved submission, she feels that she will "never again expect anything else" (ch. 42). When George Eliot's characters reach the third stage of moral development, they often become enslaved by the wishes of others and incapable of asserting their own. Once they become aware that others have an equivalent center of self, they tend to give in when there is a conflict of interests. Dorothea tries not to have desires merely for herself, "because they may not be good for others" (ch. 39). This is hardly the least partial good.

When Casaubon asks her to promise to carry out his wishes in case of his death, Dorothea is "crushed by opposing fears" (ch. 48). Some of her fears are for herself, and some are for her husband. She had wished to marry him so that she could help him in his work: "But she had thought the work was to be something greater, which she could serve in devoutly for its own sake. Was it right, even to soothe his grief—would it be possible, even if she promised—to work as in a treadmill fruitlessly?" (Dorothea wished to serve, of course, not purely for the sake of the work but to fulfill her need for glory.) Balanced against the prospect of a long and futile servitude is the pain a refusal would cause Casaubon. She pictures his lonely labor, "the ambition breathing hardly under the pressure of self-distrust, the goal receding," and "now at last the sword visibly trembling above him!" If "she were to say, 'No! if you die, I will put no finger to your work'—it seemed as if she would be crushing that bruised heart."

Dorothea is torn between the fears of crushing her husband and of ruining her own life. Neither she nor George Eliot seems able to envision a response to Casaubon other than cruel refusal or complete surrender. Neither can imagine saying No in a sympathetic manner, showing concern for the other person's feelings but refusing to be governed by them. This illustrates the flaw in George Eliot to which I referred earlier: the characters of whom she approves are often incapable of self-assertion and feel compelled to submit to the unreasonable demands of other people. George Eliot's philosophy leads in the direction of self-abandonment. For her, the meaning of life lies not in self-realization, of which she seems to have no conception, but in being of value to others. If they need us to serve their irrational needs by behaving in ways that are destructive to ourselves, we must do what they want if we are not to feel selfish and useless.

Dorothea is described as being compelled by her husband's nature. She asks if it would be "right, even to soothe [Casaubon's] grief" to promise "to work as in a treadmill fruitlessly" (ch. 48). This is a good question to which she does not have a good answer. It would be a crime against herself to give her husband the promise for which he asks. She feels that it would be cruel not to content his "pining hunger," but he has no right to ask her to sacrifice herself to him. Neither Dorothea nor George Eliot seems to have a position from which it is possible to assess the demands that others are making and to refuse to satisfy them when they are illegitimate. Neither sees that we do not have a moral obligation to submit to other people's claims and that we have a right to defend ourselves against them. Dorothea feels compelled to give Casaubon what he wants, and Lydgate is similarly compelled by Rosamond's demands. In neither case can George Eliot see any alternative to submission.

I do not mean to suggest that had Dorothea been capable of healthy self-assertion it would have been easy for her to say No to Casaubon. The whole meaning of his life depended on his "Key to All Mythologies," and he would have been deeply distressed if she had refused to complete it. Still, he had no right to ask her to choose his needs over hers, and if she had had a clear sense of this she might have been able to decline in a compassionate manner. Instead of saying "No! if you die, I will put no finger to your work," which is the only kind of refusal she can imagine, she might have been able to tell him that she understood his feelings and did not wish to hurt him but could not surrender her autonomy. I realize that *Middlemarch* is set in a patriarchal society in which wives are expected to obey their husbands; but, as George Eliot observes, Dorothea's intended submission is well beyond what "law," "the world's opinion," and "the real yoke of marriage" would require (ch. 48).

It is very difficult to behave as I am proposing. My favorite exemplar of healthy self-assertion is Sir Thomas More in Robert Bolt's *A Man for All Seasons*. Sir Thomas is able to say No to all kinds of demands without anger, stridency, or defensiveness because he knows what he thinks and feels and what he must do to preserve his selfhood (see Paris 1986b). Bolt describes him as a man "with an adamantine sense of his own self" who "knew where he began and where he left off." He knew "what area of himself he could yield to the encroachments" of others, but when he was asked "to retreat from that final area where he located his self," he "set like metal, was overtaken by an absolutely primitive rigor, and could no more be budged than a cliff" (Bolt n.d., xi–xiii). More resists not only the demands of the king and his agents but also the pleas of friends and family that he save himself by swearing a false oath. He chooses truth to himself over the needs of wife and daughter, but he is able to say No in such a way that they part on loving terms.

Unlike Sir Thomas, Dorothea has no adamantine sense of self to defend, only a compensatory solution to protect. George Eliot portrays her as being caught between the fear of crushing Casaubon and of having to devote her life to his meaningless work. These are not her greatest fears, however. As we have seen, she is going to say yes to her own doom because she is "too full of *dread* at the thought of inflicting a keen-edged blow on her husband to do anything but submit completely" (ch. 48; my emphasis). What does Dorothea dread? I think it is less her husband's pain than the self-hatred and despair she would feel if she violated her inner dictates and shattered her idealized image of herself.

Even after she begins to see that Casaubon is a failure, Dorothea tells Will that she "cannot help believing in glorious things in a blind sort of way" (ch. 22). The days of "that active wifely devotion which was to strengthen her husband's life and exalt her own" would never begin "as she had preconceived them; but somehow—still somehow" (ch. 28). Dorothea is forced to relinquish her dream of helping a great man with his work; but once she becomes aware of Casaubon's frustrations and sorrows, she constructs a new idealized self-image as a noble, devoted person who has no desires for herself. Now she will strengthen her husband's life and exalt her own by succoring him.

Casaubon's demand that she promise to complete his work puts Dorothea's idealized image to the test. If she accedes, she may destroy her future chances for happiness; but if she does not, she will have to abandon her search for glory and will hate herself for the rest of her life. No unhappiness resulting from submission to her husband could equal the despair she would feel if she violated her inner dictates by "crushing that bruised heart" (ch. 48). Such an act would make her feel like her despised self. By submitting, she not only escapes self-hatred but becomes a noble person who sacrifices herself for the good of others. Casaubon's demand gives her a magnificent opportunity for heroic self-sacrifice. George Eliot so arranges things that Dorothea can receive credit for her nobility without paying the price. Casaubon dies before she makes her promise, but George Eliot celebrates her readiness to do so, ascribing it to her compassion and fidelity to the ideal of marriage.

DOROTHEA AND WILL

After the death of Casaubon, Dorothea's story focuses on her relationship with Will Ladislaw and her continuing effort to find something worthwhile to do with her life. These two strands come together at the end when, in what George Eliot describes as "a self-subduing act of fellowship" (ch. 82), Dorothea overcomes her anger at finding Will with Rosamond and acts in a way that makes possible her marriage, which finally gives her a life filled with "beneficent activity which she had not the doubtful pains of discovering and marking out for herself" (Finale). Dorothea becomes a mother, and Will becomes an "ardent public man" to whom she gives "wifely help" in his struggle for political reform.

Despite Dorothea's having found emotional fulfillment and a meaningful life with Will, the novel concludes on a mournful note. Her marriage is described as "not ideally beautiful," and George Eliot continues to bemoan the social conditions that are responsible for Dorothea's lapses and her inability to do something of historical importance (Finale). Dorothea always feels there was "something better which she might have done," and George Eliot describes her fate as a sad sacrifice. Many who knew Dorothea "thought it a pity that so substantive and rare a creature should have been absorbed into the life of another, and be only known in a certain circle as a wife and mother."

Many critics have been uncomfortable with Dorothea's marriage to Will, who they feel lacks, as Henry James puts it, "the concentrated fervor essential in the man chosen by so nobly strenuous a heroine" (1953, 165). I believe we are meant to be dissatisfied with this marriage, but I do not think that George Eliot's rhetorical treatment of Dorothea and Will is any more reliable than was her treatment of Dorothea and Casaubon. In both cases, her psychological portrayal of the relationship is obscured by her authorial commentary.

In *Experiments in Life*, I argued that Dorothea's attraction to Will must be understood in light of the change in her needs brought about by her unhappy marriage: "Before marriage she had longed chiefly for an epic life, while now she required most of all an affectionate and understanding response from another to mitigate the isolation and positive hardness of her lot. In Will alone she found a look which recognized and reflected her own humanity" (188). I still think that Dorothea is drawn to Will by her needs for affection and understanding. She had imagined Casaubon to be someone who could enter into her thoughts and feelings, as no one had done before; but he has no interest in her experience and makes no response to her affection. Like Lydgate, Dorothea has "two selves" within her (ch. 15), one of which aspires to greatness while the other longs for love. As with Lydgate, her need for greatness is initially paramount, but the love need becomes stronger as her aspirations are thwarted. Frustrated in every respect by Casaubon, she feels "an immense need of some one to speak to"; and she has "never before seen any one who seemed [as] quick and pliable, [as] likely to understand everything" as Will (ch. 21). What I failed to see before is that Will is so important to Dorothea not only because he fulfills her needs for affection and understanding but also because he helps to restore her injured pride.

Before we can appreciate what Will brings to Dorothea, we must first understand her role in his life. When Will first encounters Dorothea at Lowick, he decides that she "must be an unpleasant girl"; for she professes ignorance about art and is going to marry Casaubon. He assumes that she thinks "his sketch detestable" and is laughing at him (ch. 9). Soon after he meets her in Rome, however, he is ready "to embrace her slippers, and tell her that he would die for her" (ch. 22). What brings about the radical change in Will's attitude?

Like Dorothea, Will is searching for glory but does not know how to attain it. After being educated at Rugby, he studies at Heidelberg instead of attending an English university; he then refuses to choose a profession but wishes to go abroad again, "for the vague purpose," says Mr. Casaubon, "of what he calls culture" (ch. 9). "Genius," Will holds, "is necessarily intolerant of fetters: on the one hand it must have the utmost play for its spontaneity; on the other, it may confidently await those messages from the universe which summon it to its peculiar work, only placing itself in an attitude of receptivity towards all sublime chances" (ch. 10). Will tries various attitudes of receptivity, but "the superadded circumstance which would evolve the genius had not yet come; the universe had not yet beckoned." Will sees himself as a special person who is marked out for a great destiny, but he has not yet found a calling that will enable him to demonstrate his genius, and he will settle for nothing less. When he meets Dorothea at Lowick, he is trying to become a painter.

When Will visits Dorothea in Rome, he announces that he has made up his mind against painting, which is "too one-sided a life" (ch. 21). He does not want to get into the painter's "way of looking at the world entirely from the studio point of view." Will sounds here like a potential Mr. Brooke, a person who looks into many things but does not want to go too far with any of them. His loss of interest in painting has a more specific cause, however. He has been studying under the German artist Naumann, who has described him as dilettantish and dismissed his work as "*pfuscherei*" (ch. 22). Will defends himself against this blow to his pride by rejecting the painter's life as too narrow. He has not yet discovered wherein his genius lies.

Will's attitude toward Dorothea begins to change when he sees her through Naumann's eyes in the Vatican Museum. Naumann calls her "the most perfect young Madonna" he has ever seen and describes her as "a sort of Christian Antigone—sensuous force controlled by spiritual passion" (ch. 19). This extravagant praise from a man he admires influences Will's perception; and when he calls on Dorothea he decides that she is "not coldly clever and indirectly satirical, but adorably simple and full of feeling" (ch. 21). He sees her now as "an angel beguiled": "She must have made some original romance for herself in this marriage. And if Mr Casaubon had been a dragon who had carried her off to his lair with his talons simply and without legal forms, it would have been an unavoidable feat of heroism to release her and fall at her feet." He has an inclination to fall at her feet when she poses for Naumann as Santa Clara, and he becomes exasperated at the artist's presumption when he mentions "any detail of [her] beauty," for "the ordinary phrases which might apply to mere bodily prettiness were not applicable" to Dorothea (ch. 22).

Will has discovered his calling, the worship of the divine Dorothea. Discouraged by Naumann's dismissal of his painting and unable to find a path to glory, he will become Dorothea's knight and dedicate his life to her service. He does not wish to come between her and Casaubon, but he does want her to take notice of his devotion. "The remote worship of a woman throned out of their reach plays a great part in men's lives," observes George Eliot, "but in most cases the worshipper longs for some queenly recognition, some approving sign by which his soul's sovereign may cheer him without descending from her high place" (ch. 22). Dorothea's concern for her husband is part of her divinity: "she would have lost some of her halo if she had been without that duteous preoccupation."

It is part of the romance Will makes for himself that he is devoted to a woman throned out of his reach for whom he feels a pure and unselfish love. He casts Dorothea as the perfect object of devotion and himself as the perfect lover. Instead of being frustrated by the obstacles to fulfillment, he experiences "unspeakable content" at being "in the presence of a creature worthy to be perfectly loved" (ch. 37). It would sully his image of both Dorothea and himself if there were any sexual component in their relationship or any disloyalty to Casaubon. At the same time, he feels that her marriage "is the most horrible of virgin-sacrifices" and determines never to "lose sight of her: he would watch over her—if he gave up everything else in life he would watch over her, and she should know that she had one slave in the world." This is a gloriously romantic role in which he cannot fail.

Will's idealizations are endorsed by George Eliot, who proclaims his feelings toward Dorothea to be "perfect": "for we mortals have our divine moments, when love is satisfied in the completeness of the beloved object" (ch. 37). To remove any hint of sexuality from the relationship, Eliot tells us that Will and Dorothea look at each other "as if they had been two flowers which had opened then and there" (ch. 37) or "two fond children who were talking confidentially of birds" (ch. 39). Critics have felt that Will lacks the concentrated fervor that would make him a fit partner for Dorothea, but George Eliot presents him as fervent indeed by comparing his love for Dorothea to that of Dante for Beatrice and Petrarch for Laura (ch. 37). Unlike Casaubon, Will finds what the poets have said about love to be true. The epigraph from Donne at the head of chapter 39 is authorial rhetoric designed to influence our view of Will and Dorothea:

> If, as I have, you also doe,
>   Vertue attired in woman see,
> And dare love that, and say so too,
>   And forget the He and She;
>
> And if this love, though placed so,
>   From prophane men you hide,
> Which will no faith on this bestow,
>   Or, if they doe, deride;
>
> Then you have done a braver thing
>   Than all the Worthies did,
> And a braver thence will spring,
>   Which is to keep that hid.

Dorothea is "Vertue attired in woman," and Will the brave lover who conceals his pure devotion.

Will's veneration of Dorothea makes him an important part of the vindication pattern of her story. Before his appearance no one but the narrator has truly appreciated Dorothea; but Will sees her as George Eliot feels she ought to be seen, as "an angel beguiled"; and his worship contributes to her epic stature.

It is also, of course, a major part of his appeal to Dorothea. Dorothea becomes the focus of Will's life because devoting himself to her saves him from a sense of aimlessness and failure and gives him a splendid role to play. Dorothea, too, is suffering from injured pride and a frustrated search for glory. Will's worship restores her pride and confirms her sense of herself as an extraordinary person who stands out from the crowd. His promise never to do or say anything of which she would disapprove makes her feel that she will "have a little kingdom" where she will "give laws" (ch. 37). Will is a wonderful antidote to Casaubon. Instead of making Dorothea feel stupid and useless, he sees "more in what she [says] than she herself" does. Dorothea cannot help wanting to be with the man who thus confirms her sense of her own value; there is nothing more intoxicating than such recognition.

Once the mutual attraction between Will and Dorothea is established, their story is largely about the obstacles that keep them apart.

After Casaubon's death, Will is no longer content with worshiping Dorothea from afar; but even before he knows of the codicil that will disinherit her if she marries him, his pride revolts at the thought that others might see him "as a needy adventurer trying to win the favour of a rich woman" (ch. 51). He entertains a fantasy of going away to make his fortune and then returning with "such distinction that he would not seem to be asking Dorothea to step down to him." But he is no Heathcliff. When he does not leave even after he learns of the codicil, he begins to seem like the insufficient creature of whom critics complain. His "indefinite visions of ambition are weak against the ease of doing what is habitual or beguilingly agreeable," and he begins to dream of a miracle (ch. 60). He resembles Fred Vincy not only in the expectation of a miracle but also in his feelings of hopelessness about himself unless he has an assurance that he is loved. Dorothea does love him but is afraid to let him know how she feels; this reticence is one of the obstacles that must be overcome. Will's dependency on Dorothea seems pathetic, as does his inability to resist the spell of Rosamond. He seems to have the weaknesses of Fred Vincy and Lydgate combined.

Dorothea accepts her frustrations in relation to Will as "part of her marriage sorrows" and entertains "no visions of their ever coming into nearer union" (ch. 77). She takes great comfort in Will's love, however, and in his "delicate sense of honour." She can "bear that the chief pleasures of her tenderness should lie in memory." The misfortunes of Will's lot, the murkiness of his background and social position, which others wish "to fling at his back as an opprobrium," only give "something more of enthusiasm to her clinging thought." Dorothea is as loftily romantic now as Will had been when Casaubon was alive. She envisions a future in which, although they cannot be united, they will cling to one another "with silent love and faith." (Could this possibly have worked had George Eliot put it to the test by not bringing Dorothea and Will together? He does not seem to be a flesh-and-blood man for Dorothea.) Her image of Will is shattered when she comes upon him with Rosamond in what appears to be a love scene. This throws her into despair and sets the stage for her grand "self-subduing act of fellowship."

SAVING ROSAMOND

Chapter 80 is the climax of Dorothea's story. After experiencing her rage and despair, Dorothea accepts "her own irremediable grief" and determines once again "to see and save Rosamond." In discussing this chapter in *Experiments in Life*, I followed George Eliot's view of Dorothea, as most critics have done. On waking from her night of anguish, Dorothea stops seeing the event of the preceding day simply in terms of how it affects her and begins to think of the other people involved. Moved by Lydgate's account of his marital problems, she had set out with a longing to help the young pair. She now puts aside the "jealous indignation and disgust" that was her initial reaction to finding Will with Rosamond and remembers how she had pictured to herself "the trials of Lydgate's lot." Her "sympathetic experience" asserts "itself as acquired knowledge asserts itself and will not let us see as we saw in the day of our ignorance." Because of her own troubles, she is able to envision those of Lydgate and Rosamond, and her sympathy makes her want to relieve their suffering. She asks herself how she should act if she "could clutch [her] own pain, and compel it to silence, and think of those three."

Dorothea's second visit to Rosamond improves the Lydgates' marriage, as she had hoped, and is instrumental in saving Will from a life of "discontented subjection" (ch. 82). George Eliot observes that it is "given to us sometimes even in our everyday life, to witness the saving influence of a noble nature, the divine efficacy of rescue that may lie in a self-subduing act of fellowship." Dorothea's unselfish act also facilitates her marriage to Will when Rosamond tells her that it is she whom he loves.

The action is so arranged that Dorothea can attain personal happiness only after she has learned to do without it and found meaning in life through living for others. After Will tells her that he "thought it was all over with [him], and there was nothing to try for" when she doubted his fidelity, Dorothea formulates what she has learned from her experience: "If we had lost our own chief good, other people's good would remain, and that is worth trying for. Some can be happy. I seemed to see that more clearly than ever, when I was the most wretched. I can hardly think how I could have borne the trouble, if that feeling had not come to me to make strength" (ch. 83). Dorothea has arrived at George Eliot's Religion of Humanity, in which self-despair can be reconciled "with the rapturous consciousness of life beyond self" (Prelude). Her sense of religious orientation in the cosmos rests on a firm foundation, for it comes from loving rather than from being loved.

I now think that while this interpretation is faithful to George Eliot's thematic intentions, it is not fully adequate to the mimetic portrayal of Dorothea's character. The experience-vision-sympathy pattern fits Dorothea's behavior well, but it leaves out other motivations that make Dorothea seem less unselfish and noble than George

Eliot would have us believe. We shall better understand Dorothea's behavior in chapter 80 and beyond if we place it in the context of her search for glory.

While Casaubon is still alive, Dorothea says to Lydgate, "How happy you must be, to know things that you feel sure will do great good! I wish I could awake with that knowledge every morning" (ch. 44). She married Casaubon because she thought she could make a great contribution by helping him, but this turns out to be an illusion, and she is still frustrated at not having found "work which would be directly beneficent like the sunshine and the rain" (ch. 48). When she becomes aware of Casaubon's sorrows, she tries to succor him, but this is not the "great good" she longs to do.

After her husband's death, Dorothea's desire to be greatly beneficent continues to be frustrated; and she feels herself to be one of those people who have "slipped below their own intention" (ch. 50). She "used to despise women a little for not shaping their lives more, and doing better things" (ch. 54); but she has almost given up the effort to shape her own life and suffers from a sense of failure. She is frightened by the prospect of a life "full of motiveless ease—motiveless, if her own energy could not seek out reasons for ardent action." She makes plans to drain land and set up a utopian colony where everyone will work and work well and she will be everyone's friend. Nothing comes of this, however, because although she has far more money than she needs, she has "too little for any great scheme" (ch. 76).

Constantly looking for ways to do good, Dorothea welcomes the opportunities afforded by the difficulties of people like Farebrother, Ladislaw, and Lydgate to extend patronage, faith, and moral support. Farebrother is another of those who have "slipped below their own intention," and Dorothea hopes to "rescue" him "from his chance-gotten money" by offering him a living (ch. 50). She receives a tribute for doing this from Farebrother's mother: "They say Fortune is a woman and capricious. But sometimes she is a good woman and gives to those who merit, which has been the case with you, Mrs. Casaubon" (ch. 54).

This is one among many such tributes that Dorothea receives in the second half of the novel and is part of the vindication pattern. She supports Will in the face of ugly gossip in the community by continuing to believe he is honorable. Her high estimation of him binds him "over to rectitude and purity" and helps to sustain his morale (ch. 77). Although Dorothea was wrong about Casaubon, her faith in Farebrother and Will is not misplaced. "That simplicity of hers," says George Eliot, "holding up an ideal for others in her believing conception of them, was one of the great powers of her womanhood." Dorothea continues to feel that she has nothing worthwhile to do with her life; but others, including the author, celebrate her as a saving influence.

Dorothea's most exciting opportunity to do good occurs when Lydgate is suspected of accepting a bribe from Bulstrode and colluding in the death of Raffles. Farebrother does not know how to help his friend in such a complicated matter, but Dorothea has "an ardent faith" that "efforts of justice and mercy" will "conquer by their emotional force." "What do we live for," she asks, "if it is not to make life less difficult to each other?" (ch. 72). If Lydgate's character has become "diseased," as Farebrother fears, "then," says Dorothea, "it may be rescued and healed." "People glorify all sorts of bravery," she observes, "except the bravery they might show on behalf of their nearest neighbors." She almost welcomes Lydgate's difficulties because they give her a chance to display moral heroism. As she imagines his marital problems, her thoughts are "like a drama to her, and [make] her eyes bright" (ch. 76).

Lydgate did not have a high opinion of Dorothea when he first met her, and his change of attitude is an important aspect of the vindication pattern. Whereas he felt that Rosamond was "what a woman ought to be" (ch. 11), he found Dorothea "a little too earnest," the sort of woman who is "always wanting reasons" but is "too ignorant to understand the merits of any question" (ch. 10). He later contrasts Rosamond's lack of sympathy with his work with Dorothea's passionate concern for Casaubon: "He has been all his life labouring and looking forward. He minds about nothing else—and I mind about nothing else" (ch. 58). Lydgate sees Dorothea as having "a genius for feeling nobly" and ranks her with the "dead and sceptered" geniuses whose ideas have inspired him.

Lydgate becomes a complete convert to the worship of Dorothea when she affirms her faith in his innocence in the Raggles affair and wants to help him continue with his projects. He cannot accept her offer of financial support because he has lost faith in himself and feels he must do what will please Rosamond, but he venerates Dorothea: "This young creature has a heart large enough for the Virgin Mary. She evidently thinks nothing of her own future, and would pledge away half her income at once, as if she wanted nothing for herself but a chair to sit in from which she can look down with those clear eyes at the poor mortals who pray to her" (ch. 76).

This remarkable passage is another tribute to Dorothea, and one of the most eloquent. It contributes to her sanctification by comparing her to a holy figure once more. Lydgate has arrived at a view of Dorothea as lofty as that of the author. I think that George Eliot means this passage to reinforce our perception of Dorothea as a large-hearted, generous woman who does not think about herself but is ready to make great sacrifices in order to help other people. There is something else in the passage, however, that points to another aspect of Dorothea. She wants nothing for herself "but a chair to sit in from which she can look down" at "the poor mortals who pray to her." I would suggest that this is wanting a great deal. Lydgate sees Dorothea as someone who is far above ordinary people. This is also the way George Eliot sees her and, deep down, the way Dorothea sees herself. Dorothea wants to do great things for others partly for the reasons George Eliot emphasizes, such as her vision and sympathy, but also because she wishes to be a godlike being to whom those below her will pray.

We are now in a better position to understand Dorothea's behavior in chapter 80 and beyond. Dorothea's sense of herself as a morally superior person is usually repressed, along with her contempt for ordinary people. Her claims of spiritual grandeur are made by the narrator, who also gives expression to her condescending attitudes. This allows Dorothea to preserve her self-effacing modesty and her image of herself as a loving, compassionate person who just wants to make life better for her fellow human beings. She has great pride in her goodness, along with a powerful need to be humble. We can see this in chapter 2, in the scene in which she announces her intention to give up riding because she enjoys it in too pagan and sensuous a way. To Sir James's remark that Dorothea is "given to self-mortification," Celia replies, "She likes giving up." Dorothea observes that giving up would then be self-indulgence and that "there may be good reasons not to do what is very agreeable." "Exactly," says Sir James; "You give up from some high, generous motive." "No, indeed, not exactly. I did not say that of myself," Dorothea answers, "reddening." Sir James is right, of course, but Dorothea becomes anxious when confronted with her pride in renunciation.

In chapter 80, after the blow of seeing Will with Rosamond, Dorothea's repressed self-idealization and scorn of others come to the surface, giving us an unusual opportunity to see them directly rather than through their displaced expression by the narrator. Now that she feels she has lost Will, Dorothea realizes how deeply she has loved and believed in him, and she is enraged with him for deluding her. Her anger flames out "in fitful returns of spurning reproach. Why had he come obtruding his life into hers, hers that might have been whole enough without him? . . . Why had he not stayed among *the crowd of whom she asked nothing—but only prayed that they might be less contemptible*" (my emphasis)?

Dorothea represses such feelings the next morning because they are out of keeping with her image of herself as all-loving. Instead, she lives through the encounter at Rosamond's "deliberately again, *forcing* herself to dwell on every detail and its possible meaning. Was she alone in that scene? Was it her event only? She *forced* herself to think of it as bound up with another woman's life—a woman toward whom she had set out with a longing to carry some clearness and comfort into her beclouded youth" (my emphasis). Dorothea is forced to dwell on the scene and her intentions toward Rosamond by her inner dictates, the violation of which would cause her to hate herself. In her anger, she has "flung away all the mercy with which she had undertaken that visit." Her self-idealization and condescension are evident here. The "beclouded" Rosamond is a being toward whom the godlike Dorothea had intended to be merciful.

George Eliot ascribes Dorothea's return to Rosamond to her "spirit of justice" and characterizes it as a "simple inspiration (ch. 81) and a "self-subduing act of fellowship" (ch. 82). This is misleading, I think. Before her encounter with Will and Rosamond, "the long valley of her life" looked "flat and empty of way-marks," but Dorothea trusted that "guidance would come as she walked along the road, and saw her fellow-passengers by the way" (ch. 77). As we have seen, one of these fellow-passengers is Lydgate, who becomes a cause for Dorothea. "I would take any pains to clear you," she tells him. "I have very little to do. There is nothing better that I can do in the world" (ch. 76). She sees Lydgate's fate as a version of her own: "There is no sorrow" she has "thought more about than . . . to love what is great, and try to reach it, and yet to fail." She offers to finance his work as a way of redeeming her life as well as his. Perhaps she can realize her fantasy of helping a great man through him: "You may still win great fame like the Louis and Laennec I have heard you speak of." Dorothea goes to see Rosamond as part of her project of rescuing Lydgate. If she cannot transcend her anger and go to Rosamond again, she will not only experience self-hate but will miss a wonderful opportunity to become Saint Dorothea. "And what sort of crisis," she asks herself, "might not this be in three lives whose contact with hers laid an obligation on her as if they had been *suppliants bearing the sacred branch*? The objects of her rescue were not to be sought out by her fancy: they were chosen for her" (ch. 80; my emphasis).

Lydgate sees Dorothea as wanting nothing for herself but a chair from which to look down at poor mortals who pray to her, and here Dorothea sees herself as a divine figure who has an obligation to suppliants who have come to her bearing the sacred branch. This is hardly a "simple inspiration." By subduing herself, she aggrandizes herself. She has been dwelling on fantasies of moral heroism, of rescue, of doing great good but has been frustrated by the meanness of opportunity. The universe has finally beckoned. As she sets off once more to see Rosamond, Dorothea envisions herself as a savior.

DOROTHEA'S SAD SACRIFICE

Although George Eliot glorifies Dorothea almost beyond measure at the end, the novel concludes on a somber note. We are told that Dorothea herself "had no dreams of being praised above other women, feeling that there was always something better which she might have done, if she had only been better and known better" (Finale). Dorothea has engaged in numerous acts of everyday heroism that have had a saving influence on others, and she has found love and a life of beneficent activity with Will, but she feels dissatisfied because she has not attained the grand life of which she had dreamed.

The humble Dorothea blames herself rather than others, but George Eliot places the blame on society. Dorothea's "young and noble impulse" has struggled "amidst the conditions of an imperfect social state, in which great feelings will often take the aspect of error, and great faith the aspect of illusion" (Finale). The foil to Dorothea is Lydgate, who, as a man, had an opportunity to lead an epic life but wasted it because of his flaws of character. Lydgate could have triumphed over circumstance, but Dorothea is the victim of an age in which women have no opportunities for heroism. The medium that permitted the "ardent deeds" of an Antigone or a Saint Theresa "is for ever gone" (Finale).

It is not only the fault of the age but of people like you and me that women like Dorothea are so frustrated. In a sentence that startles me now, George Eliot turns on her readers: "But we *insignificant* people with our daily words and acts are preparing the lives of many Dorotheas, some of which may present a far sadder sacrifice than that of the Dorothea whose story we know" (Finale; my emphasis). George Eliot includes herself among the insignificant people, but she is really talking about the rest of us. I did not find this sentence offensive when I was writing *Experiments in Life* because I identified with Dorothea as a superior being and felt exempt from George Eliot's criticism.

Looking at the novel from my current perspective, I find the claims for Dorothea's heroic stature to be excessive and at odds with the mimetic portrait of her character. Lydgate wants to do something great; but in addition to his desire for glory, he has an intellectual passion and the capacity to pursue it. Dorothea craves an epic life; but, unlike Lydgate, or, for that matter, George Eliot, she has no special calling or ability. Her story is what George Eliot's might have been had she not been able to become a great novelist. It is certainly true that, as a woman, Dorothea had no opportunity to develop her talents and discover a calling, because a good education and a choice of vocation were denied to her. It does not necessarily follow, however, that under different conditions she would have been able to do something grand.

Because Dorothea does not have a chance to develop her abilities, we can only speculate about her potential; but like some other characters in the novel, she seems to have the desire but not the capacity to do something of world-historical importance. Dorothea is of above-average intelligence, but she is not a mental giant and has difficulty learning languages that George Eliot mastered rather easily. The rhetoric seems to insist that in a more heroic age she could have become another Saint Theresa, but Theresa had more than a genius for noble feeling. Perhaps she could have become another Antigone if she had had the right opportunity for spectacular self-sacrifice.

What distinguishes Dorothea from ordinary people is her ardor and the loftiness of her aspirations. While George Eliot sees these qualities as the product of spiritual grandeur, I see them as manifestations of a compensatory search for glory. In any event, it takes more than ambition, ardor, and above-average intelligence to make a memorable contribution to the world, even for a male in a patriarchal society. If Lydgate had not been derailed by his personal weaknesses, it still seems unlikely that he would have made a great discovery, for, as George Eliot points out, he had not framed his question correctly. In addition to being ardent and enamoured of greatness, Dorothea is an unusually loving, caring, empathetic person; but this does not make her the potentially heroic figure George Eliot claims her to be.

It is instructive to compare Dorothea not only with Lydgate but also with Ladislaw. As a male, Will does not suffer from her disadvantages, but he is no more successful than she in leading an epic life. Like Dorothea, he thinks himself an extraordinary person but does not know how to actualize his potential for greatness. He has an inner insecurity comparable to Dorothea's and an emptiness he can fill only by attaching himself to someone else. Dorothea does not need Will as desperately as he needs her; but she, too, seems to have no inner core and depends on others for her sense of direction and worth. On the morning of the day on which she becomes engaged, Dorothea is distressed because everybody is well in the village and "nobody's pig [has] died" (ch. 83). George Eliot is still capable of making fun of her heroine. Dorothea needs other people to be in trouble so that she can rescue them. Although both Will and Dorothea find a focus for their lives through their attachment to each other, George Eliot presents Will as having been rescued by Dorothea, whereas she has been sacrificed to the "meanness of opportunity." Presumably, Will's fate is adequate to his deserts but Dorothea's sharing it is a disappointing result. Is Dorothea really so much superior to Will?

Dorothea, Casaubon, Lydgate, and Will are all searching for glory in their own way. Although they are all driven by an underlying need for self-aggrandizement, they are treated very differently by George Eliot. Dorothea is treated the most sympathetically because she is the most self-effacing. Her search for glory seems nobly unselfish because she wants to do something for other people. She does not consciously aggrandize herself—that is left to her sacred poet. Lydgate, too, has an ideal of service that George Eliot admires, but he is treated less sympathetically because he has conventional ideas about women and a sense of arrogant superiority far more perceptible than Dorothea's. Casaubon's search for glory is satirized as both futile and egoistic, but is it really more egoistic than the others? If he had been on the right track, his "Key to All Mythologies" would have been a great contribution. Will is presented at first as a somewhat comic figure who is waiting for the universe to tap his genius, but he settles down nicely to the worship of Dorothea and finds a vocation through his desire to remain close to her.

All of these characters slip below their intentions, Lydgate the most cruelly, it seems to me. It is Dorothea's disappointment, however, for which George Eliot mourns most deeply, partly because Lydgate is presented as having brought his downfall on himself, whereas Dorothea's frustrations are entirely the fault of an imperfect social order and the daily words and acts of insignificant people like you and me.

At the end, George Eliot seeks both to celebrate Dorothea and to lament her sad sacrifice. Dorothea's "finely-touched spirit" has "its fine issues," but they are "not widely visible." The effect of her being is "incalculably diffusive"; she has made things better for ordinary folks and has contributed to "the growing good of the world." The problem is that this is not enough for George Eliot, or presumably for Dorothea. However fine Dorothea's acts, they are "unhistoric." She will leave "no great name on the earth" but will live "a hidden life" and rest in an "unvisited tomb." Her "not ideally beautiful" marriage to Will is a "lapse" because it does not bring her the fame she was seeking or, according to George Eliot, which she deserves. Dorothea must be dissatisfied, and the author on her behalf, in order to maintain her claims.

I observed at the beginning of this chapter that George Eliot's "lamentation on the darkness of life without fame," to which Calvin Bedient responds so favorably (1972, 86), is just as disturbing to me as her celebration of living for others. One reason for this is that her obsession with leaving a great name on earth (see Bedient, 86–87) stirs up the craving for glory I have worked so hard to outgrow and threatens my efforts to feel good about my own life without it.

George Eliot criticizes society because it will not honor Dorothea's claims. I have suggested that a more appropriate criticism is that society's frustration of a number of Dorothea's basic psychological needs, partly because of her gender, leads her to develop a compensatory search for glory that dooms her to feel discontented with herself and her life. In a discussion of the novels of Harriet Beecher Stowe, George Eliot complained about their idealization of the slaves: "If the negroes are really so very good, slavery has answered as a moral discipline. But apart from the argumentative suicide involved in this one-sidedness, Mrs. Stowe loses by it the most terribly tragic element in the relation of the two races—the Nemesis lurking in the vices of the oppressed" (1856, 573). A similar complaint can be made about *Middlemarch*. It is a novel of social criticism that shows the depreciation of women and the constriction of their life producing a saintly creature like Dorothea.

This contradiction exists only in the rhetoric, however. The mimetic portrait of Dorothea shows both the ways in which she has been damaged by adverse conditions and the self-defeating nature of the defenses she has adopted to cope with them. Dorothea is not only dissatisfied with herself and her life but has been ready to acquiesce in her own doom. George Eliot portrays the "Nemesis lurking in the vices of the oppressed" not in Dorothea's story, but in the destruction of Lydgate by Rosamond.

In concluding, I wish to emphasize that my quarrel throughout has been with George Eliot's view of Dorothea, not with her concrete portrayal of Dorothea or with Dorothea herself. When we understand Dorothea as an imagined human being, she is a less exalted but more human, complex, and sympathetic figure. She also provides a better illustration of the ills of a patriarchal society.

3

The Two Selves of Tertius Lydgate

LYDGATE AS FOIL TO DOROTHEA

Lydgate's story is a companion and foil to that of Dorothea. Both are stories of exceptional young people, anomalies in Middlemarch, who aspire to lead benevolent lives of world-historical importance but whose aspirations are thwarted and who end with a sense of failure. Although it is Dorothea's sad sacrifice over which George Eliot lingers, I have come to feel that Lydgate's fate is far worse than Dorothea's; indeed, I have found it so painful that I have shied away from writing about it for years.

As mimetic characters, Dorothea and Lydgate have a great deal in common, much more than George Eliot seems to recognize. Her rhetoric presents them as a study in contrast, Dorothea's problems being caused by the flaws in her society but Lydgate's by his personal deficiencies. Although Dorothea makes many mistakes, the chief of which is marrying Casaubon, her blunders are the product of her spiritual grandeur ill-matched with the meanness of opportunity. Lydgate also makes many mistakes, the chief of which is marrying Rosamond; but he is held responsible for them and their consequences. Because society provides no suitable vocation for a woman like Dorothea, she cannot possibly achieve an epic life, despite her noble, ardent nature. As a gifted medical man living in a time of great discoveries, Lydgate might find an epic life within his reach; but he loses his opportunity because of his arrogant conceit, class prejudices, and conventional ideas about women. George Eliot's rhetoric focuses our attention on the ways in which Lydgate's faults contribute to his destruction.

Although Dorothea's tale ends on a note of frustration, it is essentially a story of vindication, in which Dorothea receives tribute after tribute from the people around her, including those who initially failed to appreciate her. Lydgate's story has a tragic education plot. His heroic qualities are subverted by his deficiencies, and by the time he learns his lessons it is too late to put them to use. He is not physically destroyed, as many protagonists are in such plots; but he is doomed to what is for him a living death.

As is the case with Dorothea, the mimetic portrait of Lydgate is best appreciated independently of the rhetoric. I think that George Eliot is less frequently wrong about him, but she is often vague or superficial in her interpretations and judgments. The reasons she adduces for his vulnerability to Rosamond, both before and after their marriage, are valid as far as they go; but her mimetic portrait provides a much fuller and subtler picture of Lydgate's plight and motivations. In *Experiments in Life*, I based my understanding of Lydgate on George Eliot's rhetoric and failed to see how complex a creation he is. The rhetoric works best in explaining how he becomes entrapped by Middlemarch politics and by Rosamond, although it fails to plumb the psychological sources of his vulnerability. The rhetoric is least adequate in accounting for Lydgate's inability to extricate himself once he is ensnared. George Eliot's mimetic portrait of the collapse of Lydgate's morale and his compulsive submissiveness to Rosamond is one of her most brilliant achievements. These aspects of Lydgate's story have not been sufficiently appreciated.

PRELUDE TO LYDGATE

The Prelude to *Middlemarch*, which deals only with Dorothea, is pure rhetoric, as we have seen. We have no corresponding purely rhetorical prelude for Lydgate, but the extended introduction in chapter 15 gives us the shape of his story as George Eliot wants us to see it, along with such information as we have about his past.

Lydgate experiences the birth of an "intellectual passion" at the age of ten and grows up knowing that "there is some particular thing in life" he would "like to do for its own sake" and not because he is following in his family's footsteps. Dorothea never finds that particular thing to do which Lydgate discovers while still a child. He is attracted to medicine not only because it excites him intellectually but also because it provides opportunities for social service and is a profession in need of reform. After being educated in London, Edinburgh, and Paris, he decides to practice in Middlemarch, rather than in London, to avoid temptations that might deflect him from his lofty objectives.

Lydgate's goals are "to do good small work for Middlemarch and great work for the world." His good small work is to make improvements in medical practice, for the sake of his patients and of the profession; his great work will be to "make a link in the chain of discovery" by identifying the "primitive tissue" from which all other tissues are formed. Just as Dorothea has a pantheon of great men by whose teachings she tries to live, Lydgate venerates heroes of medical discovery, especially those who have laid the foundation for his own research. Unlike Dorothea, Lydgate is not looking for someone in whose monumental project he can assist; his objective is to become a great man himself—to have a "glorious career" and to achieve "everlasting fame."

George Eliot treats Lydgate's desire for an epic life as sympathetically as she does Dorothea's. She solicits our interest in his passion for medicine as she does for Dorothea's unusual love story: "Is it due to excess of poetry or of stupidity that we are never weary of describing what King James called a woman's 'makdom and her fairnesse,' never weary of listening to the twanging of the old Troubadour strings, and are comparatively uninterested in that other kind of 'makdom and fairnesse' which must be wooed with industrious thought and patient renunciation of small desires?" In the story of this passion too "the development varies: sometimes it is the glorious marriage, sometimes frustration and final parting. And not seldom the catastrophe is bound up with the other passion, sung by the Troubadours." This is a clear foreshadowing of the frustration of Lydgate's ambition as a result of his marriage to Rosamond.

Lydgate's is to be the story of a man who "once meant to shape [his] own deeds and alter the world a little" but who comes "to be shapen after the average and fit to be packed by the gross." He becomes one of the ordinary people toward whom he, Dorothea, and George Eliot feel such condescension. The stories of such failures are "hardly ever told," even their own consciousness, for there is "nothing in the world more subtle than the process of their gradual change"; but in her portrayal of Lydgate, it is precisely such a story that George Eliot wishes to tell and such a process she wishes to trace.

George Eliot tells us that "Lydgate did not mean to be one of those failures," but she then goes on to spell out the faults that will make his downfall inevitable. He has a "fearless expectation of success" that is based on a "contempt for petty obstacles or seductions of which he [has] had no experience." Lydgate is too fearless, "too self-confident and disdainful." He is actually a naive, inexperienced man who overestimates his strength and underestimates the impediments with which he must contend. He is "benevolently contemptuous" of ordinary people and can be tactless in his dealings with them, for he feels that he should not have to humor "everybody's nonsense" (ch. 17). He intends "to do a great deal" for "noodles" and feels "quite sure that they could have no power over him." He does not envision the effects of his behavior on others or the resistance of both patients and fellow practitioners to his reforms. Because of his conceit, Lydgate is out of touch with reality and unprepared to deal with its challenges.

Lydgate is also plagued by what George Eliot calls "spots of commonness" that lie "in the complexion of his prejudices," which are similar to those of "ordinary men of the world" (ch. 15). His "distinction of mind" as a scientist does not "penetrate his feeling and judgment about furniture, or women," or his pride in his high birth. The most serious of his spots of commonness have to do with his careless attitude toward money and his conventional views of women. Coming from an aristocratic background, he takes it as a matter of course that he should have the best of everything, without giving much thought to the relation between income and expenditure. His expensive tastes and careless spending lead him to incur a crippling debt. A great deal of Lydgate's story has to do with his money troubles. These are brought on by his marriage to Rosamond, who is even more self-indulgent and less responsible than he. The marriage is presented as a direct result of Lydgate's conventional attitudes toward women, which lead him to see Rosamond as what a woman should be. When he first meets Dorothea, he finds her "too earnest" and concludes that she is not his "style of woman," but George Eliot observes that he "might possibly have experience before him which would modify his opinion as to the most excellent things in woman" (ch. 10). As we have seen, his opinion will indeed be modified.

George Eliot presents many of Lydgate's faults as characteristic of men of his time and class. He is extraordinary in some ways but ordinary in others, and his ordinariness prevents him from fulfilling his promise. A fault that is more personal to him is his proneness to "fitful swerving of passion" in relation to women (ch. 15). This proclivity, though it has something to do with such conventional attitudes as his view of women as weak and in need of protection, is not a mere product of them. George Eliot illustrates Lydgate's inclination toward "impetuous folly" by telling the story of his relationship with Laure, the French actress who seems accidentally to have stabbed her husband in the course of a play. After she leaves Paris, Lydgate finds her in Avignon and asks her to marry him. He knows that this is "like the sudden impulse of a madman," but it is the one thing he is "resolved to do." He is saved from himself when Laure tells him that the stabbing was not accidental—she had become tired of her husband. He returns to his medical studies, "believing that illusions were at an end for him": from now on, "he would take a strictly scientific view of woman, entertaining no expectations but such as were justified before-hand." This is excruciatingly ironic. Instead of putting him on guard against his vulnerability, Lydgate's experience with Laure has the opposite effect; for it fosters the illusion that it has made him proof against such folly in the future.

George Eliot does not minimize the retarding friction Lydgate encounters in his environment: "Oh, sir, the loftiest hopes on earth / Draw lots with meaner hopes; heroic breasts / Breathing bad air, run risk of pestilence" (epigraph to ch. 18); but the moral of his story is that if he had been greater, circumstances would have been less strong against him.

LYDGATE'S TWO SELVES

Having described Lydgate's lofty aspirations and the flaws that will thwart them, George Eliot sets his story in motion by showing how he is gradually ensnared by Middlemarch politics and Rosamond's wiles, until he becomes enmeshed in a tangle of problems from which he is unable to extricate himself. In accounting for Lydgate's fate, George Eliot's rhetoric is more illuminating than it was in the case of Dorothea; but it is often inadequate to her mimetic portrait of his character. She depicts much better than she explains the psychology of a man who is undone, at least in part, by his powerful emotional needs and psychological conflicts.

We get our first glimpse of Lydgate's inner conflicts in the story of Laure, when he compulsively declares his love and asks her to marry him, despite the incongruity of these actions with his habitual behavior and his entire plan for his life: "He had two selves within him apparently, and they must learn to accommodate each other and bear reciprocal impediments" (ch. 15). One of these selves is Lydgate the ambitious scientist and reformer who, through "industrious thought and patient renunciation of small desires," aspires to take his place among the "Shining Ones." But what is the other self? George Eliot tells us that Lydgate is prone to "fitful swerving of passion," that he is capable of "impetuous folly," and that his proposal to Laure "was like the sudden impulse of a madman." With respect to Lydgate's other self, the authorial commentary tends to remain at this level of vagueness and generality; yet this other self is even more responsible for his downfall than his arrogance, class prejudices, and conventional ideas about women.

After the affair of Laure, Lydgate's other self does not surface again until the fateful moment of his engagement to Rosamond. Lydgate is attracted to Rosamond, who has, he thinks, just the kind of "refined, docile" intelligence "one would desire in a woman" (ch. 16); but he only wishes to play at being a little in love and does not mean to become her "captive" (ch. 27). He has the naive belief that if a man "could not love and be wise, surely he could flirt and be wise at the same time." He breaks off the flirtation when Rosamond's aunt, Mrs. Bulstrode, warns that he should stay away if he is not intending to marry because his attentions are discouraging possible suitors; but his absence deeply distresses Rosamond, who has been dreaming of escaping her provincial middle-class life through marriage to this socially superior man. When Lydgate sees her distress during a chance meeting, he forgets everything else, as he did with Laure, and makes another impulsive proposal. After he declares his love, Rosamond makes "her little confession, and he [pours] out words of gratitude and tenderness with impulsive lavishment. In half an hour he left the house an engaged man, whose soul was not his own, but the woman's to whom he had bound himself" (ch. 31).

George Eliot explains Lydgate's behavior by reminding us that this "ambitious man" was "very warm-hearted and rash" (ch. 31), but this characterization is no more illuminating than telling us that he was prone to fitful swerving of passion. The word that leaps out at me in her account of Lydgate's behavior is *gratitude*. Why should this overconfident, benevolently contemptuous man impulsively pour out words of gratitude on hearing Rosamond's confession? And why, after he becomes engaged, is his soul "not his own, but the woman's to whom he [has] bound himself"? Why does Lydgate so easily fall under Rosamond's sway and later find it impossible to emancipate himself? Rosamond is a master manipulator, to be sure; but not every man would lose his soul to her, just as not every woman would be ready, like Dorothea, to say yes to her own doom.

I think Lydgate's behavior toward Laure and Rosamond indicates that a suppressed need for love overpowers him when a triggering event allows it to emerge. George Eliot gives us almost no information about the sources of his emotional hunger, and her rhetoric tends to obscure this side of his personality, but she depicts its effects quite vividly. Perhaps it derives from a childhood in which he experienced little warmth and did not develop a sense of being personally valued. All we know is that his father was a military man, that Lydgate was orphaned when he was only freshly out of public school, and that he was placed in the care of guardians to whom he does not seem to have mattered a great deal and for whom he has little respect. This sketchy biography does not tell us very much, but it does not suggest a warm family life. Lydgate has two siblings, but we never hear that he gives them a thought.

Although Lydgate had already displayed a sense of intellectual superiority by the age of ten and seems immensely confident of his abilities as physician and scientist, he appears to have been a rather isolated person who has not received much affection and is insecure about being lovable. He tries to get his emotional needs met in a safe and indirect way, through service to his fellows for which they will be grateful. He likes medicine because it both calls forth "the highest intellectual strain" and keeps him "in good warm contact" with his neighbors (ch. 16). He has an interest not only in finding the primitive tissue but also in helping John and Elizabeth—especially, we are told, Elizabeth. His medical practice enables him to gain a feeling of human connection, particularly with women, while keeping his distance and avoiding exposure to personal frustration or injury. It is a way of satisfying his two selves at once, although his emotionally needy self receives only meager nourishment.

Lydgate's buried need for love emerges full force, under rather similar conditions, first with Laure and then with Rosamond, both of whom are beautiful, sexually appealing women. He becomes enamored of Laure when he sees her on stage while he is a student in Paris, but he is in love with her "as a man is in love with a woman whom he never expects to speak to" (ch. 15). Here, as later with his patients, he enjoys a sense of emotional connection at a distance. His "remote impersonal passion for her beauty" passes "into personal devotion" after she stabs her husband, who is playing her lover, in what seems to be an accident. When Laure swoons, Lydgate leaps onto the stage, finds a contusion on her head, and lifts her "gently in his arms." George Eliot characterizes this as "the chivalrous kindness which helped to make him morally lovable." Lydgate is indeed chivalrous toward women, finding in their weakness opportunities for getting close to them through service. He "vehemently contend[s]" for Laure's innocence and dwells with "tender thought" on her lot. She is "melancholy" and "grateful," and Lydgate finds her "more and more adorable."

Having come to Laure's rescue gives Lydgate a claim on her, in his own mind at least, that permits him to abandon his detachment and experience his desire for love. He becomes "madly anxious about her affection," afraid that someone else might ask her to marry him (ch. 15). When Laure disappears, no one takes much trouble to find her except Lydgate, who imagines her as a sorrow-stricken wanderer who can find "no faithful comforter"—the role he has assigned to himself. Putting his studies aside, he traces her to Avignon and impulsively asks her to marry him. His adoration does not survive her confession that she "meant to do it" because her husband had wearied her by being "too fond." Feeling chastened by his experience, Lydgate returns to his studies, convinced that he will not make such a mistake again.

That Laure does not, in fact, reciprocate his love restores Lydgate's detachment. He once again suppresses the emotional neediness that threatens his sense of self-worth and his search for glory. His need for love is undiminished, however, and is poised to reemerge when he finds himself in a situation that promises fulfillment.

Such a situation occurs when Lydgate becomes engaged to Rosamond. His proposal is triggered by his sense of Rosamond's need for him. When Mrs. Vincy asks Lydgate to tell her husband that she wants him to come to Stone Court, where she has been nursing Mr. Featherstone, Lydgate calls at the Vincy home rather than at the warehouse because, although he has no intention of courting Rosamond, he wants to receive some assurance that she has missed him. Embarrassed by her agitation in his presence, he becomes quite reserved and speaks of his reason for calling in a manner that crushes Rosamond's hopes. Mortified, she drops her chain work, and when Lydgate raises his eyes after picking it up, he sees "a certain helpless quivering which touched him quite newly, and made him look at Rosamond with a questioning flash" (ch. 31). In a "moment of naturalness," Rosamond lets her tears fall, and an idea thrills "through the recesses within him" that has "a miraculous effect in raising the power of passionate love lying buried there in no sealed sepulchre, but under the lightest, easily pierced mould." Lydgate is "completely mastered by the outrush of tenderness at the sudden belief that this sweet young creature depended on him for her joy." He folds her in his arms "gently and protectingly—he was used to being gentle with the weak and suffering—and kiss[es] each of the two large tears."

Here, as with Laure, what liberates Lydgate's "power of passionate love" is a damsel in distress who depends on him for her rescue. In both cases, his sense of the weakness and dependency of the woman is a large part of her appeal because it makes him feel that he is needed and that his love will be returned. Laure does not want him for a husband, but Rosamond does. The signs of her attachment allow his longings for love to emerge; and once they do, they sweep away everything else, as they did before, and lead him to behave in a way that runs counter to his carefully laid plans.

When Rosamond makes her "confession," Lydgate pours out "words of gratitude and tenderness with impulsive lavishment" because he has been rescued from his emotional isolation and his doubts about being lovable. He feels such tenderness toward Rosamond because he loves her for loving him. One reason Lydgate's soul is no longer his own is that he has allowed himself to experience his hunger for love and he needs Rosamond to gratify it.

LYDGATE'S DEMORALIZATION

As we have seen, Lydgate's is the story of a man who meant to shape his own deeds and alter the world but who comes to be shaped after the average. George Eliot's object is to trace the subtle process of his gradual change. She shows Lydgate losing control of his life because of his involvement with Bulstrode, his marriage to Rosamond, and his descent into debt. These intertwined events are products of both character and circumstance, and they lead to a demoralization that renders Lydgate incapable of coping with his problems. One reason he is mastered by external forces is that his self-confidence is not as robust as it seemed. He thought he had mastery and strength, but when difficulties arise, his resolution slackens, and he is unable to maintain his belief in himself.

We are introduced to Lydgate as a man who has "a fearless expectation of success," a "contempt for petty obstacles," and a "pleasure in fighting" (ch. 13). His conceit is "massive in its claims and benevolently contemptuous" (ch. 15). George Eliot does not explain why Lydgate is this way, but she provides some clues about which we can speculate. By the age of ten, he is displaying a sense of intellectual superiority. It has "already occurred to him that books [are] stuff, and that life [is] stupid." He does not excel in his studies because knowledge seems "a very superficial affair, easily mastered; judging from the conversation of his elders, he had apparently got already more than was necessary for mature life." He looks down on the adults in his world and is ready to pass judgment on life, which seems pointless to him. Such attitudes in one so young seem defensive.

Lydgate may be defensive because he occupies a disadvantaged position in his family and needs to look down on those who he senses are looking down on him. His father, a younger son who had to pursue a military career while his brother became a baronet, dies, having made but little provision for his children, so that Tertius is left dependent on his uncle for his education. When Lydgate asks to be trained as a doctor, it seems "easier to his guardians to grant his request" than "to make any objections on the score of family dignity" (ch. 15). His pursuit of a profession that lowers him socially reinforces the marginality of his position, and the lack of objection may contribute to his feeling of not being regarded as the equal of his cousins. He becomes aloof from his family and scornful toward them.

Lydgate no longer regards knowledge as a superficial affair after he develops an intellectual passion, but that passion only reinforces his contempt for his family and other ordinary mortals. He identifies with the heroes of medical discovery and adopts them as his models, much as Dorothea adopted religious figures as models for herself. Both Lydgate and Dorothea see themselves as belonging to a sublime tradition of their own choosing that sets them apart from the petty concerns of ordinary people.

Like Dorothea, Lydgate wants to achieve something of world-historical importance, with the difference that an epic life seems a real possibility for him. I am not questioning the genuineness of his intellectual passion, but that passion serves many needs, including his need to compensate through self-idealization for his marginal position and emotional insecurity. Lydgate's professional aspirations give shape to his search for glory. He will belong not to the frivolous aristocracy represented by Sir Godwin, but to an aristocracy of talent, of great discoverers and benefactors of humankind. He will become one of the immortals. George Eliot seems to be as much in sympathy with Lydgate's need for glory as she is with Dorothea's.

Although Lydgate rejects the values and way of life associated with his family, he is not as free of the attitudes of his class as he thinks himself to be. He wants it to be "known (without his telling) that he was better born than other county surgeons," and he feels that "there would be an incompatibility in his furniture not being of the best" (ch. 15). An incompatibility with what? He wants to succeed by his own efforts and on his own terms, in a way that will show him to be vastly superior to the other members of his family; but he continues to have a sense of entitlement that is a reflection of his upper-class origins. He has never had to be concerned about money, which he regards as a matter "of no importance to a gentleman" (ch. 18); hence, he incurs excessive expenses in connection with his marriage "without any notion of being extravagant" (ch. 36). He is a radical in "medical reform and the prosecution of discovery," but "in the rest of practical life he walk[s] by hereditary habit." His habits would not tell against him if he had inherited the money required to sustain them, but they are out of keeping with his economic situation and professional objectives.

George Eliot's commentary does much more justice to the way Lydgate's hereditary habits contribute to his undoing than to the role of his self-idealization, which is of at least equal importance. Lydgate's self-idealization leads to his massive claims, to the pride that alienates so many people from him and prevents him from seeking help, and to his inability to assess his situation realistically and rectify his mistakes. It is a principal cause of his demoralization, for it makes him more vulnerable than he would otherwise be, and its collapse leads to rage, self-hatred, and despair.

In his idealized version of himself, Lydgate is a strong, masterful man who is kind to "noodles," for whom he feels sorry and who can have no power over him. He is not only more intelligent than other medical men but more scrupulous as well. He is going to reject the "venal decorations and other humbugs" of his profession (ch. 15) and "set up a disinfecting apparatus within" (ch. 17). When he describes his project to Farebrother, the vicar comments on the difficulty of carrying it out: "You have not only got the old Adam in yourself against you, but you have got all those descendants of the original Adam who form the society around you." Lydgate pays no heed to Farebrother's warnings because he has the illusion that he is free of personal vulnerabilities and impervious to external influences. He will not have to "wear the harness" and go where his "yoke-fellows" pull him, as Farebrother fears he might, because he has "made up [his] mind some time ago to do as little of [that] as possible"; and he feels he has taken adequate measures to protect his independence. Lydgate has an unrealistic belief in his sagacity and the power of his intentions. When Farebrother observes that the world has been too strong for him, that first resolves are not enough, Lydgate feels that the "low estimate of possibilities" by the vicar is the result of his own failure and that he is displaying "a pitiable infirmity of will" (ch. 18).

As we have seen, Lydgate's ideal scenario for his life includes not only the assiduous practice of his profession but also the pursuit of a great idea, and he models himself on the great discoverers who are his inspiration. He wants to make "his life recognised as a factor in the better life of mankind—like other heroes of science who had nothing but an obscure country practice" (ch. 16). He will "keep away from the range of London intrigues, jealousies, and social truckling, and win celebrity, however slowly, as Jenner had done, by the independent value of his work" (ch. 15). He anticipates having to fight his way against people's "ignorance and spite," like his hero Vesalius (ch. 45), and is confident of achieving a similar result.

Lydgate has a fearless expectation of success partly because he believes in his strength and mastery and partly because he feels that he is living up to his lofty values. These things are interrelated: he feels that his strength is as the strength of ten because his heart is pure. He has resolved "that his action [will] be benevolent" (ch. 15), that he will not work for "either place or money" (ch. 46), that he will avoid all temptations to dishonesty, and that he will not "truckle to lies and folly," as so many other do, in the practice of his profession (ch. 17). On the basis of his exalted conception of himself and his obedience to his inner dictates, he makes what George Eliot describes as his massive claims on the world. He should not have to give his mind to practical affairs; he should not have to be attentive to professional etiquette; he should not have to take the feelings and follies of other people into account; he should not even have to be prudent. "How am I to be prudent?" he asks Farebrother. "I just do what comes before me to do.... It isn't possible to square one's conduct to silly conclusions which nobody can foresee" (ch. 45).

Lydgate has made a bargain with fate, according to which his claims will be honored if he lives up to his ideals. This is a purely intrapsychic transaction that has no basis in reality, for the world has not signed on to his deal. Because he is maintaining high standards and is pursuing beneficent goals, his life should work out as he has planned. His problem is not simply that he walks by hereditary habit and does not bring the same kind of intelligence to his human relations that he does to science. He engages in magical thinking that fosters unrealistic expectations and self-defeating behaviors.

Lydgate lives in an illusory world that is gradually invaded by reality. In the Tyke affair, he feels for the first time "the hampering threadlike pressure of small social conditions, and their frustrating complexity"; and he resents "the subjection" that has "been forced upon him": "It would have seemed beforehand like a ridiculous piece of bad logic that he, with his unmixed resolutions of independence and his select purposes, would find himself at the very outset in the grasp of petty alternatives, each of which was repugnant to him. In his student's chambers, he had prearranged his social action quite differently" (ch. 18). Lydgate's resentment derives from a sense of injustice that someone with his resolutions and purposes should be subject to "petty degrading care[s]" (ch. 58). The world is not arranged according to the logic of his magic bargain, as he imagined it to be.

As Lydgate falls into debt and begins to be dunned for payment, he has difficulty facing his situation and dealing with it effectively in part because he is outraged at finding himself "assailed by the vulgar hateful trials" of a man who owes money (ch. 58). He is "amazed, disgusted, that conditions so foreign to all his purposes, so hatefully disconnected with objects he cared to occupy himself with, should have lain in ambush and clutched him when he was unaware." He sees his troubles not as something he has brought on himself but as unfairly imposed from without. He expends so much energy seething at the unfairness of his lot, at how different it is from what he expected, that he has not enough of it left to deal with his problems effectively.

Other factors as well contribute to Lydgate's inability to extricate himself from his situation. One is "his intense pride—his dislike of asking a favour or being under an obligation to anyone" (ch. 58). We must remember, George Eliot tells us, that "he was one of the proudest among the sons of men" (ch. 73). Lydgate's pride is not simply a hereditary habit, a reflection of class; it is a product of his self-idealization, with its accompanying claims.

Perhaps because he felt humiliated as a child by his position in his family, Lydgate has a compelling need for independence and a profound aversion to any form of dependency or subjection. He does not expect to get much from other people, and he does not want to need them for anything. He has protected his pride in part through detachment. His idealized image of himself is that of a man who will avoid getting into a position in which he relies on other people or puts himself in their power, and he has determined to make the necessary renunciations. But then, because of emotional needs over which he has no control, he marries Rosamond Vincy, a woman who also wants the best of everything, and finds himself burdened with debt.

It might have helped if Lydgate could share his problems with friends and family, but his pride prevents him from doing so. He has enabled Farebrother to resolve his money problems by recommending him to Dorothea, who appoints him vicar of Lowick; but when Farebrother senses that Lydgate is in trouble and invites his friend's confidences, Lydgate shrinks "into unconquerable reticence" (ch. 63). It is unbearable to him to discuss "his case," to "imply that he wanted specific things. At that moment, *suicide seemed easier*" (my emphasis). This is a powerful statement. Suicide seems easier than asking for help, because any breach in his pride exposes Lydgate to unbearable self-hatred, which is the other pole of self-idealization.

Lydgate is enraged with Rosamond for having written to Sir Godwin, but he has considered making an application himself and has shrunk from doing so. His self-hatred would be so great if he applied to his uncle that he has rejected the idea, and once Rosamond has written to Sir Godwin, it is too late to turn in that direction for help. If Lydgate had been able to seek assistance sooner, he might not have become so ruinously entangled with Bulstrode. Even the thought of seeking assistance has caused a "reaction of anger that he—he who had so long ago determined to live aloof from such abject calculations, such self-interested anxiety about the inclinations and pockets of men with whom he had been proud to have no aims in common, should have fallen not simply to their level, but to the level of soliciting them" (ch. 64). Lydgate's anger here is not only with the world for having put him in such a position but also with himself for being tempted to sink so far below his lofty conception of himself.

When Lydgate tries to take measures to reduce his expenses, he is repeatedly thwarted by his wife. I shall discuss the dynamics of his relationship with Rosamond in the following section, but I should observe here that this is another situation in which reality turns out to be the opposite of what Lydgate has anticipated. Feeling himself "amply informed" about "the complexities of love and marriage . . . by literature, and that traditional wisdom which is handed down in genial conversation" (ch. 15), Lydgate spins the "gossamer web" of "young love-making," despite his experience with Laure, and expects to find "ideal happiness" in marriage (ch. 36). Relying on conventional ideas about the relation of goose to gander, he expects Rosamond to admire his work without understanding it, to devote herself to fulfilling his needs, and to defer to his masculine wisdom and authority. What he finds is that "his superior knowledge and mental force, instead of being . . . a shrine to consult on all occasions, was simply set aside on every practical question" (ch. 58). He has "an amazed sense of his powerlessness over Rosamond." Here, as elsewhere, he is amazed when his claims are denied, when his version of reality turns out to have been false. He had expected to be master in his marriage, but Rosamond masters him, and Lydgate finds himself in the hateful position of dependency and subjection. Instead of being in control, he begins to feel a "half-maddening sense of helplessness" (ch. 65).

George Eliot emphasizes that Lydgate cannot cope with Rosamond not only because of her insensibility to his point of view, her conviction of absolute rightness, her deviousness, and her imperviousness to reason, but also because of his "wavering resolve" (ch. 64), his "creeping paralysis," his "slackening resolution" (ch. 58). His slackening resolution is partly the result of "her torpedo contact" (ch. 64), but it is also the product of a demoralization of which Rosamond is only one of the causes.

Lydgate collapses very quickly. In a rather short time, he goes from being a supremely self-confident man with very ambitious goals and a fearless expectation of success to being to an "intensely miserable" man (ch. 58), enfeebled by his frustrations. After having lived in a dream world all through his years as a student, he finds his illusions being shattered almost as soon as he embarks on his career. When his claims are not honored, his idealized image of himself is called into question; and self-doubt weakens his sense of potency and of the inevitability of success. He takes pleasure in fighting and zestfully engages in a feud with other medical men, but only while he still believes in his star. He is rapidly drained by conflict when no easy victory is in sight and others are not obeying the logic of his bargain with fate.

Lydgate's initial response to his frustrations is amazement, disgust, and anger with the world for betraying his expectations; but he soon begins to react similarly toward himself. His idealized image collapses not only because the world fails to honor his claims but also because once he gets into trouble, he can no longer live up to his inner dictates. The arrogant, self-satisfied man begins to experience a "creeping self-despair" (ch. 64), a "self-discontent" that, George Eliot observes, makes "more than half our bitterness under grievances, wife or husband included" (ch. 58). Lydgate's demoralization is in large part the product of his emerging self-hatred, of his sense of how far he has fallen below his own expectations of himself. Having swung from self-idealization to self-contempt, he now feels like his despised self. He suffers from a "sense of mental degeneracy" (ch. 66). He takes a dose or two of opium in an effort to escape his pain. He tries gambling, which he had formerly despised, and subsequently feels disgusted with himself. He has become helpless, dependent, self-interested, anxious about the inclinations and pockets of men like his uncle, and subjugated to the will of a woman from whom he had expected veneration and obedience.

LYDGATE AND ROSAMOND

Lydgate's submission to Rosamond is one of the most important causes for the frustration of his ambitions. Even after he has been mired in Bulstrode's disgrace, he has a chance to continue his work at the fever hospital and to resume his research once Dorothea proffers her moral and financial support. She tells him that he can "still win a great fame," but Lydgate no longer trusts himself enough to accept her offer: "I meant everything to be different with me. I thought I had more strength and mastery" (ch. 76). He is afraid of sinking "into the degradation of being pensioned" for work never achieved. Moreover, he knows that he may have to leave town, despite his desire to stay and see himself vindicated, because that is what Rosamond wants. He feels "despair as to his being able to carry out any purpose that Rosamond had set her mind against." He tells Dorothea: "It is impossible for me now to do anything—to take any step without considering my wife's happiness. The thing that I might like to do if I were alone, is become impossible to me. I can't see her miserable." " 'I know, I know—you could not give her pain, if you were not obliged to do it,' " Dorothea replies, "with keen memory of her own life."

Lydgate feels that it will be difficult to keep his "soul alive" in the kind of life he will now have to lead but that he must relinquish his professional objectives if he is not to make Rosamond miserable. Apparently, keeping his soul alive is not a sufficient reason to cause his wife pain. Like Dorothea, Lydgate is prepared to say yes to his own doom. Dorothea cannot disapprove, and neither can the author, who seems to feel that Lydgate is doing what he should. From a psychological point of view, Dorothea and Lydgate do not look so different as the rhetoric suggests. Both are drawn into disastrous marriages by emotional hunger and illusions about the partner, both become disenchanted, and both are unable to resist the partner's demands. Lydgate's fate gives us an idea of what Dorothea's would have been had the author not intervened on her behalf.

Even though Lydgate's misreading of Rosamond may be largely the result of conventional attitudes that he shares with other men of his time and class, his inability to say no to her, even in order to preserve his precious vocation, must be understood in light of his individual psychology. His inability derives in part, of course, from the emotional neediness that led to his impulsive proposal. After marriage, he can no longer live in the "dreamland" in which Rosamond Vincy "appeared to be that perfect piece of womanhood who would reverence her husband's mind" without really understanding it (ch. 58). He soon realizes that Rosamond cares nothing for "the more impersonal ends of his profession and his scientific study," both of which she finds to be disagreeable. His disenchantment is expedited by the visit of Captain Lydgate, which makes him aware that Rosamond wishes he were more like his fashionable relatives. He begins to distinguish between the "adoration" he has imagined her to feel "and the attraction towards a man's talent because it gives him prestige, and is like an order in his button-hole or an Honourable before his name." He has an "amazed sense of his powerlessness" when Rosamond, having gone riding against his orders, loses her baby as a result, and he is "astounded" to find "that affection [does] not make her compliant"—as it does him. Once again, Lydgate's astonishment is a response to the failure of reality to conform to his expectations.

For a while Lydgate remains confident of Rosamond's affection, despite her lack of compliance; but he cannot help doubting it in the face of her growing aloofness. He tries desperately to maintain his belief in her love and to be tender toward her despite his misgivings, because he "dread[s] a future without affection" (ch. 64). This dread, combined with her lack of an equivalent emotional engagement, gives Rosamond tremendous power over him. When Lydgate begins to have "an alarmed foresight of her irrevocable loss of love for him, and the consequent dreariness of their lives," he is held, "as with pincers," by the "need of accommodating himself to her nature" (ch. 65). George Eliot attributes Lydgate's dread of losing Rosamond's love to "the ready fullness of his emotions," a very vague explanation.

What is most striking to me about Lydgate is not that his need for love makes him compliant but that his compliance continues after it becomes clear that Rosamond has little or no affection to give him. When he realizes that his wife no more "identif[ies] herself with him than if they had been creatures of different species and opposing interests," he thinks that he must find his satisfactions in his work and looks at her with "a despairing acceptance of the distance she [is] placing between them" (ch. 58). However, later he tells her: "You and I cannot have opposite interests. I cannot part my happiness from yours" (ch. 65). Since Rosamond cannot identify herself with his interests, the only way Lydgate can preserve their union is to identify himself with hers. His only hope for keeping his soul alive is to separate his happiness from hers, to stand up for his own legitimate needs, but he cannot do it. Instead, he sacrifices himself without any real hope of reciprocated affection.

There are a number of reasons, I think, for Lydgate's behavior. George Eliot describes him as "bowing his neck under the yoke like a creature who had talons, but who had Reason too, which often reduces us to meekness" (ch. 58; see also the epigraph to chapter 65). It is not reason that produces Lydgate's meekness, though his understanding is far greater than Rosamond's. He can comprehend her situation and enter into her feelings, whereas she is devoid of empathy and can entertain only her own point of view. As with Dorothea and Casuabon, the partner who becomes aware of the other's equivalent center of self feels compelled to submit to that person's unreasonable demands. This is not a case of the domination of the rational partner by the irrational one, as George Eliot's rhetoric suggests, but of the self-effacing partner's giving in to the aggressive one, who has no scruples about exploiting the other in order to get what he or she wants. George Eliot cannot entertain the idea that it may be necessary to frustrate the excessive claims of another when fulfilling them will ruin one's life. But again, though I may quarrel with her endorsement of her protagonists' self-sacrificial behavior (not only Dorothea's and Lydgate's but also Mary Garth's), I think that her mimetic portrayals are brilliant and that her characters behave as they must.

Lydgate behaves as he does toward Laure not only because his belief in her emotional need allows him to experience his own, but also because her ostensibly helpless position appeals to the chivalric component of his idealized image, which he seeks to actualize by coming to her rescue. He has a similar fantasy when he proposes to Rosamond, whose tears and evident misery move him. He will be the comforter of this woman whose happiness depends on him. George

Eliot tells us that "this rather abrupt man had much tenderness in his manners towards women, seeming to have always present in his imagination the weakness of their frames and the delicate poise of their health in both body and mind" (ch. 64).

I find it difficult to locate the author's attitude here. Is Lydgate's tenderness a mark of the "chivalrous kindness" that makes him "morally lovable" (ch. 15) or of his conventional, condescending attitude toward women, who turn out to be much tougher than he? Rosamond, Dorothea, and Mary Garth are far less fragile psychologically than Lydgate, Will, and Fred; and Mrs. Garth is a tower of strength. This is a novel about strong women and rather pathetic men. The other weak men make out better than Lydgate because they fall in love with good women rather than with Rosamonds. In *Middlemarch*, men's fates lie in women's hands.

In any event, Lydgate's submissiveness toward Rosamond even after he realizes that he was mistaken about her affection is partly motivated by his sense of her vulnerability and his assumption of the role of protector. He cannot risk frustrating her to protect his own interests, because if she does not get what she wants, she may be destroyed. Signs of her unhappiness make him intensely uncomfortable. When he tells her that men will come to make an inventory of their possessions, "her tears cut him to the heart" (ch. 58); and when she later expresses the wish that she had died with the baby, George Eliot says that her "words and tears" were "omnipotent over a loving-hearted man" (ch. 65).

I think it is less Lydgate's loving-heartedness than his guilt that is responsible for Rosamond's omnipotence. He marries her because she depends on him for her joy, and now she wishes she were dead. Lydgate had meant everything to be different. Rosamond touches "him in a spot of keenest feeling by implying that she [was] deluded with a false vision of happiness in marrying him" (ch. 64). Because of his sense of her feminine weakness and his masculine strength, Lydgate takes far too much responsibility for Rosamond and the failure of the marriage and feels that he must do whatever it takes to make his wife happy. "It is part of manliness," says George Eliot, "for a husband to feel keenly the fact that an inexperienced girl has got into trouble by marrying him" (ch. 58). The author seems here to be endorsing the chivalric ideal, which though protective of women treats them as lesser beings. She presents Lydgate as undone not only by his faults but also by what she regards as his virtues. Rosamond senses Lydgate's feeling of responsibility and plays brilliantly on his guilt. It becomes "more bearable" for Lydgate "to do without tenderness for himself than to see that his own tenderness could make no amends for the lack of other things to her" (ch. 69).

Another reason Lydgate sacrifices himself to Rosamond without any hope of receiving her affection is that he must prove to himself that he loves her. He realizes that for him "the tender devotedness" of "the ideal wife must be renounced, and life must be taken up on a lower stage of expectation, as it is by men who have lost their limbs"; but Rosamond still has "a hold on his heart, and it [is] his intense desire that the hold should remain strong. In marriage, the certainty, 'She will never love me much,' is easier to bear than the fear, 'I shall love her no more' " (ch. 64). I am not sure about the general validity of this strange pronouncement, but it clearly applies to Lydgate. He needs to maintain a loving stance toward his wife, whatever her treatment of him, because he will hate himself if he cannot. His idealized image dictates that he *should* love this poor, weak creature whose happiness depends on him.

As Lydgate becomes demoralized and his resolution weakens, it is no longer possible for him to resist Rosamond or to fight for himself. He feels her needs to be more important than his, and relieving her misery becomes the motive that governs his life. The pain of "foreseeing that Rosamond [will] come to regard him chiefly as the cause of disappointment and unhappiness to her" is "more acute" than "the sufferings of his own pride from humiliations past and to come" (ch. 69).

George Eliot is referring to the blows to Lydgate's pride from his financial and professional humiliations, but his pride is suffering in his relations with Rosamond also, and he needs to vindicate himself as a husband and to live up to his chivalric ideals by making her happy somehow. The more hopeless he becomes about realizing his professional and scientific ambitions, the more important it becomes not to fail as a husband. Rosamond's frustration of Lydgate's ambitions gives her more power over him, for the collapse of his dream of glory makes him all the more desperate to maintain his marriage. If that fails, he will have nothing at all. He cannot free himself from Rosamond emotionally, but feeling that he loves her ennobles his enslavement and makes it more tolerable.

LYDGATE'S SAD SACRIFICE

Middlemarch ends on a somber note as George Eliot mourns Dorothea's sad sacrifice. She bestows much less sympathy on Lydgate, presumably because he brought his misery on himself through his arrogance and spots of commonness; but it seems to me that he is just as much a victim of his compensatory needs and the attitudes of his society as Dorothea is and that his fate is far sadder than hers. Lydgate is caught in a crossfire of conflicting shoulds and is bound to hate himself, whatever he does. To save himself professionally, he must cause Rosamond pain; but if he does that, he will hate himself for failing to love and protect her. To make Rosamond happy, he must abandon his professional goals, a choice that not only frustrates his search for glory and thwarts self-actualization but makes him despise himself for his lack of strength and mastery. Full of rage, self-hatred, and despair, he is an intensely miserable man.

Lydgate's final surrender occurs in the scene in which Dorothea offers her support. Dorothea is shocked at the change in his face, the result of "the persistent presence of resentment and despondency" (ch. 76). The resentment is directed at the world and at Rosamond, and the despondency is the result of the collapse of both his marriage and his hopes for medical discovery and reform. Instead of envisioning himself as taking his place among the immortals, Lydgate has been "seeing all life as one who is dragged and struggling amid the throng." Because of his close association with Bulstrode, whose "character has enveloped" him, and the widespread suspicion of his complicity in the death of Raffles, Lydgate feels that he is "simply blighted—like a damaged ear of corn—the business is done and can't be undone." When Dorothea offers to help undo the damage, Lydgate cannot accept, partly because he has lost confidence in himself and partly because he cannot do anything of which Rosamond would not approve.

Dorothea feels somewhat discontented with herself and her lot, but she finds emotional fulfillment in marriage and motherhood and a life filled with "beneficent activity" (Finale). She has no regrets about having married Will. Despite her frustration at not having attained an epic life, she is much better off than Lydgate, who does not merely fail to actualize his idealized image but becomes its opposite. "I must do as other men do," he tells Dorothea, "and think what will please the world and bring in money" (ch. 76). This is precisely what he had determined not to do, so that he could pursue his research and carry out his reforms.

Having relinquished his dream of glory, Lydgate now has a depressing new scenario for his life: "[I must] look for a little opening in the London crowd, and push myself; set up in a watering-place, or go to some southern town where there are plenty of idle English, and get myself puffed,—that is the sort of shell I must creep into and try to keep my soul alive in." Dorothea assures him that she can clear his name: "I can say of you what will make it stupidity to suppose that you would be bribed to do a wickedness." " 'I don't know,' " Lydgate replies, "with something like a groan in his voice. 'I have not taken a bribe yet. But there is a pale shade of bribery which is sometimes called prosperity.' " Lydgate achieves prosperity, thus doing what Rosamond wants, but at the expense of his professional goals and ideals. He becomes a fashionable physician and writes a treatise on gout, "a disease which has a good deal of wealth on its side" (Finale). Others view him as a success, but he "always regard[s] himself as a failure," suffering a lifetime of self-contempt because he has abandoned his lofty objectives and taken the bribe.

Lydgate's sad sacrifice preserves his marriage, thereby saving him from the self-hatred he would feel if he had failed in what he regards as his duty to Rosamond; but he never comes to terms with his anger and bitterness. When it looks as though their possessions will be sold to pay his debts, Lydgate begs Rosamond to forgive him "for this misery. Let us only love one another" (ch. 69). Rosamond plans to return to her parents until he can provide a comfortable home but says that she will not leave until tomorrow: " 'Oh I would wait a little longer than to-morrow—there is no knowing what may happen,' said Lydgate, with bitter irony. 'I may get my neck broken, and that may make things easier to you.' " George Eliot observes that "it was Lydgate's misfortune and Rosamond's too, that his tenderness towards her . . . was inevitably interrupted by these outbursts of indignation," which are "in danger of making the more persistent tenderness unacceptable." Lydgate's oscillation between tenderness and indignation persists through the remainder of the marriage, until he dies prematurely of diphtheria. He sacrifices himself to Rosamond but blames her bitterly, partly because he is externalizing his hatred of himself. Afraid that his rage will crush her and destroy their marriage, he tries mightily to suppress it, but his "despairing resentment" (ch. 75) keeps bursting out in his bitter comments.

George Eliot shows us Lydgate struggling to adjust to his situation but failing to do so. Before his meeting with Dorothea, he has "almost learned the lesson that he must bend himself to [his wife's] nature, and that because she came short in her sympathy, he must give the more" (ch. 75). As a result of the meeting, Dorothea goes to see and save Rosamond, persisting even after she finds her with Will. She assures her of Lydgate's innocence in the Raffles affair and reports that Lydgate has told her "that he could not be happy in doing anything which made you unhappy" (ch. 81). Having been thus reassured by Dorothea and rebuffed by Will, Rosamond is "meek enough to nestle under the old despised shelter. And the shelter was still there: Lydgate had accepted his narrowed lot with sad resignation. He had chosen the fragile creature, and had taken the burthen of her life upon his arms. He must walk as he could, carrying that burthen pitifully" (ch. 81). It is difficult to distinguish between rhetoric and mimesis here, but George Eliot seems to be endorsing Lydgate's sad sacrifice.

From the author's point of view, Lydgate has no choice but to bend himself to Rosamond's nature and carry the burden pitifully. I am not a clinician, but I have often had fantasies about being Lydgate's therapist and exploring some better options with him. There is no better option that would not involve frustrating Rosamond, but she is not as fragile as Lydgate thinks; and, in my view, he is not morally obliged to sacrifice himself to satisfy her narrow demands. Why must he be the only one to suffer for her pettiness and egocentricity? Dorothea and Lydgate cannot stand up for themselves if it means causing pain to their partner, not because they are noble but because to do so would threaten an important component of their idealized conception of themselves and generate a self-hatred even more un- bearable than the spoiling of their lives.

In Lydgate we see the price of the kind of self-sacrifice George Eliot glorifies but that she saves Dorothea from having to make. He does not accept his constricted lot with sad resignation, for his resent- ment and rage keep erupting. The self-righteous Rosamond is reason- ably happy as long as she gets her way, but Lydgate is in agony for the rest of his life. As the years go by, he "oppose[s] her less and less whence Rosamond conclude[s] that he [has] learned the value of her opinion" (Finale); but Lydgate has simply become more and more hopeless about his ability to reach her in any way. To the last, he occasionally lets "slip a bitter speech which [is] more memorable than the signs he had made of his repentance. He once called her his basil plant; and when she asked for an explanation, said that basil was a plant which had flourished wonderfully on a murdered man's brains." The reference, of course, is to Keats' "Isabella," a poem in which the heroine keeps the head of her murdered lover in a pot in which a basil plant flourishes on the nutriment thus supplied. This is a memorable speech indeed. It is hard to imagine a bitterer remark.

4

"A Dreadful Plain Girl": Mary Garth

A FOIL TO THE EGOISTS

In *Experiments in Life* I argued that George Eliot was profoundly influenced by positivist epistemology, which distinguished between two fundamentally different approaches to reality, the subjective and the objective, the metaphysical and the empirical. From the positivistic point of view, the essential characteristic of the subjective or metaphysical approach is that it converts the internal into the external, thereby making the subjective and objective orders identical. There is no clear distinction between self and nonself; the world is an extension of the ego. Abstractions—mental constructs—are reified. The desires of the heart, the preconceptions of the intellect, and the qualities of human nature are projected onto outer phenomena and then assumed to have an external existence. For the positivists, the external world possesses an autonomous order that does not necessarily correspond to the order of thought; to pursue truth, it is necessary to submit the mind to the world in such a way that the order of ideas reflects the order of things.

I further observed that the great division among George Eliot's characters is between those who approach the world subjectively and those who approach it objectively. In her view, we are all born egoists, taking the world as an udder to feed our supreme selves. Maturation is the process of recognizing the independent existence of outer phenomena (including other people) and yielding up the supremacy of the self. Eliot's egoists see things in their relation to the self rather than in their relations to one another. Egoists tend to assume that the order of things corresponds to their desires; and instead of cultivating a true vision of causal sequences, they delight in imaginatively shaping the future to accord with present wishes. Egoists are often gamblers. They may engage in actual games of chance, or they may be worshipers of Fortune and live in hope that the realization of their desires, or escape from punishment, will somehow be granted to them. They frequently have a love of power, a craving for mastery over other people. Sometimes they have the illusion that others must want to do what they desire, and sometimes they deliberately contrive to have them act as they wish. They give the feelings of others no importance.

George Eliot's novels repeatedly show that the subjective approach to reality is unsatisfactory both as an ethical choice and as a means to personal satisfaction. Egoists do not regard others as fellow beings with an equivalent center of self but either as extensions of themselves or as objects to be manipulated. This often brings great suffering to those so regarded. Because egoists' wishes are not chastened by submission to necessity and their actions are not governed by a true vision of the relations of things, such people remain at the mercy of circumstances, and their desires are more often frustrated than fulfilled. The comfortable illusions with which they surround themselves may be shattered at any moment; and because their self-centeredness has cut them off from genuine contact with the world and their fellows, egoists, if disillusioned, have no relief from their loneliness and despair. The claims they make for themselves can never be satisfied; and they may find the world to be a dull, drab, frustrating place.

For George Eliot, the second stage of moral development is one in which the egoist is subject to painful disenchantment, which makes the world seem alien and the self insignificant. The third stage entails developing a realistic assessment of oneself and one's place in the world and a sense of belonging to the human community, which gives meaning and value to life.

I argued in *Experiments in Life* that one of George Eliot's chief interests in *Middlemarch* is the presentation on a large scale of the roles which the subjective and objective habits of mind play in shaping human destiny. The extreme egoists in the novel include Casaubon, Fred Vincy, Rosamond, Bulstrode, and Featherstone. Dorothea, Lydgate, and Ladislaw are mixed cases. They have egoistic traits, especially early in the novel, but grow out of them as a result of painful experience; and they are not extremely subjective to begin with. Lydgate exemplifies the objective approach to reality in his scientific work, while Dorothea comes to exemplify it in her human relations.

In this context, the Garths play an important illustrative role in the novel, for they all stand in contrast to the egoistic characters. Caleb's idealism and unselfishness contribute to his poverty and make him seem naive and impractical at times; but he understands the nature of things, does excellent work, and gains a sense of impersonal immortality through his contribution to future generations. His skill and conscientiousness are eventually rewarded, and he achieves financial success without having to compromise himself. Mrs. Garth has "that rare sense which discerns what is unalterable and submits to it without murmuring" (ch. 24).

Mary Garth is perhaps the chief foil to the egoists. Unlike them, she "neither trie[s] to create illusions nor indulge[s] in them for her own behoof" (ch. 12). Whereas Fred and Rosamond are spoiled and become selfish and discontented as a result, Mary, whose lot has been much harder, experiences no great frustration: "for, having early had strong reason to believe that things were not likely to be arranged for her peculiar satisfaction, she wasted no time in astonishment and annoyance at that fact" (ch. 33). Not only Fred and Rosamond but all the egoists have the illusion that things are arranged for their particular satisfaction. Here one can include the early Dorothea, who sees Casaubon as her means of leading an epic life, and Casaubon, who sees her as being providentially provided to assist him in completing "The Key to All Mythologies." Unlike the egoists, Mary has "learned to make no unreasonable claims" (ch. 33). As a result, she is less vulnerable to frustration and less likely to be destructive to others. Instead of ruining the man who loves her through selfish demands, as does Rosamond, Mary is instrumental in saving Fred from a wasted life and helping him to mature. In the Finale, George Eliot draws a striking contrast between the marriages of Fred and Mary on the one hand and Lydgate and Rosamond on the other.

Mary's story is a variation on the vindication plot, as is Caleb's, too, in a way. Her virtues are appreciated from the beginning by her father, Fred, and the narrator; but she is undervalued by Mrs. Vincy, looked down on by Rosamond, ignored by Lydgate, and abused by Featherstone. In time she is cherished not only by Fred but also by Farebrother, whose family wants him to marry her. The outcome of the action and the judgment of the community mirror the narrator's praise.

As I have reread *Middlemarch* over the years, I have become more and more interested in Mary, who is far more complicated than a thematic reading suggests, and have found myself increasingly troubled by her relationship with Fred. Critics have generally regarded her as a normative character, a "near perfect creature" (Karl 1995, 497), as I did in *Experiments in Life*; but I have come to see that, like Lydgate and Dorothea, Mary is in danger of ruining her life because of her psychological vulnerabilities. As she does with Dorothea, George Eliot celebrates her heroine's potentially self-destructive behavior and saves her from its consequences by authorial manipulations. While the rhetoric presents Mary as a nearly perfect creature, the mimesis shows her committing herself to a man of whom she does not approve and risking her happiness on his not very probable reformation. George Eliot attributes many of Mary's virtues to her "hard experience" (ch. 25), which has freed her from claims and illusions and made her sensitive to the feelings of others; but the author fails to see the extent to which Mary's hardships have damaged her psychologically.

MARY'S HARD LIFE

George Eliot tells us that Mary has suffered from hard experience, that she has had strong reason to believe that things are not likely to be arranged for her satisfaction, and that "if a belief flatter[s] her vanity" she dismisses it "as ridiculous, having early had much exercise in such dismissals" (ch. 57). These are striking statements, but exactly what are the tribulations Mary has endured and how have they affected her? As childhoods in Victorian fiction go, hers was a relatively fortunate one. She grows up in a loving but not overindulgent family and is the favorite of her father, who is proud of her. The Garths are poor and lead a humble existence, but we are told that they do "not mind it" (ch. 24). Caleb and Susan get on well together, despite Caleb's failure in business. "Adoring her husband's virtues," Susan "had very early made up her mind to his incapacity of minding his own interests, and had met the consequences cheerfully." Mary's parents are not embittered by their difficulties but are confident of their values and free from envy, competitiveness, and resentment. Their relationship with Mary is marked by mutual love and esteem. "I consider my father and mother," she tells Featherstone, "the best part of myself" (ch. 25). Mary lives up to her parents' high standards, to which she subscribes, and they approve of her. What, then, is the "hard experience" that might have made Mary "cynical if she had not had parents whom she honoured, and a well of affectionate gratitude within her" (ch. 33)?

Mary's severest hardship seems to have been her lack of beauty. Almost the first thing we hear about her is Mrs. Vincy's remark that she is "a dreadful plain girl" (ch. 11), and it is clear that Mary is very conscious of her physical unattractiveness. When Fred says that he thinks John Waule, another of Featherstone's nephews, is in love with her, Mary replies: "I should have thought that I, at least, might have been safe from all that. I have no ground for the nonsensical vanity of fancying everybody who comes near me is in love with me" (ch. 14). This bitter remark may contain a jab at Mary's opposites, women like Fred's sister, Rosamond.

We first meet Mary when Rosamond comes to Stone Court in hopes of encountering Lydgate; and the narrator's comparison of the two girls occasions an important, though somewhat mystifying, passage. Rosamond has "hair of infantine fairness" and "eyes of heavenly blue, deep enough to hold the most exquisite meanings an ingenious beholder could put into them."

> Mary Garth, on the contrary, had the aspect of an ordinary sinner; she was brown; her curly dark hair was rough and stubborn; her stature was low; and it would not be true to declare, in satisfactory antithesis, that she had all the virtues. Plainness has its peculiar temptations and vices quite as much as beauty; it is apt either to feign amiability, or, not feigning it, to show all the repulsiveness of discontent: at any rate, to be called an ugly thing in contrast with that lovely creature your companion, is apt to produce some effect beyond a sense of fine veracity and fitness in the phrase. At the age of two-and-twenty Mary had certainly not attained that perfect good sense and good principle which are usually recommended to the less fortunate girl, as if they were to be obtained in quantities ready mixed, with a flavour of resignation as required. Her shrewdness had a streak of satiric bitterness continually renewed and never carried utterly out of sight, except by a strong current of gratitude towards those who, instead of telling her that she ought to be contented, did something to make her so. (ch. 12)

This passage suggests both Mary's pain at being regarded as ugly and its effect on her psyche. Although the narrator goes on to say that "advancing womanhood had tempered her plainness" and that "Rembrandt would have painted her with pleasure," it is clear that Mary has been badly hurt by her sense of her own unattractiveness and that George Eliot is consciously aware of some of the damaging consequences. That she is not conscious of all of them is not surprising, for Mary's problem was very close to her own. She portrays the consequences mimetically, however.

In describing the "peculiar temptations and vices" of "plainness," the narrator remarks that "it is apt either to feign amiability, or, not feigning it, to show all the repulsiveness of discontent." I find this observation puzzling because, whatever its general truth, it does not seem to apply to Mary Garth, at least as the author would have us perceive her. Mary does not feign amiability, and she is favorably contrasted with the egoists because she makes no unreasonable claims and therefore feels no annoyance when things are not arranged for her satisfaction. I do not think that George Eliot wants us to see Mary as showing "the repulsiveness of discontent."

Yet the passage as a whole makes it clear that Mary *is* discontented. She has a streak of satiric bitterness and resents people who tell her she ought to be contented, without doing something to make her so. Mary has not attained the required resignation but feels rage at the hardship of her lot, at not being properly valued and treated with kindness. "If you made her angry," George Eliot tells us, "she would not raise her voice, but would probably say one of the bitterest things you had ever tasted the flavour of" (ch. 40). In Mary is a good deal of aggression just waiting to come out.

The Garths are often thought of as a group, and they have many traits in common, but it is important to recognize the differences between Mary and her parents. Whereas Mrs. Garth discerns what is unalterable and submits to it without murmuring, Mary is simmering with indignation. Her mother was not "inclined to sarcasm and to impulsive sallies, as Mary was" (ch. 24). When Farebrother quotes Mary's remark that Fred "would be one of those ridiculous clergymen who help to make the whole clergy ridiculous," Caleb laughs and says, "She gets her tongue from you, Susan." " 'Not its flippancy, father,' said Mary quickly, fearing that her mother would be displeased" (ch. 40). Mary knows that her parents do not share her acerbity and that they would not wish it ascribed to them. They are in no danger of becoming cynics, as Mary would be, were it not for the few people who have won her respect and gratitude.

The fact that she is in danger of becoming a cynic suggests that Mary feels unfairly treated by life. Although this feeling seems to arise from experiences outside her family, the Garth's poverty and low social status may be contributing factors. We are told that these conditions do not bother her parents, but I think they do bother Mary, especially in conjunction with her homeliness. They reinforce her sense that others regard her as insignificant, undesirable, and unworthy of notice, consideration, or respect.

Mary's sense of injustice may have been exacerbated by the experience of growing up in the shadow of Rosamond Vincy. There is a slight family connection between the Garths and the Vincys, in that Peter Featherstone's first wife was the sister of Caleb Garth and his second was Mrs. Vincy's sister. The Vincys feel too superior, socially and financially, to want to have much to do with the Garths, but the children become friends and play together. Mary and Rosamond go to the same provincial school, Mary as an articled pupil. Mary is consistently inferior to Rosamond in terms of social position, money, and beauty. It is Rosamond who has all the advantages and receives admiring attention, while people seem hardly aware of Mary's existence. When Rosamond asks Mary how she likes Lydgate, Mary replies: "There is no question of liking at present. My liking always wants some little kindness to kindle it. I am not magnanimous enough to like people who speak to me without seeming to see me" (ch. 12). Whereas Lydgate makes Mary feel like a nonentity, he is immediately attentive to Rosamond. As the wedding of Lydgate and Rosamond approaches, we find Mary sewing handkerchiefs for the bride.

Although George Eliot does not portray Mary's hard life in detail, we can get a sense of it if we pay close attention to the information she provides. Mary seems comfortable in the bosom of her family but unhappy in the world outside. Although she no doubt feels herself to be more sensitive and intelligent than most of the young women with whom she associates, she is at a disadvantage in relation to them because of her poverty, plainness, and low social station. Mary's remark to Rosamond that she takes Fred's part because "he is the only person who takes the least trouble to oblige me" (ch. 12) suggests that she has lived in a world in which she has been made to feel last and least, like Jane Austen's Fanny Price. Except for her family and Fred, no one shows concern for her feelings. Her resentment of Lydgate's manner toward her may be a result of her having often been spoken to without seeming to have been seen. When, late in the novel, she becomes aware of Farebrother's interest, she cannot help having "fleeting visions of . . . new dignities and an acknowledged value of which she had often felt the absence" (ch. 57). Unlike her parents, Mary deeply craves status and recognition.

Part of the hardship in Mary's life, though not in its earliest phases, derives from the abuse she has to endure from Peter Featherstone. Featherstone wanted Rosamond to live with him, but she refused; and Mary accepts the post because, as Rosamond puts it, "she likes that better than being a governess" (ch. 11). Although Mary is his niece, Featherstone orders her about like a servant, flaunts his favoritism toward Fred and Rosamond, and constantly injures her feelings. Fred is distressed to see Mary's red eyes. When he tells her that it is a shame she "should stay here to be bullied in that way," she replies: "Oh, I have an easy life—by comparison" (ch. 14). The comparison is with being a teacher or governess. It is one of the puzzles of Mary's character that she finds living with Featherstone easier than doing the work for which she has been trained. Given the indignities of her position at Stone Court, her preference is difficult to understand.

Mary's is another story in *Middlemarch* that has to do with a problem of vocation. Because of her family's financial position, Mary must make a contribution, a duty she accepts without question. But what is she to do? She tells Fred that she has "tried being a teacher" but does not feel fit for it because her "mind is too fond of wandering on its own way" (ch. 14). She says that she prefers caring for Featherstone because "everything here I can do as well as any one else could; perhaps better than some." She continues, "I think any hardship is better than pretending to do what one is paid for, and never really doing it." It is difficult to believe that Mary lacks the competence to be a good teacher. Has she really not done her job? If her mind wanders, it may be because of an aversion to teaching that is related to her character and experience. As an articled pupil, she no doubt had to render some service in exchange for her education, perhaps as a teacher's apprentice. She may have resented her disadvantaged position and the lack of consideration with which she was treated by comparison with the other girls.

It is striking that Mary has so little to offer by way of explanation of her distaste for the only career for which she is qualified. After Featherstone's death, she decides to accept a position in a school at York, rather than become a governess, because she feels "less unfit to teach in a school than in a family" (ch. 40):

> "Teaching seems to me the most delightful work in the world," said Mrs. Garth [who had taught before her marriage], with a touch of rebuke in her tone. "I could understand your objection to it if you had not knowledge enough, Mary, or if you disliked children."
>
> "I suppose we never quite understand why another dislikes what we like, mother," said Mary, rather curtly. "I am not fond of a school-room: I like the outside world better. It is a very inconvenient fault of mine." (ch. 40)

Mary's testiness suggests that this is a sensitive issue for her and that she cannot explain her dislike, either because she feels that her mother would not understand or because she does not comprehend it herself.

Her objection *is* difficult to understand, and her dislike of teaching *is* a very inconvenient fault; for it leaves her not only without an occupation, but without a way of fulfilling her duty to her family in a manner that she does not find painful. Teaching is more disagreeable than caring for Featherstone, which seems a dreadful occupation; and for Mary, being a governess is worse yet, perhaps because the position of a governess in a family is even more uncomfortable than that of a teacher whose pupils are better-off than she. Mrs. Vincy is afraid that by caring for Featherstone, Mary will earn a place in his will, something of which she is not worthy, because Featherstone's first wife brought him no money, as her sister had, and because "Mary Garth is a dreadful plain girl—more fit for a governess" (ch. 11). Mary may be resisting what seems to be the inevitable sad fate of ill-favored girls with no money.

Mary says that she likes "the outside world" better than a schoolroom, but there is no evidence that she likes the outside world at all. When Caleb becomes the agent for Sir James and Mr. Brooke, his financial troubles are over; and it immediately occurs to him that now Mary need not leave home: "Mary, write and give up that school. Stay and help your mother. I'm as pleased as Punch, now I've thought of that" (ch. 40). Mary is also delighted, for this is just what she wants. She tells Fred: "Everything seems too happy for me all at once. I thought it would always be part of my life to long for home" (ch. 40). Home is the only place where Mary feels valued; in the outside world, she is a poor, plain, insignificant girl. She may have preferred living at Stone Court to being a teacher or a governess because at least there she would be a member of the family and would be close to her parents.

I have had to be somewhat speculative about the hardships of Mary's life because George Eliot's mimetic portrait of this aspect of her experience is sketchy. The psychological consequences of the hardships are presented in greater detail. As we have seen, they include a streak of satiric bitterness, a sense of injustice that inclines Mary toward cynicism, and an embeddedness that involves a preference for the safe, the known, and the familiar and which may have something to do with her dislike of teaching.

Another important consequence is Mary's detachment. The rhetoric praises Mary's freedom from illusion and vanity, qualities of which she is proud herself. Because of her hardships, she anticipates little from life; and she looks down on people who expect things to be arranged for their satisfaction. This enables her to feel superior to those who treat her with indifference or condescension. They may regard her as insignificant, but she regards them as fools. During a night watch at Featherstone's bedside, she sits by the fire "revolving, as she was wont, the scenes of the day, her lips often curling with amusement at the oddities to which her fancy added fresh drollery: people were so ridiculous with their illusions, carrying their fool's caps unawares" (ch. 33). Mary identifies herself with the fire, which, "with its gently audible movement," seems "like a solemn existence calmly independent of the petty passions, the imbecile desires, the straining after worthless uncertainties, which were daily moving her contempt."

Mary seeks a sense of calm independence from the slings and arrows of outrageous fortune by distancing herself from passions and desires, which she regards as follies, given the nature of life. She would feel contempt for herself if she strained after worthless uncertainties, and she despises ordinary mortals who do so. For Mary, as for the Preacher in Ecclesiastes, all is vanity and a striving after wind. She tries to cope with her frustrations by taking "life very much as a comedy" (ch. 33) and laughing at painful situations, which, after all, cannot matter very much. We are told that she does not suppose other people to be looking at her but that she looks at them with "a certain expression of amusement in her glance which her mouth keeps the secret of" (ch. 40). She is a detached observer whose lips often curl with amusement as she sees through other people's self-delusions and who has "plenty of merriment within" (ch. 33). When she is in a good mood, she has "humour enough . . . to laugh at herself" (ch. 12). Although Mary is searching for calm, there is a good deal of anger in all this. Her aggression expresses itself not only in her streak of satiric bitterness, but also in her regarding other people as ridiculous and in the scorn she feels for them.

Another manifestation of Mary's detachment may be her lack of ambition. She asks Fred, "How can you bear to be so contemptible, when others are working and striving, and there are so many things to be done—how can you bear to be fit for nothing in the world that is useful?" (ch. 25). I suppose this is to be taken as an example of the "honesty," the "truth-telling fairness," that we are told is Mary's "reigning virtue" (ch. 12). I am hard put to find other instances of this virtue, and I am not sure that this is one, for Mary's remarks do not seem entirely fair, given the fact that we do not see her working and striving and trying to make a contribution to the world. She could not bear to be a useless creature like Fred, for she has a sense of duty to her family and feels she must earn her way. Indeed, she contributes her savings to help pay off the note that Caleb has signed for Fred; and if she had taken a teaching position after Featherstone's death, part of her earnings would have gone toward the education of one of her brothers. As we have seen, however, Mary does not want to teach, although this is one of the most socially useful things she could do; and we do not see her pining, like Dorothea Brooke, to make some lasting contribution. When the Garths' finances improve and she no longer must work, Mary stays home or visits the Farebrother family at Lowick Parson-

age. She has "a proud, nay a generous resolution not to act the mean
or treacherous part" in the comedy of life (ch. 33), but she has no
particular goals for herself and seems rather aimless. Perhaps she does
not chafe more at her position at Stone Court because she feels that
what she does with her life does not greatly matter as long as she does
not behave ignobly or fail in her duty.

Although Mary tries to regard life as a comedy and to be amused
by human folly, some things she takes quite seriously. She honors her
parents, cherishes their approval, and tries to live up to their standards.
She has a sense of superiority to her ridiculous fellow creatures, but she
is also profoundly insecure about her own worth and is inordinately
grateful to those who show that they value her. Apart from her parents,
the chief person to whom she is grateful is Fred Vincy, who has always
been fond of her and treated her with kindness. She enjoys the self-
delusions of the hangers-on at Featherstone's, but Fred's illusions are
"not quite comic to her" (ch. 33). On the basis of her close observation
of her uncle, she is convinced that the Vincys are as likely as everyone
else to have their expectations disappointed: "She could make a butt of
Fred when he was present, but she did not enjoy his follies when he
was absent." The intensity of Mary's bond to Fred is another consequence of her hard experience. It leads her to behave in ways that are
potentially self-destructive and requires close examination.

MARY AND FRED

So far I have been looking mainly at Mary's character—with its dis-
parate components of satiric bitterness, clinging gratitude, lofty standards, and detachment—and its relation to her experience. George
Eliot shows Mary's character in action principally in the story of her
relationship with Fred Vincy. That story has the shape of a romance in
which various blocking forces must be removed before the lovers can
be united. We know from the start that Fred and Mary love each other,
but their love seems hopeless through most of the novel. The chief
obstacle is that Fred is "an idle frivolous creature" whom Mary finds
"contemptible" (ch. 25). His defaulting on the note Caleb has cosigned
adds a further complication. Mary knows that her parents would never
approve of marriage to such a man, and it is inconceivable to Mary
herself. When Caleb tells her that he and her mother would "think it a
pity for anybody's happiness to be wrapped up" in someone who is "not
to be trusted," Mary replies: "Don't fear for me father. . . . Fred has always
been very good to me; he is kind-hearted and affectionate, and not false,
I think, with all his self-indulgence. But I will never engage myself to one
who has no manly independence, and who goes on loitering away his

time on the chance that others will provide for him. You and my mother have taught me too much pride for that."

The only way the impediments to a union between Fred and Mary can be removed is through a major change in Fred's character. From their earliest appearance in the novel, the lovers are at an impasse: Fred says he can change for the better only if he is sure Mary loves him, and Mary replies that she can make no such commitment until he shows himself worthy of her love. Mary is in a very difficult situation. Marriage is her best chance for fulfillment, given her lack of a vocation; and she feels that Fred is the only man who would ever want to marry her. She cannot accept him, however, unless he meets the standards she shares with her parents; and for most of the novel it seems highly unlikely that he will do so. When Fred gets the commitment he wants by using Farebrother as an ambassador, Mary places herself in a very vulnerable position. She says she will not marry Fred unless he straightens up, but she will not marry anyone else, and Fred is free to marry whom he chooses. If Fred does not reform, Mary's life is ruined, much as Dorothea's would have been had Casaubon not died before she could make the promise. Fortunately, Fred is at the center of a comic education plot in which a variety of forces combine to overcome what seem to be insuperable obstacles.

Mary's and Fred's stories seem fairly straightforward when we look at them in formal and thematic terms. Mary's is a story of vindication and Fred's is one of education. Unlike Lydgate's, Fred's story has a happy ending, for he learns his lessons in time to benefit from them. Thematically, Mary illustrates an unself-centered approach to reality that is characterized by freedom from illusions and unreasonable claims, whereas the egoistic characters, including Fred, illustrate the opposite. Fred is the only extreme egoist in *Middlemarch* to undergo a successful transformation, one that makes him a foil to his sister Rosamond, who confronts some hard realities but remains essentially unchanged. Mary is also a foil to Rosamond—the unspoiled versus the spoiled child. She is Fred's salvation, whereas Rosamond destroys Lydgate.

When I look at Mary and Fred not only as aesthetic and illustrative characters but also as imagined human beings, questions arise that make their stories more complex, more interesting, and more problematic. If Mary despises Fred, how can she be so deeply attached to him? Since she feels she could love no one else, why won't she give Fred the encouragement for which he begs? Indeed, why are the lovers at such loggerheads, Fred demanding something Mary cannot give and Mary refusing the very thing Fred says he must have? Why does she finally give in when Fred sends Farebrother as an ambassador?

And why does she then offer so much, binding herself to Fred, while leaving him free, at a time when his reformation seems highly uncertain?

I also have questions concerning Fred. Why is he so attached to Mary, when they are such opposites? He has a need for unconditional acceptance, while Mary, as he explains to Mrs. Farebrother, "has such severe notions of what people should be that it is difficult to satisfy her" (ch. 57). This seems an unpromising combination. And why is Fred so emotionally dependent on Mary, much more than she is on him? He feels that if Mary will never have him, he "might as well go wrong in one way as another," that if he "had to give her up, it would be like beginning to live on wooden legs" (ch. 52). Fred eventually wins the approval of Mary and her parents, but George Eliot has to deploy so many forces to bring this about that I sometimes feel she is making it happen because the resolution of the comic plot requires it. How plausible is Fred's transformation, given his shallowness and deeply-rooted egoism, and how thorough is the change in his character?

The main reason Mary loves Fred seems to be gratitude. As we have seen, she has both a tendency toward bitterness and cynicism because the world has treated her badly and a "strong current of gratitude" toward those who have been kind to her. Especially outside her family, she expects to be neglected or looked down on, and she is overly grateful to anyone who shows her consideration. Fred observes that she regards it as a "great service . . . if anyone snuffs a candle" for her (ch. 14). Fred has always been very good to her, and her gratitude to him is immense. When Farebrother approaches her on Fred's behalf, Mary says that she could never be happy if she thought Fred was unhappy for the loss of her: "It has taken such deep root in me—my gratitude to him for always loving me best, and minding so much if I hurt myself, from the time when we were very little" (ch. 53).

We usually think of Mary as Fred's savior, but he plays a similar role in her life. Their relationship goes back to when they were play-mates in childhood. When he is six, Fred thinks Mary "the nicest girl in the world" and makes her "his wife with a brass ring which he had cut from an umbrella" (ch. 23). As Mary grows up, Fred is an exception to her sense that people regard her as insignificant and undesirable. He gives her the respect, the esteem, the sense of being cherished as woman that she receives from no one else. He tells Rosamond that he cares "so very much what Mary says" because she is "the best girl I know" (ch. 12). When Rosamond observes that she "should never have thought [Mary] was a girl to fall in love with," Fred replies: "How do you know what men would fall in love with? Girls never know." The Vincy women give us a sense of the view of Mary to which Fred is the antidote. To them she is a dreadful plain girl, fit to be a governess, who is not likely to be an object of love. Despite both the opposition of his family and his university education, which "exalt[s] his views of rank and income" (ch. 14), Fred's love for Mary increases as he becomes a young man. He is constantly telling her that he likes her "better than anyone else," that he'll never be good for anything unless she encourages him, and that he'll do anything she wants if she'll only say she loves him. He makes it clear that he desperately needs her. This would be intoxicating even for a woman who did not think of herself as "a brown patch" (ch. 40). Since she cannot imagine "that any man could love her except Fred" (ch. 52), it is no wonder that Mary is profoundly grateful to him, and deeply attached.

The problem is that Mary cannot openly respond to Fred's affection because he represents the opposite of everything for which the Garths stand. He is fit for nothing, unreliable, and self-indulgent. Whereas they have a work ethic, Fred would be quite content to lead the life of an idle gentleman. They have a realistic sense of their place in the scheme of things and eschew illusions and unreasonable claims. Fred believes that things are arranged for his satisfaction and expects "the wisdom of providence," "the mysteries of luck," or the "still greater mystery of [his] high individual value in the universe" to "bring about agreeable issues" (ch. 23). The Garths do their duty, however unappealing, while Fred feels that he has "a right to be free from anything disagreeable." They are independent, self-reliant, and industrious; he is always "hanging on others, and reckoning on what they will do for him" (ch. 25).

Fred pleads with Mary to tell him she loves him, but she cannot do so because she would be ashamed to say she loved a man with his failings. She has internalized the values of her parents and judges Fred by them, much as she judges herself. Indeed, she demands more of Fred than she does of herself; for she expects him to work and strive and do something valuable, whereas she has no such ambitions. She is holding him, presumably, to a masculine standard, the model for which is her father. As we have seen, Fred complains about the severity of Mary's notions of what people should be. Her severity is inspired, I think, not only by her idealization of her father, but also by her mother's "rigorous judgment" (ch. 24). Mrs. Garth is "disproportionately indulgent toward the failings of men, and [is] often heard to say that these [are] natural"; but she is "apt to be a little severe toward her own sex," including Mary. Mary cannot see why she should demand less of Fred than her mother demands of her. She has a profound inner resistance to giving the unconditional love for which he asks because she is accustomed to earning the approbation she receives.

Another obstacle to Mary's telling Fred that she loves him before he proves himself is that she fears she will lose the approval of her parents if she does. Mrs. Garth has "a motherly feeling" toward Fred and has "always been disposed to excuse his errors," but "she would probably not have excused Mary for engaging herself to him, her daughter being included in that more rigorous judgment which she applied to her own sex" (ch. 24). Mary repeatedly cites her parents when resisting Fred's pleas. She quotes her father to Fred as saying that "an idle man ought not to exist, much less be married" and he "would think it a disgrace to me if I accepted a man who would not work!" (ch. 14). Since Mary loves Fred, no doubt a part of her longs to give him the reassurance he seeks; but the idea of doing so fills her with a fear of shame and disgrace. Not only will she not tell him she loves him, but she asserts that "it would be wicked" to marry him even if she did (ch. 14). After she confesses to Farebrother that she does love Fred, she says: "I should like better than anything to see him worthy of every one's respect. But please tell him I will not promise to marry him till then: I should shame and grieve my father and mother" (ch. 53).

The only way Mary can accept Fred and be comfortable with both her parents and herself is for him to become worthy of everyone's re-spect, and Fred feels that the only way he can become worthy is to be sure Mary loves him and will marry him if he lives up to her standards. The biggest obstacle to their union is Fred's flaws of character; but before he can change, Mary must provide the reassurance he requires, despite her resistance to doing so. He appears absolutely to need what Mary feels it would be disgraceful to give. The impasse is resolved when Fred asks Farebrother to be his emissary. The scene between Farebrother and Mary is crucial and calls for close examination.

After having earlier failed his examination, Fred has taken his degree and must decide whether he should become a clergyman, as his parents wish. He has no inclination for the profession and has hoped to be saved from it by an inheritance from Featherstone. Mary has always passionately opposed the idea because she really wants to marry Fred and feels that this would be impossible if he entered the church: "I could not love a man who is ridiculous. . . . I can never imagine him preaching and exhorting and pronouncing blessings and praying by the sick, without feeling as if I were looking at a caricature. His being a clergyman would be only for gentility's sake, and I think there is nothing more contemptible than such imbecile gentility" (ch. 52). As we have seen, Mary is amused by human folly, except in Fred. Fred is torn between a desire to satisfy his father, who has invested a great deal in his education, and a fear of losing Mary should he do so. Feeling that if he has no chance at Mary, it does not matter which way he goes wrong, he asks Farebrother to sound her out. As Farebrother explains: "Fred will not take any course which would lessen the chance that you would consent to be his wife; but with that prospect, he will try his best at anything you approve" (ch. 52). Fred has no other career in mind, but he will do whatever Mary says.

Farebrother brings a great deal of pressure to bear on Mary during their interview. After Mary says that she certainly never will be Fred's wife if he becomes a clergyman, Farebrother asks: "But if he braved all the difficulties of getting his bread in some other way—will you give him the support of hope? May he count on winning you?" (ch. 52). Mary responds with some "resentment" that Fred ought not to put such questions until he has "done something worthy, instead of saying that he could do it." This has been her position all along, for reasons I have explored. Farebrother presses on. "Either your feeling for Fred Vincy excludes your entertaining another attachment, or it does not: either he may count on your remaining single until he shall have earned your hand, or he may in any case be disappointed." This does not seem quite fair. Mary's feeling could be that she would marry Fred if he proved himself worthy but would be open to entertaining another attachment if he did not. Farebrother's concern seems to be not at all for Mary, whom he is boxing in, but for Fred, who wants to be assured that he will not be braving difficulties without a reward. Fred knows perfectly well how Mary feels about his becoming a clergyman.

George Eliot presents Farebrother's speaking to Mary on Fred's behalf as a noble, self-sacrificial act. He loves Mary himself but agrees to be the emissary of his rival and then presses Fred's cause so vigorously that he succeeds in overcoming Mary's resistance to confessing her love. When I examine Farebrother's motives, however, his concern seems at least as much for himself as it is for Fred; and this may be why he pushes Mary so hard. He wants to know if he has a chance with her. He had resigned himself to not being able to marry because of his family responsibilities and poverty, but now that he has a better living, thanks to Dorothea, he finds himself thinking of Mary. It is not only Fred's possible frustration about which he is concerned, but his own. He would rather give up the idea of marriage to Mary right away and resume his resignation than live in uncertainty and continue to hope, perhaps only to be disappointed. He is no more willing to take his chances fighting for Mary than is Fred.

Mary senses that Farebrother has a personal stake in their conversation, but she is too diffident to allow herself to register its import. Farebrother overcomes her resistance to acknowledging her love for Fred by saying that "when the state of a woman's affection touches the happiness of another life—of more lives than one—" it is "the nobler course for her to be perfectly direct and open" (ch. 52). Mary wonders at Farebrother's "tone, which had a grave restrained emotion in it"; and the idea flashes "across her mind that his words [have] reference to himself"; but she is "incredulous, and ashamed of entertaining" this idea. She has "never thought that any man could love her except Fred . . . ; still less that she could be of any importance to Mr. Farebrother, the cleverest man in her narrow circle."

What opens Mary's lips is Farebrother's statement that it is the nobler course for her to be direct and open. "Since you think it my duty," she replies, "I will tell you that I have too strong a feeling for Fred to give him up for anyone else." The key word here is "duty." Mary has felt it to be her duty to her parents and herself not to encourage a man as irresponsible as Fred, but Farebrother's statement allows her to feel that to be direct and open is the nobler course. No one can now reproach her, nor need she reproach herself, for acknowledging her feelings toward Fred. The impasse has been resolved; and, given Fred's dependence on her acknowledgment, a major obstacle to the happy ending has been removed.

We still must ask why Mary promises so much. The narrator shows no discomfort at her having done so; but I feel a good deal, especially seeing that Fred has not yet shown any capacity for change. Farebrother has done well for Fred, but he has led Mary to make a commitment that could turn out to be self-destructive. Her commitment is conditional, in that she says she will not promise to marry Fred until she sees him worthy of everyone's respect, but it is unconditional in that she says she has "too strong a feeling for Fred to give him up for anyone else" and that she could not be happy if she "thought he was unhappy for the loss" of her (ch. 53). She will love him, and only him, even if he does not reform; but she will marry him only if he does. Where does this leave her if Fred fails to change? She says that "he is free to choose someone else," but she does not claim a similar freedom for herself. The rhetoric indicates that the author means us to find Mary's behavior quite admirable—she is nobly open, loving, and generous, and still she maintains her values. I think that Mary puts herself in such a vulnerable position because of her insecurity, excessive gratitude, and feelings of unlovableness.

In part, of course, she is responding to Farebrother's pressure and his formulation of her options. Yet though Farebrother gets her to admit what she has so far withheld, I do not think he gets her to say anything she does not feel. Mary has known all along that her love for Fred excluded her entertaining another attachment and that she would remain single until he earned her hand. It must be a relief to her to be able to express this. Mary cannot imagine herself loving someone else, in part because she has never thought any man but Fred could love her. She has envisioned herself remaining single all her life because there was no man for her but Fred and he would never meet her standards. Inwardly, she has already made the commitment for which Farebrother asks, but in a spirit of hopelessness that contributes to her detachment. She does not expect Fred to remain single because she will not marry him, and so she feels that he should be "free to choose someone else" (ch. 53). It only makes sense that he might look for someone less demanding.

There is in fact another possibility open to Mary, but she is "incredulous and ashamed of entertaining" the idea that Farebrother is interested in her (ch. 53). Because of her negative feelings about herself and her pessimistic outlook, she dismisses anything that seems to flatter her, and so she regards her intuitions about Farebrother as "perhaps illusory." In her determination not to delude herself, and thus become like the fools she ridicules, she fails to register the true situation. But even if she understood Farebrother's feelings, she would still cling to Fred, despite the unpromising outlook. To appreciate the significance of Mary's behavior, we must take a closer look at the man to whom she has committed herself.

FRED VINCY

Fred Vincy may be the most problematic character in *Middlemarch*. As we have seen, he is in many ways a typical George Eliot egoist, given to taking the world as an udder to feed his supreme self. The pierglass image used to describe Rosamond's egocentricity applies just as well to her brother. The surface is scratched in all directions, but place "a lighted candle as a centre of illumination, and lo! the scratches will seem to arrange themselves in a fine series of concentric circles round that little sun. . . . The scratches are events, and the candle is the egoism of any person now absent" (ch. 27). Like Rosamond, Fred has the illusion that life has been providentially arranged for his satisfaction. He has been as spoiled by his parents as she, perhaps as the first-born, a son, and his mother's favorite, even more (ch. 14). And he is just as much drawn to the life of the upper classes, to which he feels he should belong.

Fred, though, is presented as more honest, affectionate, and good-natured than Rosamond, although there is no effort to account for the difference; and he is in love with Mary Garth, who seems a strange choice for him, whereas Rosamond loves no one, other than herself. I can readily understand what attracts Dorothea and Casaubon, Dorothea and Ladislaw, and Lydgate and Rosamond to each other, and Mary to Fred. But what attracts Fred to Mary, given her plainness, low social position, different values, and critical attitude toward him? Completely lacking the self-containment of his sister, Fred has an emotional neediness that binds him to Mary and makes him dependent on her, again without explanation. He evolves in a way that Rosamond cannot, despite a similar narcissism. In the case of Fred, I have problems not only with George Eliot's rhetoric but also with her mimetic portrait, which seems in some respects to be insufficiently realized. I shall try to fill in some of the blanks by making inferences from the information we have.

Fred appears to be as much a product of his family as is Rosamond. The Vincys live "in an easy, profuse way," and the children have no sense of limitations or "standard of economy" (ch. 23). Both Fred and Rosamond get into trouble because of their careless spending. The Vincys are social climbers who try to boost their family status by sending Rosamond to finishing school and Fred to university. Bulstrode reproaches his brother-in-law for having destined Fred for the church "entirely from worldly vanity" and devoted more than he could afford to "an expensive education which has succeeded in nothing but in giving him extravagant idle habits." His university education does not provide Fred with a vocation, since being a clergyman does not appeal to him, but it exalts his views on rank and income. Rosamond goes to school with girls of higher position, and Fred is "thought equal to the best society at college" (ch. 11). Both are left with the feeling that they are out of place in their own class and that they deserve better than the station into which they have been born.

Fred has expectations of Featherstone but dislikes "courting an old fellow for his money," because he holds "himself to be a gentleman at heart" (ch. 14), and gentlemen should not have to do such things. He does not regard his expectations, moreover, as "anything so very magnificent" (ch. 12). He would be ashamed to confess the smallness of his prospects, and of his "scrapes," to his college companions. "Such ruminations," we are told, "naturally produced a streak of misanthropic bitterness. To be born the son of a Middlemarch manufacturer . . . while such men as Mainwaring and Vyan—certainly life was a poor business, when a spirited young fellow, with a good appetite for the best of everything, had so poor an outlook." Featherstone understands Fred's appetites and uses them to manipulate him: "You want to cut a figure in the world, and I reckon Peter Featherstone is the only one you've got to trust to." "Yes, indeed," replies Fred: "I was not born to very splendid chances. Few men have been more cramped than I have been" (ch. 14). His parents' indulgence and his university experience have led Fred to feel sorry for himself. He judges not only his lot but also his behavior by comparing himself to the men he knows at school. When Mary calls him selfish after he has defaulted on his debt, Fred objects: "It is hardly fair to call me selfish. If you knew what things other young men do, you would think me a good deal off the worst" (ch. 25).

Fred's discontent with the meanness of his lot is similar to Rosamond's, but it is apt to be overlooked because it is obscured by the dominant picture of him as a man who feels like the favorite of fortune, rather than its step-child. As we have seen, he has an expectation that providence, "will bring about agreeable issues" (ch. 23). Fred sees his place in the universe in the light of his experience in his family and has a sense of entitlement. He believes in his good fortune and regards Featherstone as "an incorporated luck." He is not a gambler, George Eliot tells us, but engages in "a joyous imaginative activity which fashions events according to desire." He doesn't worry about his debt because, although he has no idea of how he can pay it, his optimism leads him to expect that things will somehow work out in his favor. When he needs a cosigner in order to obtain a renewal, he asks Caleb Garth rather than someone who could afford to pay, because the easygoing Caleb will not subject him to any discomfort; and Fred feels he has a right to be free from anything disagreeable. Besides, he does not see himself putting Caleb at risk—Fred is confident the universe will take care of him.

Fred's claims give him a feeling of confidence, but they are out of touch with reality and increase his vulnerability, for they lead him to rely on a magical hope rather than practical measures to deal with his difficulties. His claims and his bitterness may be related to each other, in that he feels aggrieved when any frustration of his expectations violates his sense of entitlement. Most of the time Fred believes in his star; but when he compares himself with his more privileged friends or doesn't get what he wants, his faith is shaken. He counts on a gift of money from Featherstone to clear his debt, but the gift actually presents "the absurdity of being less than his hopefulness had decided that [it] must be. What can the fitness of things mean, if not their fitness to a man's expectations? Failing this, absurdity and atheism gape behind him" (ch. 14). George Eliot mocks Fred's private religion, but she also presents it as an important feature of his psychology.

This, then, is the man with whom Mary Garth is in love. We can understand her disapproval of his character, which is in so many ways the opposite of her own. She wants him to work and strive, like her father, to be fit for something useful; but Fred is waiting for Featherstone to die so that he can lead the idle life he feels should belong to a gentleman. As he explains to Farebrother, if Fred does not want to enter the church, it is simply because he does not like it: "I don't like divinity, and preaching, and feeling obliged to look serious. I like riding across country, and doing as other men do" (ch. 52)—the other men in question being his upper-class friends at college. It is no wonder that he is "utterly depressed" when he learns the terms of Featherstone's will: "Twenty-four hours ago he had thought that instead of needing to know what he should do, he should by this time know that he needed to do nothing: that he should hunt in pink, have a first-rate hunter, ride to cover on a fine hack, and be generally respected for doing so" (ch. 36).

George Eliot's depiction of Fred's egoism is the most successful part of her portrait, and that Mary loves so unsuitable a man is intelligible when we understand the depth of her insecurity and the immensity of her gratitude. What is more difficult to comprehend is Fred's love for Mary. George Eliot simply tells us that having become attached to Mary at a very early age, Fred always remained kind and admiring and that he fell more and more "in love with his old playmate" as he grew "from boy to man" (ch. 14). The author provides little information about the nature of his attraction to a woman who seems just as unsuited to him as he is to her, and what she does provide requires a good deal of interpretation. Fred adores Mary, while she calls him a variety of hard names and would prove a most uncomfortable companion in the life he envisions for himself.

The puzzling quality in Fred's behavior toward Mary is evident in the first extended scene between them, which occurs just after Fred has received the gift of money from Featherstone. Fred defends himself against what he knows to be Mary's view of him as "idle and extravagant" by saying: "Well, I am not fit to be a poor man. I should not have made a bad fellow if I had been rich" (ch. 14). When Mary says that she doesn't want to quarrel with him because "however naughty you may be to other people, you are good to me," Fred replies: "Because I like you better than any one else. But I know you despise me." He then pleads with Mary to say she loves him so that he can improve:

> "When a man is not loved, it is no use for him to say that he could be a better fellow—could do anything—I mean, if he were sure of being loved in return."
>
> "Not of the least use in the world for him to say he *could* be better. Might, could, would—they are contemptible auxiliaries."
>
> "I don't see how a man is to be good for much unless he has some one woman to love him dearly."
>
> "I think the goodness should come before he expects that."

"You know better, Mary. Women don't love men for their goodness."

"Perhaps not. But if they love them, they never think them bad."

"It is hardly fair to say I am bad."

"I said nothing at all about you."

"I never shall be good for anything, Mary, if you will not say that you love me—if you will not promise to marry me—I mean when I am able to marry."

Fred says he could be a better fellow if Mary would assure him of her love, but it is difficult to imagine what he has in mind. In what way does he see himself as deficient or as able to improve? He feels that his idleness and extravagance would be acceptable if he were rich; and he expects to be rich, though in a more modest way than he would like, when he inherits from Featherstone. On the basis of his observation of his college companions, he thinks that his conduct is better than that of other young gentlemen. Even now, he feels it unfair of Mary to say he is bad.

Why is Fred behaving as he does in this scene? Is he just trying to manipulate Mary into pledging her love without his having to deserve it, and thereby satisfy his claim to indulgence? Because she indicates that she will not marry him unless he earns her respect, is he promising that he'll be a better fellow if she encourages him, without really intending to change? He acknowledges that he doesn't make a good poor man, but he thinks he'll be seen as a good fellow when he is rich and that Mary will then accept him. After he defaults on his debt, he again promises to reform if Mary will say she loves him. She again refuses, condemning him severely; but Fred still feels that when he inherits Stone Court, she can "no longer have any reason for not marrying him. And all this [is] to come without study or other inconvenience, purely by the favour of providence in the shape of an old gentleman's caprice" (ch. 36). It is to come, that is, without his having to modify his behavior. Does Fred pretend to feel he is deficient and eager to reform because he thinks that is what Mary wants to hear?

Fred may be trying to manipulate Mary in the way I have suggested, but something deeper seems to be at work in his pleading. He is not only saying that he could be a better fellow if he were sure of Mary's love; he is also saying that he'll never be good for anything if she won't promise to marry him. The implication is that he doesn't feel good for much and that he is looking to Mary to save him. He may be so desperate for her commitment in part because he feels that she represents a standard of goodness to which he could measure up if she gave him encouragement and that measuring up to that standard would alleviate his feeling of worthlessness. Without her love, he has only her disapproval, which corresponds to his buried self-contempt, and no guidance on what he should do to escape it. A man with no center of self, despite his egoism, Fred is completely dependent on Mary to tell him how to be and feels lost and hopeless without her. When Mary repeats her father's remark that "an idle man ought not to exist, much less, be married," Fred responds: "Then I am to blow my brains out?" (ch. 14).

This scene, and others like it, lead me to infer that an important source of Fred's attraction to Mary may be her disapproval. Fred has an inflated sense of his importance in the universe that is based on his having been a spoiled child; however, he has never done anything—has never *had* to do anything—to earn his sense of worth and give it a solid foundation. He has an idealized image of himself as a favorite of fortune, on the basis of which he makes unreasonable claims, but underlying it are feelings of worthlessness and inadequacy. These are brought to the surface when his claims are frustrated. Although Mary activates Fred's discomfort with himself, by refusing to honor his claims and judging him instead, she also offers him a means of escaping his self-hatred that he can find nowhere else. The approval of his family is of little value because he has never had to deserve it. Mary loves him but tells him truths that speak to his suppressed sense of uneasiness about himself. He thinks that if he gains her approval, he can feel worthwhile at last.

Even though he is his mother's favorite, Fred seems insecure not only about his worth but also about his lovability. Like Mary, he needs confirmation from outside his family, and he has sought from childhood to win it from Mary through kindness. In the scene at Stone Court, he expresses fears that Mary cannot love him because of his idleness and extravagance, because he is not a "stupendous fellow" who has "wise opinions about everything," and because "a woman is never in love with any one she has always known" (ch. 14). To allay his anxiety, he pleads for her love in a wheedling, submissive fashion and is ready to promise anything if only she will reassure him. After he defaults on his debt, he is afraid that Mary will never think well of him again and begs her not to give up on him: "I will try to be anything you like, Mary, if you will say that you love me" (ch. 25). As we have seen, until Farebrother's intervention, Mary refuses to give Fred the unconditional love he requires if he is to try to meet her conditions. I think that he really wants to meet them, for reasons I have proposed, at the same time that he hopes all difficulties will disappear, without any effort on his part, when Featherstone dies. With his high expectations and self-doubts existing side by side, Fred is full of inconsistencies.

It is important to recognize that part of the dynamic between Fred and Mary is his putting the burden of his rescue on her shoulders. His message is that he is not good for much, that he will become better if she gives him encouragement and worse if she does not, and that he will despair if she does not love him. His fate is in her hands. This feeds Mary's pride and leads her to adopt, at times, an almost "maternal" attitude (ch. 25). When Fred tells her about the trouble he has brought to her family by defaulting on his debt, Mary criticizes him severely. Fred's response is to whine about how miserable he is, to ask Mary to feel sorry for him, and to beg again for her love. Mary cannot give him the commitment he wants, but when she sees "his dull despairing glance, her pity for him surmount[s] her anger." In view of her gratitude to Fred, her need of him, and his need of her, Mary is under tremendous pressure to give him the confession of love he seeks; and she does so as soon as Farebrother assures her that to be direct and open is her duty.

We have seen how important it is to Mary that Fred reform, but it might be even more important to Fred, for he is more dependent on her than she is on him. Mary has a sense of virtue that exists independently of Fred, while he needs her approval to alleviate his feeling of not being good for anything. She defends herself through detachment against her frustration in love, whereas Fred has no defenses at all. Exchanges between the two are marked by ironic distance and playfulness on Mary's part, when she is not being critical; but Fred is openly needy and desperate. It seems that he will be lost without Mary, much as Will would be lost without Dorothea. It should be kept in mind, of course, that Mary finds emotional support in knowing that Fred loves her, whether they can marry or not, whereas Fred is in doubt about Mary's sentiments.

THAT HAPPY ENDING

At the center of Mary and Fred's story is an education plot, which traces the breakdown of Fred's egoism and the resulting process of moral development that makes him an acceptable suitor. George Eliot's initial portrait of Fred's deficiencies is so compelling that she has a challenging task convincing the reader that the change in Fred is plausible and adequate, that the happy ending not only rounds out the plot but represents a genuine possibility.

If we are to believe Fred capable of significant change, we must see him as having a potential for growth that is absent in his fellow egoist, Rosamond. George Eliot does not *show* us this potential in concrete detail but has the narrator and various characters testify to it. Fred is described as open, affectionate, kind-hearted, truthful, and sincere. Mrs. Vincy dotes on him, and the narrator tells us that "the mother's eyes are not always deceived in their partiality: she at least can best judge who is the tender, filial-hearted child" (ch. 14). His mother's belief that "Fred will turn out well" (ch. 36) is shared by others and confirmed by events. Before Fred defaults on his debt, Caleb Garth thinks he has "a good bottom to his character—you might trust him for anything" (ch. 23). Garth subsequently warns Mary against trusting him but repeats his belief that Fred is "good at bottom" when he hires him (ch. 56). After the default, Mary accuses Fred of selfishness and asks how he can bear not to be fit for anything useful. Even then she tells him, however, that "with so much good in [his] disposition" he "might be worth a great deal" (ch. 25). Farebrother wishes that "Fred were not such an idle dog," but says that "he has some very good points" and excuses him because of Featherstone's "delusive behaviour" (ch. 40).

I think that George Eliot treats Fred with surprising indulgence. She presents a vivid picture of him as a self-deluded egoist with almost no sense of responsibility and then tries to counterbalance that with vague words of praise, faith, and exculpation. Where is the "good bottom" of which Caleb speaks? What "very good points" does Farebrother have in mind? I am more impressed by such mimetic details as Fred's feeling "something like the tooth of remorse" *for the* *"first time"* when he realizes that by defaulting on his debt he is robbing Mrs. Garth and Mary of their savings and preventing Alfred from going to school (ch. 23). This suggests a rather considerable moral obtuseness, especially for someone who is supposed to have a great deal of good in his disposition. Indeed, even after his realization, Fred feels only "something like" remorse, and he resists the idea that he is "selfish" or "bad." Fred has a very long way to go in his development, and George Eliot's efforts to suggest his educability seem feeble to me.

George Eliot's characters enter the second stage of moral development when they undergo frustrations that force them to confront reality. Much of Fred's story is devoted to the breakdown of his illusory picture of himself and the universe and his subsequent effort at finding a place for himself in the world. One of the biggest blows he suffers is receiving no inheritance from Featherstone; but he experiences frustrations before that, when Featherstone's gift of money is not large enough to pay off his debt, when his horse-trading fails, and when he must confront the harm he has done the Garths by having asked Caleb to cosign his note. Moreover, Mary serves as a check on his unreasonable claims all along.

Fred receives another major blow when he realizes that Farebrother is in love with Mary and that Mrs. Garth feels he is standing in Mary's way: "Fred's light hopeful nature had perhaps never had so much of a bruise as from this suggestion that if he had been out of the way, Mary might have made a thoroughly good match" (ch. 57). The narrator tells us that this experience is a "discipline for Fred hardly less sharp than his disappointment about his uncle's will." Having Farebrother as a rival makes Fred much less "easy about his own accomplishments" (ch. 63). No doubt it does, but I find this description somewhat misleading, for, as we have seen, Fred has not felt very easy about himself before. He vacillates throughout between self-satisfaction and feelings of insecurity about his worth.

George Eliot presents Fred's growth as being fostered not only by events that challenge his illusions about himself but also by the support he receives from his fellows. His is another story of rescue. He is saved, as it were, by Caleb Garth's faith and "ardent generosity" (ch. 56); by Farebrother's noble self-sacrifice, first in speaking to Mary on Fred's behalf and then in warning him away from gambling when he might have let him ruin himself (ch. 66); and by Mary's loving him before he deserves it and setting "a watch" on her affection and constancy when she becomes aware of Farebrother's interest. "Fred has lost all his other expectations," she tells herself; "he must keep this" (ch. 57). Caleb feels that Fred's "soul is in [his] hands" and that it is his "duty" to "do the best [he] can for him" (ch. 56). He resolves to take Fred into the business "and make a man of him." Farebrother's "fine act" in warning Fred away from gambling "produces a sort of regenerating shudder through the frame, and makes [him] feel ready to begin a new life" (ch. 66). Fred resolves to try to be worthy of both Farebrother and Mary, whose hand it is "a discipline" to have won. Caleb tells his wife that "a true love for a good woman is a great thing. . . . It shapes many a rough fellow" (ch. 56).

I think we are supposed to see Fred as being full of illusions at first and as gradually accommodating himself to reality with the help of various "disciplines" and the support of his friends. Fred does change enough to make him acceptable to Mary, but just barely, it seems to me. He gives up many of his claims and his dreams of an idle life and begins to work at a job that is not the gentlemanly calling he and his parents had envisioned. Although Fred comes to terms with reality to a certain extent, the process is made much easier by the author's tailoring reality to his needs (and to Mary's as well).

Fred must learn that the universe is not "arranged for his peculiar satisfaction," but he turns out to be the favorite of fortune after all, because the author arranges events so that his story will end happily. His being disappointed by Featherstone is the best thing that could have happened, because Mary could never have accepted him if an inheritance had permitted him to remain idle and frivolous (and her conflict between love and respect for her family's values could not have been resolved). Fred has been indulged by his mother and expects to be indulged by the universe. He is, in fact, indulged by Mary, Caleb, and Farebrother, who play parental roles in his life. They all feel sorry for the poor fellow because of his disappointment and believe in the goodness of his disposition, without much visible basis for doing so. Fred stumbles into a vocation when Caleb's assistant is injured in the altercation between laborers and the surveyors for the railway and Caleb asks Fred to help complete the day's task. He ends up at Stone Court, which he had expected to inherit, as a result of Bulstrode's downfall and Caleb's proposal that he become tenant. "And it would be as pretty a turn of things as could be," says Caleb to Susan, that Fred "should hold the place in a good industrious way after all—by his taking to business" (ch. 68). A pretty turn of events indeed, and one that allows Fred and Mary to marry. Caleb's words give the impression that Fred has somehow earned his place at Stone Court through industry, whereas it has fallen into his lap, much as he expected it to do in the first place. He must work to keep it, of course.

All this good fortune creates the impression of a greater change in Fred than actually takes place. If Fred does not enter the church, Farebrother asks Mary, but "brave[s] all the difficulties of getting his bread in some other way. . . . may he count on winning you?" (ch. 52). Fred is not interested, however, in braving difficulties: "What secular *avocation* on earth was there for a young man (whose friends could not get him an 'appointment') which was at once gentlemanly, lucrative, and to be followed without special knowledge?" (ch. 56; my emphasis).

Fred is attracted to working with Caleb because he likes having "to do with outdoor things" (it's a bit like riding across country), but he is tempted to give up the job when he finds that it entails record-keeping and learning to write a legible hand: "He had not thought of desk-work—in fact, like the majority of young gentlemen, he wanted an occupation which should be free from disagreeables" (ch. 56). No braving of difficulties here. George Eliot says she does not know what the consequences might have been had Fred not been looking forward to telling Mary that he was engaged to work under her father. Fred's need of Mary barely keeps him in line. He finds a place in the world because he clings to her, much as Will finds a place because he must be near Dorothea.

After working steadily for only six months, Fred begins to back-slide by going to the Green Dragon, where he is tempted to gamble, and this despite his knowledge of Farebrother's interest in Mary. George Eliot tells us that discovering he has a rival is "a discipline for Fred. . . . The iron had not entered into his soul, but he had begun to imagine what the sharp edge would be" (ch. 57). The iron never enters his soul, any more than does real remorse, although he does feels genuinely sorry for himself. Fred's "light hopeful nature" does not change, however much it is bruised. Farebrother's warning keeps him from going astray again, and his rectitude is made much easier by his getting to live at Stone Court. It is difficult to say how Fred would have borne up if things had not gone his way. Not very well, I suspect.

That things work out so prettily obscures not only Fred's real course of development but also the relationship between Mary and Fred. George Eliot makes them all seem better than I find them to be. I proposed earlier that Mary is in danger of ruining her life because of her psychological vulnerabilities but that, through authorial manipu-lations, George Eliot saves her from the consequences of her poten-tially self-destructive behavior. Fred *must* reform if Mary is to be saved, and I have tried to show what elaborate machinery the author em-ploys to make him an acceptable mate. Although he is better than he was, he hardly measures up to the high standards of the Garths.

Fred tells Mary that women don't love men for their goodness. That is certainly true of Mary. Although Fred must become good enough for her to be able to accept him, she is bound not by his worthy qualities, such as they are, but by her insecurity, which is the primary source of her gratitude. She does not have enough confidence in her own worth to feel deserving of a better man. She is thrilled by Farebrother's interest but also frightened by it, I think. When after their marriage Fred concedes that Farebrother was "ten times wor-thier" of her, Mary replies: "To be sure he was . . . and for that reason he could do better without me. But you—I shudder to think what you would have been." (Finale). Fred's neediness and haplessness put Mary in the position of savior and assuage her fears of inad-equacy—remember that she stays with Featherstone partly to avoid a sense of failure in a more demanding position. Mary is only half joking when she tells her father that she would "never like scolding anyone else so well" and that "husbands are an inferior class of men, who require keeping in order" (ch. 86). This is not a role she could play with Farebrother.

Moreover, Fred feels safer to Mary than Farebrother because of her long history with Fred. Both Mary and Fred cling to the known, to what is familiar from the past. Mary tells Caleb: "I don't think either of us could spare the other, or like anyone else better, however much we might admire them [a reference to Farebrother]. It would make too great a difference to us—like seeing all the old places altered, and changing the name of everything" (ch. 86). For Mary, marrying the tamed Fred is the closest thing to never having to leave home. And Fred, despite his experiences at university and his dreams of the gentleman's life, clings to his childhood playmate, without whom he will be the most miserable devil in the world. There is between Fred and Mary a mutual dependency, borne of their fears and insecurities, that we are supposed to regard, I think, as the basis for a healthy relationship.

This is not to say that their marriage is unsuccessful. With a lot of help from the author in arranging things to suit them, they are able to achieve "a solid mutual happiness" (Finale). At the beginning of the novel, neither Fred nor Mary has a sense of vocation. When Fred says that he would not have made a bad fellow if he had been rich, Mary observes:

> "You would have done your duty in that state of life to which it has not pleased God to call you."
>
> "Well, I couldn't do my duty as a clergyman, any more than you could do yours as a governess. You ought to have a little fellow-feeling there."
>
> "I never said you ought to be a clergyman. There are other sorts of work. It seems to me very miserable not to resolve on some course and act accordingly." (ch. 14)

Neither Fred nor Mary can resolve on a course, and both are at sea. They find a satisfying life through each other, Fred as the industrious tenant of Stone Court and Mary as wife and mother. Fred remains "unswervingly steady" and becomes a responsible husband and father, hunting occasionally but not taking risks at the fences (Finale). Lydgate is shocked that affection does not make Rosamond compliant; it does Fred. Caleb, promoting the union, observes to Susan, "Marriage is a taming thing. Fred would want less of my bit and bridle" (ch. 68). If Fred needs further managing, he always has Mary to scold him. In some ways, however, he retains his light, hopeful nature. "The yield of crops or the profits of a cattle sale usually fell below his estimate, and he was always prone to believe that he could make money by the purchase of a horse which turned out badly" (Finale). This does not grieve Mary too much, for she maintains an ironic detachment. When Fred makes a bad bargain, she observes that this "was of course the fault of the horse, not of Fred's judgment."

Unlike Dorothea, Mary seems well satisfied with her life, which is even more confined to the domestic sphere. She is not frustrated at not having done something better, because she has never expected great things of life or herself but has embraced resignation early. Her life has turned out better than she hoped, whereas Dorothea is disappointed not to have found a high destiny. Mary, still sensitive about being dreadfully plain, has the good fortune to bring forth men-children only. Fred wishes to have "a girl like her," but Mary is "not discontented" with boys. She tells Fred that having a daughter (who might resemble her) "would be too great a trial to your mother" (Finale). Her streak of satiric bitterness has not disappeared.

5

"This Problematic Sylph":
Gwendolen Harleth

GREAT ACHIEVEMENTS AND GREAT PROBLEMS

According to my perspective in *Experiments in Life, Daniel Deronda* is about characters who exemplify the subjective and objective approaches to reality and the movement of those characters' through the stages of moral development. Gwendolen is George Eliot's most fully realized egoist, while Deronda, her opposite, comes closer than any other character to attaining the unself-centeredness George Eliot glorifies. Both characters undergo a process of development, as a result of disillusioning experiences. Deronda's development is completed early in life; he has already attained moral maturity when we first encounter him. The central action of the novel is Gwendolen's education, with Deronda as her mentor. George Eliot's attempts to tell such a story in *Felix Holt* and *Middlemarch* had not been entirely successful; and *Daniel Deronda* is her final, most elaborate effort to portray the transformation of an egoist through a relationship with a more fully evolved individual.

Like most critics before and since, in *Experiments in Life* I saw Gwendolen as having been "saved," partly through the influence of Daniel Deronda, who, George Eliot assures us, had "not spoiled his mission" (ch. 44). As a result of error and consequent suffering, Gwendolen attains vision and sympathy, a version of George Eliot's Religion of Humanity. I felt Deronda's problem to be one of rootless cosmopolitanism, exacerbated by his paralyzing capacity to entertain a variety of perspectives and resolved by his finding a vocation through

111

the discovery of his Jewish identity. I described Deronda as "the most fortunate of George Eliot's characters" because he "has an opportunity to lead an epic life, like St. Theresa's—the kind of life that Dorothea so yearned for but could not find" (209).

I now question George Eliot's celebration of her heroine's development; for Gwendolen seems held together at the end by a compulsive need to escape her self-loathing through living up to the dictates of her internalized Daniel Deronda, who preaches duty, self-sacrifice, and the value of remorse. She is no longer a selfish narcissist, but she has no center of self to give direction to her existence. Neither does the much glorified Deronda. Although George Eliot presents him as a virtually perfect altruist who is a source of salvation to others, Daniel leads an aimless life from which he needs to be rescued by the imposition of duties. He points Gwendolen not in the direction of psychological growth, as George Eliot would have us believe, but toward his own ways of coping with anger and guilt, a sense of inner vacuity, and doubts about his vocation. He is damaged by the adverse conditions of his childhood, which result in self-alienation. Apart from his aimlessness, however, the form the damage takes is one the author admires. George Eliot seems to confuse being driven to live for others out of emptiness, guilt, or despair with moral excellence and emotional well-being.

In recent years, *Daniel Deronda* has been celebrated as George Eliot's greatest psychological novel, largely because of the portrait of Gwendolen, who is widely regarded as the author's finest creation. More psychoanalytical studies have been done of Gwendolen than of any other George Eliot character, and the relationship between Gwendolen and Daniel has frequently been compared to that of patient and therapist. F. R. Leavis's view of the novel as having a splendid Gwendolen half and a rather awful Deronda one has largely prevailed, but I think there are great achievements and great problems in both parts. Despite the idealizations in the Deronda half of the novel, I find Daniel to be a very interesting character, more fully realized than critics have generally thought, while certain aspects of the portrait of Gwendolen, fine as it is, seem discordant or implausible. However much I may now disagree with George Eliot's interpretations and judgments of such characters as Maggie Tulliver and Dorothea Brooke, her intuitive understanding of them always seems right. I find myself questioning some aspects of her mimetic portrayal of Gwendolen.

As in *The Mill on the Floss* and *Middlemarch*, the concrete depiction of character often subverts George Eliot's rhetoric. Her celebration of Deronda's altruism, of Gwendolen's transformation, and of Daniel's role as Gwendolen's savior is called into question by the mimesis—as

I now interpret it. Moreover, I think there are conflicts not only between authorial rhetoric and mimesis but within the rhetoric itself, especially in the Gwendolen story. While I find the rhetoric surrounding Dorothea to be misleading, it is clear and consistent, whereas George Eliot's view of Gwendolen seems murky. Gwendolen is such a "problematic sylph" (ch. 1) in part because the author's treatment of her is inconsistent. This is one of the reasons why, as Harold Bloom says, the novel "will go on confusing" its readers (1986, 5).

A CONFUSING PICTURE OF GWENDOLEN

As Martin Price has observed, Gwendolen's "growth into moral life" is in some ways "the most complex single story that George Eliot wrote" (1983, 166); but what exactly is the shape of that story? How does George Eliot want us to see it? I do not think she was clear about this herself, and at times I find her presentation of Gwendolen bewildering. Although it is brilliant in parts, I am not sure that it comes together as a whole. The different versions of Gwendolen often seem incompatible with each other.

We are given conflicting rhetorical signals from the very beginning. One shape to Gwendolen's story is suggested by the epigraph to the novel and another by the title of Book I. The epigraph indicates that this is to be a story of crime and punishment:

> Let thy chief terror be of thine own soul:
> There, 'mid the throng of hurrying desires
> That trample on the dead to seize their spoil,
> Lurks vengeance, footless, irresistible
> As exhalations laden with slow death,
> And o'er the fairest troop of captured joys
> Breathes pallid pestilence.

The reference is to Gwendolen's trampling on others to take what she wants, particularly on Mrs. Glasher and her children in order to marry Grandcourt. Her hurrying desires lead to moral violations; she is then punished, and transformed, by her tormented conscience. Vengeance is visited on her not from without but from within. Hers is a story of psychomachia, of a struggle between good and evil in her soul. The opening words of the novel reinforce this view. As he sees Gwendolen at the gaming table, Deronda wonders what gives "the dynamic quality to her glance": "Was the good or the evil genius dominant in those beams? Probably the evil." (ch. 1). Gwendolen's sinister quality is reinforced by her having "got herself up as a sort of serpent" and being described by an onlooker as possessing a kind of "Lamia beauty." After chapter 1, however, this view of Gwendolen disappears until her marriage to Grandcourt, except for a reference in chapter 7 to her "undefinable stinging quality—as it were a trace of demon ancestry— which made some beholders hesitate in their admiration" of her.

Book I of the novel is entitled "The Spoiled Child," and it is primarily as an egoist that we are invited to see Gwendolen until she marries Grandcourt, almost halfway through the novel. Then she becomes a guilty woman who is hounded by remorse and a dread of murderous impulses, against which she struggles and for which she hates herself. Before this, however, the rhetoric characterizes her as vain, narrow, and self-indulgent, full of illusions about herself and the world, but not really vicious or malign.

Gwendolen's egoism is presented as the product of her upbringing. The "pet and pride of the household," she is always treated like a "princess in exile" (ch. 3). She is fed on flattery and believes in her ability to conquer circumstance through her cleverness and in her divine right to rule. Her position in the family gives her the feeling that she is an exceptional person who cannot remain in ordinary circumstances. She believes herself to be a favorite of fortune who, on horseback, feels "as secure as an immortal goddess" and is confident that nothing bad will happen to her (ch. 7). When we first encounter her, at Leubronn, she has been winning at roulette and has visions of being worshiped as a goddess of luck.

George Eliot's rhetorical treatment of her heroine is initially quite unsympathetic. She presents her as a greedy, reckless, petty, domineering, selfish, insensitive, self-aggrandizing young woman of whom she disapproves. At the end, Gwendolen describes herself to Deronda as having been "always wicked" (ch. 64) and says that "all the wrong" she has done was in her at the time of their encounter at Leubronn (ch. 56). In the second half of the novel, George Eliot subscribes to this view. Despite the negative rhetoric, however, Gwendolen is not initially presented as wicked, but rather as an overindulged narcissist who is bound to be chastened by reality, much like Fred Vincy. Like Fred, she is subjected to a series of blows to her conception of herself and her place in the world, and she proves far more susceptible than he to having her illusions shattered and to being humbled. From a thematic perspective, she becomes the most thoroughly deflated and transformed of George Eliot's egoists.

As harsh realities close in on Gwendolen and crush her pride, the tone of the rhetoric changes. She becomes a "poor spoiled child" (ch. 26) who is deserving of our compassion—it is not Gwendolen's fault, after all, that she was indulged. She is presented more and more as the victim of her upbringing and of her woman's lot, by which she is profoundly oppressed. Shortly before her encounter with Mrs. Glasher, who illustrates some of the injustices of the feminine condition, she explains woman's plight to Grandcourt: "We women can't go in search of adventure. . . . We must stay where we grow, or where the gardeners like to transplant us. We are brought up like flowers, to look as pretty as we can, and be dull without complaining. That is my notion about the plants: they are often bored, and that is the reason why some of them have got poisonous" (ch. 13).

This brilliant passage offers a rationale for Gwendolen's being poisonous; but with a few exceptions, she has not been depicted as deliberately vicious or cruel. There *is* one early passage in which she is characterized as ruthless. How is it, George Eliot asks, that Gwendolen was able to maintain her domestic empire? Her decisiveness, her charm, and her mother's defensiveness about her second marriage all contribute to her ascendency; but the narrator suggests that she might have attained it even without these advantages. For she is one of those people who display "a strong determination to have what [is] pleasant, with a total fearlessness in making themselves disagreeable or dangerous when they [do] not get it," who have an "inborn energy of egoistic desire" and a "power of inspiring fear as to what [they] might say or do" (ch. 4).

What is most interesting to me about this passage is that it ends on a very different note. We are told that those who fear Gwendolen are also fond of her:

> the fear and the fondness being perhaps both heightened by what may be called the iridescence of her character—the play of various, nay, contrary tendencies. For Macbeth's rhetoric about the impossibility of being many opposite things in the same moment, referred to the clumsy necessities of action and not to the subtler possibilities of feeling. We cannot speak a loyal word and be meanly silent, we cannot kill and not kill in the same moment; but a moment is room wide enough for the loyal and mean desire, for the outlash of a murderous thought and the sharp backward stroke of repentance.

The passage begins with a description of Gwendolen as a determinedly single-minded person who is not afraid to make herself disagreeable or dangerous in order to get her way but ends with the suggestion that she is full of contradictory tendencies. Her aggressive impulses produce a backlash of repentance. (The reference to

Macbeth is a foreshadowing of what happens in the second half of the novel. Just as Macbeth cannot murder Duncan without suffering from an overwhelming sense of guilt, so Gwendolen cannot wrong Mrs. Glasher without feeling pangs of conscience. Both would have been able to get away with their actions had they had the courage of their crimes, and both are pursued by a nemesis that operates primarily from within [on Macbeth, see Paris 1991a]. The reference also prefigures Gwendolen's murderous impulses toward Grandcourt and her struggle against them.) Within a single paragraph, George Eliot compares Gwendolen to "unscrupulous male" domestic tyrants, whose inborn energy of egoistic desire is unfettered by scruples (Grandcourt comes to mind), and indicates that she is the very opposite of the kind of person who can make herself disagreeable or dangerous without experiencing inner qualms.

Later, in comparing Gwendolen with Grandcourt, George Eliot observes that her "will had seemed imperious in its small girlish sway; but it was the will of a creature with a large discourse of imaginative fears: a shadow would have been enough to relax its hold" (ch. 35). Here Gwendolen is presented as psychologically complex, but in the early part of the novel George Eliot does not seem to have made up her mind whether she wants us to see Gwendolen as a shallow egoist with no inner conflicts or a complicated woman beset by "contrary tendencies."

The version of Gwendolen as untouched by inner conflict is advanced most vividly in chapter 2, after she has learned of her mother's loss of fortune. She stays up all night packing for her departure from Leubronn and, as dawn arrives, she turns to gaze at herself in a mirror:

> It is possible to have a strong self-love without any self-satisfaction, rather with a self-discontent which is the more intense because one's own little core of egoistic sensibility is a supreme care; but Gwendolen knew nothing of such inward strife. She had a *naïve* delight in her fortunate self, which any but the harshest saintliness will have some indulgence for in a girl who had every day seen a pleasant reflection of that self in her friends' flattery as well as in the looking-glass. And even in this beginning of troubles, while for lack of anything else to do she sat gazing at her image in the growing light, her face gathered a complacency gradual as the cheerfulness of the morning. Her beautiful lips curled into a more and more decided smile, till at last she took off her hat, leaned forward and kissed the cold glass which had looked so warm. How could she believe in sorrow? If it attacked her, she felt the

force to crush it, to defy it, or run away from it, as she had
done already. Anything seemed more possible than that she
could go on bearing miseries, great or small.

When we first encounter this passage, it seems part of the picture of
Gwendolen as someone with such a strong belief in herself and her
star that she easily rebounds when her faith is challenged, as it is first
by Deronda's scrutiny and then by her mother's misfortune. This belief
in herself is certainly an aspect of Gwendolen's personality. As we
read on, however, the passage seems more and more discordant with
both rhetoric and mimesis. The rhetoric increasingly presents
Gwendolen as subject to internal strife, and the mimesis shows her to
be so almost from the beginning of the novel—indeed, from the very
beginning, if we take her susceptibility to Deronda's measuring gaze
as an indication of underlying insecurity. She requires constant admiration because she is not confident of possessing the superiority she
needs in order to feel worthwhile. Her "own little core of egoistic
sensibility" *is* "a supreme care."

In George Eliot's mimetic portrait of Gwendolen, her narcissism
and her insecurity are closely related: it is because she is so narcissistic
that she is so insecure. Her narcissism is, as the rhetoric suggests, a
product of her upbringing. As a favored and talented child, she was
made to feel special, remarkable, the object of everyone's attention
and deference. She emerges from childhood with an exalted conception of herself and her destiny. Her project as an adult is to maintain
the favored position she has occupied in her family, by winning a
comparable affirmation of her power and superiority from the social
world at large and, indeed, from fortune itself. She seeks to accom-
plish this by asserting her claims and exercising her charm, and her
belief in her beauty, talent, and prerogatives often has a bewitching
effect. She needs perpetual confirmation of her grandiose vision of
herself, and she has, as a result, an insatiable hunger for admiration
that manifests itself in scene after scene.

Gwendolen's incessant need for affirmation makes her extremely
dependent on the approbation of others, and hence very vulnerable. It
is difficult for her to feel secure in her high self-estimation, because it
is based on others' unearned deference and flattery rather than on
substantial accomplishments of her own. As a spoiled child and a
member of the leisure class, she has not had to submit to discipline or
prove herself, as someone like Mirah Lapidoth has had to do.
Gwendolen's sense of her own worth and position is at once very
elevated and very fragile. It is easily threatened, but because she has
been so long indulged, it is also resilient. Much like Shakespeare's

Richard II (see Paris 1991b), she has internalized the image of herself projected by her flatterers; and she alternates between it and her self-doubts, which increase as she encounters harsh realities.

George Eliot's rhetoric emphasizes the chastening of the foolishly self-confident heroine, and her moral growth as her illusions are destroyed and she confronts truths about herself and the world. Gwendolen is presented unsympathetically until her complacency begins to collapse, after which she becomes an object of pity. The mimetic portrait of Gwendolen shows her vulnerable from the beginning, as she struggles to maintain her self-image in the face of challenges. She is arrogant until her pride is crushed, but accompanying her cockiness are undertones of hopelessness, self-doubt, and anxiety.

In the opening scene of the novel, Gwendolen's conception of herself is challenged when Deronda looks at her with what she takes to be disapproval while she is gambling. If her self-love is as secure as George Eliot would have us believe, it is difficult to understand why she reacts to Deronda as intensely as she does and why she continues to be haunted by this episode. Gwendolen's self-confidence is based on the flattery of people to whom she feels superior and whose opinion she does not really respect. She may question at some level whether she is truly as wonderful as everyone says. Both the flattery she has received and the self-confidence founded on it can be subverted by a judgment that seems to have greater authority. Deronda is "young, handsome, distinguished in appearance," different from "the human dross around her" (ch. 1). He is someone whose opinion she cannot dismiss. When she feels him "looking down on her as an inferior," her belief in herself is shaken. Indeed, it seems to me that it was shaky to begin with and that Gwendolen's sense of being regarded as an inferior is in part a projection of uncertainties she has about herself.

When Gwendolen's luck at roulette abandons her, she tries to maintain her pride by losing strikingly. After her money is gone, she turns resolutely toward Deronda and looks at him: "There was a smile of irony in his eyes as their glances met; but it was at least better that he should have kept his attention fixed on her than that he should have disregarded her as one of an insect swarm who had no individual physiognomy. Besides, in spite of his superciliousness and irony, it was difficult to believe that he did not admire her spirit as well as her person" (ch.1). Gwendolen seeks to alleviate her feeling that Deronda is looking down on her by taking satisfaction in the persistence of his attention and persuading herself that he admires her. She assures herself not only of Deronda's regard but also of her superiority to the multitude, the swarm of insects that are indistinguishable from one another.

Although wincing from Deronda's measuring gaze, Gwendolen wants to learn more about him and gain an introduction, presumably so that she can charm him and in that way restore her pride. They are not introduced that evening, however; and when she returns to her room, she finds the letter from her mother announcing the family's misfortune. Gwendolen is half-stupefied at first, but her belief in her luck quickly revives, and she decides to sell a necklace containing turquoises that had once belonged to her father, and so perhaps retrieve her losses. As she debates whether to leave immediately or return to the gaming table, she is deterred from the latter course first by the image of Deronda watching her and then by his restoration of her necklace, which she finds humiliating: "No one had ever before dared to treat her with irony and contempt" (ch. 2). Instead of being able to assuage her discomfort by exerting her personal influence on Deronda, she feels herself rebuked.

The blows to Gwendolen's pride with which the novel opens lay the foundation for her psychological dependency on Deronda. They bring her underlying insecurity much closer to the surface and lead her to regard him as her moral superior. She feels uncomfortable about herself when she sees herself through his eyes, and she can relieve her discomfort only by meeting his standards. As the novel progresses, she becomes preoccupied with discovering what his standards are and trying to gain his approval. She transfers her pride from herself to him and looks to him to save her from self-hatred. None of this would have happened if Gwendolen had had the complacency, the freedom from inward strife, the naive delight in her fortunate self that George Eliot ascribes to her in chapter 2.

MORE VERSIONS OF GWENDOLEN

Despite George Eliot's description of Gwendolen as a shallow egoist with no inner conflicts, we can see from the beginning that she is a complicated woman beset by insecurities who works very hard at fending off threats to her self-image and maintaining her claims for herself. As her portrait of Gwendolen's psychological complexity deepens in the chapters that follow, George Eliot's uncertainty about the story she is telling continues to manifest itself, for while she shows us her heroine's self-doubts and anxieties, she also dwells on Gwendolen's self-satisfaction and her need to be humbled.

Although the opening chapters suggest that Gwendolen's exalted sense of herself has not been challenged before her encounter with Deronda, we find that she has already suffered blows to her pride, the first of these when she sings at the Arrowpoints and is told by Klesmer that she has not been well taught and has chosen music which "expresses a puerile state of culture" (ch. 5). Accustomed to "unmingled applause," she now experiences "a sinking of heart at the sudden width of horizon opened round her small musical performance." The imagery of widening horizons introduced here recurs in the novel as Gwendolen is shaken out of her narrow view of the world. In typical fashion, Gwendolen hopes to repair her wounded ego by finding an opportunity to win Klesmer's admiration. She develops a plan of acting in charades as a way of cutting a more striking figure in the neighborhood; but struck with terror when the panel opens to reveal the portrait of a dead face, she is mortified instead. Divining her distress, Klesmer tries to be kind by taking her reaction for good acting; and Gwendolen, eager to believe, cherishes "the idea that now he [is] struck with her talent as well as her beauty" (ch. 6). She is thus able to restore her pride through self-deception.

In commenting on Gwendolen's response to the dead face, George Eliot tells us of a "helpless fear," a "susceptibility to terror," a "spiritual dread," that sometimes overtakes her. Like the study of astronomy in school, "solitude in any wide scene" impresses her with "an undefined feeling of immeasurable existence aloof from her, in the midst of which she [is] helplessly incapable of asserting herself" (ch. 6). Gwendolen's "fits of timidity or terror" suggest that she has a good deal of anxiety and that her armor of egoistic complacency is easily pierced. Her self-confidence, like that of many spoiled children, does not rest on a solid foundation. She seems to oscillate between believing in her luck, or the magic of her will, and feeling impotent and vulnerable.

Gwendolen's grandoise conception of herself is threatened not only by Klesmer and the vast indifferent universe, but also by Catherine Arrowpoint, who lacks physical beauty but has attained a mental superiority and a level of musical accomplishment that make it "impossible to force her admiration and [that keep] you in awe of her standard" (ch. 6). I am reminded of the rivalrous feelings that Emma Woodhouse, another narcissist, has toward the more disciplined and accomplished Jane Fairfax (see Paris 1978). Despite Catherine's kindness, Gwendolen suspects her of regarding her accomplishments as of a common order. She recovers her equanimity by relishing the approval she receives from her less discriminating neighbors. The pattern is again a threat to her pride that she manages to ward off. It seems that it will require heavier blows to shatter her complacency.

Heavier blows do follow, badly bruising Gwendolen's belief in herself and her star. The proposed marriage to Grandcourt has shown a hideous flaw; her chances at roulette have not adjusted themselves to her claims; her mother has lost her fortune; Deronda has injured her pride; and she is faced with the prospect of having to become a governess. Although Gwendolen begins to sense "the close threats of humiliation,"she feels "clever enough for anything" (ch. 23) and still believes that she can master her destiny. She plans to go on stage, but Klesmer tells her that people will no longer ignore her blunders and that she will never achieve more than mediocrity. Lacerated by Klesmer's words, she has, for the first time in her life, a "vision of herself on the common level." She loses "the innate sense that there were reasons why she should not be slighted, elbowed, jostled—treated like a passenger with a third-class ticket, in spite of private objections on her own part." Gwendolen becomes disenchanted with both the world and herself—the world because it fails to honor her claims, and herself because she finds she does not have the powers she thought she possessed. When the failure of the world to accede to her expectations shatters the illusion that she is destined for easy preeminence, she feels no longer powerful and fortunate but helpless and victimized.

George Eliot has been presenting Gwendolen as a spoiled child whose delusions have been fostered by excessive indulgence and will soon present her as a sinful woman whose conscience is awakened by her marriage to a man who rightfully belongs to someone else. In chapter 26, however, we are given another version of Gwendolen: namely, as a girl who is manifesting no more than the unrealistic expectations and exaggerated frustrations of youth. She is in the "first crisis of passionate youthful rebellion" against "the absence of joy." She is experiencing "that first rage of disappointment in life's morning, which we whom the years have subdued are apt to remember but dimly as part of our own experience, and so to be intolerant of its self-enclosed unreasonableness and impiety." The suggestion here is that Gwendolen's experience is a common one, a part of growing up, and that we readers have been through the same thing and should have compassion for her. Her "amazed anguish" that she is "the smitten one" seems "absurd" from the perspective of age; but we should remember that some who have later become heroically unselfish "nevertheless began with this angry amazement at their own smart, and on the mere denial of their fantastic desires raged as if under the sting of wasps which reduced the universe for them to an unjust infliction of pain."

This observation foreshadows Deronda's assurance that Gwendolen can become one of those women who make others glad they were born. In chapter 26, however, the rhetoric has the effect of blurring the detailed portrait of the conditions in which she grew up, and the consequences of those conditions, and replacing it with generalizations about the absurdities of youth. Gwendolen's "self-enclosed unreasonableness,"

her "fantastic desires," her "angry amazement," her "rage of disappointment," and her sense of injustice are not simply products of youth;
rather, they belong to her individual psychology, which George Eliot
both brilliantly depicts and obscures.

The shape of Gwendolen's story after her marriage is predominantly one of crime, punishment, and reformation, of the awakening
of conscience after transgression. I shall examine that part of the story
in the next chapter. The chastening of her egoism is a continuing theme,
however. From Deronda, Gwendolen learns that instead of knowing
what is admirable, she is ignorant and selfish. From Grandcourt, she
learns the folly of her ideas about marriage and the impotence of her
will. Her narrowness and self-importance continue to be scourged to
the end. Her dependency on Deronda is presented as another form of
egoism that must be overcome. She has seen Daniel only from the
perspective of her own needs, without any sense of his independent
existence. When she learns of his "wide-stretching purposes," she feels
herself "reduced to a mere speck" and is dislodged at last "from her
supremacy in her own world" (ch. 69).

GWENDOLEN'S SORROWS

I have argued that in the first half of the novel, Gwendolen is portrayed primarily as an egoist who is being chastened and that George
Eliot's presentation of her is confusing. Although we are usually invited to see her as a spoiled child, in one passage her claims and
illusions are described as being typical of youth. The picture of her is
further clouded by George Eliot's depiction of her as both ruthless and
moved by compunction, simple and complex, unabashedly selfish and
full of contrary tendencies, shallowly complacent and deeply insecure.
The more closely we examine George Eliot's mimetic portrait of
Gwendolen, the more perplexing it becomes and the more dissonant
it seems with some of the rhetoric.

The most vivid account of the simple, confident, self-adoring
Gwendolen occurs in the passage I have quoted from chapter 2, in
which we are told that she feels fortunate, delights in herself, and does
not believe in sorrow. Despite her mother's loss of fortune, Gwendolen's
face becomes complacent, her lips curve into a smile, and she kisses
her image in the glass: "How could she believe in sorrow? If it at-
tacked her, she felt the force to crush it, to defy it, or run away from
it, as she had done already." However, in George Eliot's account of the
heroine's earlier history, Gwendolen believes in sorrow all too well.
She exhibits despair about her lot, a feeling that happiness is unattain-

able and that life holds nothing worthwhile. Moreover, inclined though she is toward self-adulation, she feels at times that something is wrong with her.

Gwendolen has not had a happy life. After the family settles at Offendene, Mrs. Davilow urges that her daughter be provided with a horse because she needs cheering; and Gwendolen feels that in many ways she has been "hardly dealt with" (ch. 4). She has been treated like a princess, to be sure; but she is a "princess *in exile*, who *in time of famine* was to have her breakfast-roll made of the finest-bolted flour from *the seven thin ears of wheat*" (my emphasis). For most of Gwendolen's existence, her family has experienced hard times.

After Gwendolen's father dies, while she is quite young, her mother marries Captain Davilow, by whom she has four daughters. Gwendolen regards them as "superfluous" and "unimportant," yet "from her earliest days" they are "an obtrusive influential fact in her life" (ch. 3). She wishes her mother had not remarried, resents having to share her with her sisters, and dislikes being asked to do anything for them. Her uncle observes that her mother's second family has kept Gwendolen "in the shade." Although we know little about her stepfather, it is evident that he has been an oppressive presence in her life. Her mother has inherited a fortune from the maternal side of her family; but Captain Davilow appropriates her income, sells her jewels to gain additional money, and forces the family into a life of shabby gentility that Gwendolen intensely dislikes, since it forces her to meet new people under conditions that make her "appear of little importance."

To understand Gwendolen's psychology, we must recognize that she has been both indulged and frustrated. She is treated like royalty at home but has not been able to occupy what she regards as her proper position in society. She is a princess *in exile*. Her experience in the family and her sense of superiority to other young women at school give rise to claims that are not being fulfilled by the life she has to lead. She feels that with her beauty, talent, intelligence, and charm, she should be able to conquer the world, just as she has mastered the people immediately around her; but she has not yet been able to do so on any large scale. Even though her claims on fate have been repeatedly frustrated, she keeps asserting them as a way of insisting that life must eventually give her what she deserves. She does not want to reconcile herself to things as they are, for that would mean accepting a diminished status and relinquishing the hope of fulfilling her dreams.

The death of her stepfather and the move to Offendene mark a major turning point in Gwendolen's life. With the return of her fortune to her own control, her mother can "take up her abode in a house which had once sufficed for a dowager countess." In view of the family's previous existence in "the border-territory of rank," this restitution means a great deal to Mrs. Davilow, and even more to Gwendolen (ch. 3). Despite her conviction that so exceptional a person as she could hardly remain in ordinary circumstances, Gwendolen *has* been apprehensive; but now that her mother has such a satisfactory establishment, her fears are banished. She is proud of living at Offendene, which will provide an excellent background for her triumphs.

After having long been frustrated, Gwendolen's claims are being honored at last. Her suffering pride is now being fed, and her dreams are coming true. Her belief in her star has been vindicated; she is to have the position for which she has felt destined. The family will no longer subsist in the "border-territory of rank," and she will no longer be kept in the shade. Her need to convince herself of this new reality may be responsible, to some extent at least, for her imperious behavior when we first see her at Offendene. She wants to confirm her status by asserting her prerogatives. She resists giving lessons to her sisters and refuses to help Anna in the schools, not simply because she regards these things as unpleasant, but because she needs to establish that they are beneath her, that she should not be expected to go on making sacrifices for "creatures worth less than herself" (ch. 4).

Gwendolen now has an appropriate position from which to pursue her goal of "having the world at her feet" (ch. 4), and she is determined not to allow herself to be "blown hither and thither" like other young women but to conquer circumstance through her cleverness. Her yearning for ascendancy lacks a clear focus, however. Although she knows that she does "not wish to lead the same sort of life as ordinary young ladies" do, she has no idea of "how she should set about leading any other" (ch. 6).

Gwendolen has difficulty imagining how she can fulfill her ambition within the confines of a woman's lot. In her society, as Mr. Gascoigne says, "marriage is the only true and satisfactory sphere of a woman" (ch. 13); but Gwendolen regards matrimony as "a dreary state, in which a woman could not do what she liked, had more children than were desirable," and became dull as a consequence (ch. 4). She tells Rex that girls lives are "stupid" because "they never do what they like" and that she "never saw a married woman who had her own way" (ch. 7). When he asks her what she would like to do, she replies: "Oh, I don't know!—go to the North Pole, or ride steeplechases, or go to be a queen in the East like Lady Hester Stanhope." She complains to Grandcourt that "women can't go in search of adventures—to find out the North-West Passage or the source of the Nile, or to hunt tigers in the East" (ch. 13). Like plants, they must stay where they grow or are transplanted, and thus often become bored and poisonous. Gwendolen would like to lead an adventurous life, to achieve a masculine kind of triumph. During her winning streak at Leubronn, she has visions of being worshiped as a goddess of luck by followers who would "watch her play as a directing augury. Such things had been known of male gamblers; why should not a woman have like supremacy?" (ch. 1). She craves the kind of freedom, power, and excitement that are usually available only to men.

Gwendolen can find no feminine role models, except for the exotic Lady Hester Stanhope. She is as rebellious against the constraints of her lot "as if she had been sustained by the boldest speculations; but she really had no such speculations, and would at once have marked herself off from any sort of theoretical or practically reforming women by satirising them" (ch. 6). Her "passion for doing what is remarkable" must be made consistent "with the highest breeding," and so her "pursuit of striking adventure" is "held captive by the ordinary wirework of social forms," and she "does nothing in particular."

Gwendolen is a would-be rebel who is paralyzed by her narrowness and conventionality. Like Ibsen's Hedda Gabler, she feels oppressed by her lot and wishes she were a man; but, as with Hedda, her desire to escape the restrictions of her culture is checked by an even more powerful need to conform to its codes (for a discussion of Hedda, see Paris 1997). She is like Dorothea Brooke in wanting to lead a grand life and not knowing how to do so, except that for her the grand life consists of "personal pre-eminence and *éclat*" (ch. 24). She, too, feels thwarted by the "meanness of opportunity"; but in her we discover no spiritual grandeur, no epic aspirations such as Dorothea's. Gwendolen's ambition pales alongside that of Dorothea, who wants to have an impact on the world and on history. Gwendolen's "horizon," George Eliot tells us, is "that of the genteel romance" (ch. 6). Her desire to lead dwells "among strictly feminine furniture" and has "no disturbing reference to the advancement of learning or the balance of the constitution" (ch. 4). She longs to transcend her lot; but she has no real knowledge, embraces no larger interests, and cannot imagine being anything other than a proper lady.

Thus, although her stepfather's death, her mother's independence, and the establishment of the family at Offendene seem to open the possibility of satisfying her "hunger for supremacy," there is, in fact, very little Gwendolen can do. George Eliot tells us that she "means to lead," that "such passions dwell in feminine breasts also" (ch. 4); but all Gwendolen can carry off is small social triumphs in which she eclipses other women in what she comes to regard as a mediocre neighborhood. The author's descriptions of Gwendolen as busy contriving ways to "make her life pleasant" (ch. 11) do not seem quite right. The following passage is more precise: "She meant to do what was pleasant to herself in a striking manner; or, rather whatever she could do so as to strike others with admiration and get in that reflected way a more ardent sense of living, seemed pleasant to her fancy" (ch. 4).

Gwendolen is motivated not by a search for pleasure per se but by a compulsive need to win admiration. Lacking an inner sense of worth and direction, she is dependent on the flattering image of herself that her domestic circle has always reflected. To gain reassurance and overcome her feelings of emptiness, she requires the same kind of homage from the broader social world, and especially from men. In the presence of women, who pay her no homage, she has "a sense of empty benches" (ch. 11). She sees herself as an independent spirit who can assert her will and master her fate, but her insatiable hunger for admiration puts her at the mercy of other people, whose view of her she is constantly trying to influence. Her attempts always to do something striking yield little more than a series of fleeting triumphs.

Gwendolen's big day comes at the archery meeting, where she outshines all other women. For a while she is able to lose herself in the moment and not worry about "what she should do next to keep her life at the due pitch" (ch. 11), but her euphoria does not last long. Later in the day she tells her mother that she wishes she were like Catherine Arrowpoint:

> "Why? Are you getting discontented with yourself, Gwen?"
> "No, but I am discontented with things. She seems contented."
> "I am sure you ought to be satisfied to-day. You must have enjoyed the shooting. I saw you did."
> "Oh, that is over now, and I don't know what will come next." (ch. 11)

What comes next, of course, is Henleigh Grandcourt, who revives her exultation by asking her to dance: "She was now convinced that he meant to distinguish her, to mark his admiration of her in a noticeable way; and it began to appear probable that she would have it in her power to reject him, whence there was a pleasure in reckoning up the advantages which would make her rejection splendid, and in giving Mr Grandcourt his utmost value."

Gwendolen's triumph on this day is now complete, but note that her fantasy is of achieving glory by rejecting a splendid offer rather than by accepting it. This would be a magnificent union, which is unobjectionable as far as she knows; yet she has great difficulty responding to Grandcourt's advances. If she does not want such a marriage, what is she to do with her life? Her reluctance is largely attributable to her feelings about matrimony, which have little to do with this particular man.

We are told that Gwendolen's thoughts "never dwelt on marriage as the fulfilment of her ambition" (ch. 4). It is true that marriage is "social promotion"; nevertheless, "a peerage will not quite do instead of leadership to the man who meant to lead." Gwendolen means to lead, and marriage, however grand, will subject her to "domestic fetters" and place her in a subordinate position. She wants to be "very much sued or hopelessly sighed for" as a sign of her "womanly power," but becoming a wife seems "a vexatious necessity" to which she sees no alternative. It is a triumph that would have "to be taken with bitter herbs."

Gwendolen derives her picture of marriage largely from her observation of her mother. Far from being unable to believe in sorrow, Gwendolen has difficulty believing in happiness. "Can nobody be happy," she asks her mother, "after they are quite young? You have made me feel sometimes as if nothing were of any use. With the girls so troublesome, . . . and everything make-shift about us, and you looking so dull—what was the use of my being anything?" (ch. 3). Living under makeshift conditions with a mother who is chronically depressed, Gwendolen has had a sense of futility about exercising her powers: "What is the use of my being charming, if it is to end in my being dull and not minding anything? Is that what marriage always comes to?" Although Gwendolen may have moments of naive delight in her fortunate self, she sees her mother's fate as a prefiguration of her own and fears being overcome by her lassitude and despair. When her mother complains of being old, Gwendolen remonstrates: "Please don't mamma! . . . You are hardly twenty-five years older than I am. When you talk in that way my life shrivels up before me" (ch. 14).

Gwendolen's high spirits over the move to Offendene are the result in part of new hopes for her mother. With Captain Davilow out of the way and her fortune now in her own hands, perhaps her mother will be able to be happy. On the day of their arrival, however, Mrs. Davilow's morale shows no sign of improvement. When Gwendolen expresses a wish that her nose were straight like her mother's, instead of being upturned, Mrs. Davilow, "with a deep, weary sigh" replies: "Oh, my dear, any nose will do to be miserable with in this world" (ch. 3). "'Now mamma,'" says Gwendolen, "with an air of vexation, 'don't begin to be dull here. It spoils all my pleasure. . . . What have you to be gloomy about now?'" When Mrs. Davilow says that it is enough for her to see Gwendolen happy, her daughter responds: "But you should be happy yourself." Gwendolen feels that she cannot be happy unless her mother is also, and she is quite disappointed that the new conditions of their life seem to have made so little difference.

Her mother's unhappiness in marriage has such a powerful impact on Gwendolen because the two women have an extraordinarily close relationship: they are mutually dependent, identify with each other, and are highly sensitive to each other's feelings. When younger, Mrs. Davilow was a beauty, like Gwendolen but unlike her other daughters; and she longs to see her own frustrated hopes fulfilled by this promising child. Her mother's having been a beauty intensifies Gwendolen's identification with her and contributes to the daughter's fear that she will suffer a similar fate. Mrs. Davilow has resigned herself to being unhappy but seeks vicarious fulfillment through her daughter. Gwendolen senses this and later goes to great pains to conceal her misery.

Mrs. Davilow feels guilty about having married again and subjected Gwendolen to the ills that has entailed. This is one reason she is so tender, timid, and filled with compunction. She spoils Gwendolen in part to compensate for the wrongs done her. As a spoiled child, Gwendolen is very dependent on the parent who spoils her, especially given that, except in small ways, the rest of the world is not yet honoring her claims to grandeur and happiness. Her mother is her chief source of appreciation, indulgence, and stability during the lean years of the family's exile. She is the only person Gwendolen trusts, about whom she cares, and with whom she can have an intimate relationship.

Gwendolen craves the homage of men; but she neither likes them nor envisages the possibility of marrying for emotional or sexual fulfillment. She wonders "how girls manage to fall in love"—after all, "men are too ridiculous" (ch. 7). She has a "physical repulsion to being directly made love to" and is famously frigid. She "curl[s] up and harden[s] like a sea-anemone at the touch of a finger" when Rex tries to be tender: "Pray don't make love to me! I hate it," she exclaims, looking "at him fiercely." Despite her delight in being adored, there is "a certain fierceness of maidenhood in her." George Eliot offers no explanation for this facet of Gwendolen's personality, but it does not seem out of keeping with her character. Gwendolen's life offers no admirable male figures, just as it offers no positive female role models. She sees women as misused, fettered, and dull, and men as ridiculous. She seems to have been traumatized by her mother's treatment at the hands of her stepfather and to be defending herself against her fear of men by regarding them as creatures who are not to be taken seriously. She has profound inhibitions about needing them, in view of what has happened to her mother, and about letting them get too close to her.

Despite her boldness and social ambition, Gwendolen is anxiously dependent on and attached to her family, especially in her relationship with her mother. Petted and flattered by her mother and those immediately around her, she has been otherwise under the cloud of her family's makeshift arrangements and marginal social position. Her charms and small triumphs have not made her confident of achieving happiness or receiving the treatment she feels she deserves. She needs to conquer the world, while remaining at a safe emotional distance from it, invulnerable to its potential slings and arrows. She clings to her mother, from whom she has not achieved the kind of separation that would allow her to form other close relationships. That she sleeps in her mother's bedroom is a clear indication that something has gone awry in her development, that she has not outgrown her early dependency and is afraid to be on her own.

Gwendolen knows that something is wrong with her. After the scene with Rex, her mother finds her "sobbing bitterly." She cries, "Oh mamma, what can become of my life? There is nothing worth living for!" (ch. 7). There are her competitive triumphs, of course, but at the moment these seem empty to Gwendolen, in view of her emotional sterility and fear of other people. When her mother asks why nothing is worth living for, Gwendolen replies: "I shall never love anybody. I can't love people. I hate them." More and more "convulsed with sobbing," she puts "her arms around her mother's neck with an almost painful clinging" and confides, "I can't bear any one to be very near me but you." Then her mother begins to sob, "for this spoiled child had never shown such dependence on her before: and so they clung to each other." Gwendolen seems to be saying that life is not worth living without love, but that she is incapable of it and cannot not let anyone else get close to her. She physically recoils from Rex's attempts at tenderness but fiercely embraces her mother. It seems clear that Gwendolen's dependence is sweet to her mother, who has, perhaps unconsciously, encouraged it, and who needs to be needed by her child. Gwendolen's sobbing and clinging bring back the days when Mrs. Davilow was all in all to her daughter.

Almost like lovers, Gwendolen and her mother are highly attuned to each other's feelings. Gwendolen is oppressed by her mother's sadness and wishes she could relieve it. When Gwendolen becomes listless after her hopes are dashed by Klesmer, her mother watches her "with silent distress; and, lapsing into the habit of indulgent tenderness," she begins to imagine what Gwendolen is "thinking, and to wish that everything should give way to the possibility of making her darling less miserable" (ch. 24). Gwendolen engages in a similar kind of empathic involvement with her mother. Full of self-pity, she envisions herself being even more unhappy than her mother has been, but then she realizes that now her mother's life will be still worse, and she resolves to try to earn some money for her: "And then with an entirely new movement of her imagination, she saw her mother getting quite old and white, and herself no longer young but faded, and their two faces meeting still with memory and love, and she knowing what was in her mother's mind—'Poor Gwen too is sad and faded now'—and then for the first time she sobbed, not in anger but with a sort of tender misery" (ch. 26). In her imagination what she has always feared has come to pass—she has become just like her mother. Her identification is complete, and she sobs in tender misery for them both.

We have seen that in one place George Eliot describes Gwendolen as having a strong determination to have what is pleasant and a total fearlessness in making herself dangerous or disagreeable when she does not get it. This is certainly not true in relation to her mother; for, although she does sometimes injure her through selfishness or insensitivity, she always feels very uncomfortable about it and tries to avoid a recurrence. She refuses to get medicine for her mother one night, but the next day she is "keenly conscious of what must be in her mamma's mind" and tries "to make amends by caresses" (ch. 3). When her mother shows her memorials of her father and Gwendolen asks why she married again, Mrs. Davilow says, "You have no feeling child." After this, Gwendolen, ashamed, never dares to ask a question about her father. Mrs. Davilow is a vulnerable, unhappy woman who is easily hurt, and Gwendolen is very much afraid of adding to her mother's misery by injuring her feelings. The girl can hardly be said to have had a carefree childhood. Spoiled by her mother, to be sure, Gwendolen also feels terribly burdened by and responsible for her.

An especially revealing scene between Gwendolen and her mother occurs in chapter 9, when, not having met Grandcourt as yet, they are speculating on what kind of man he is. When Gwendolen says she feels sure that "with a little murdering he might get a title," her mother attributes such ideas to the books she has been reading:

"I declare when your aunt and I were your age we knew nothing about wickedness. I think it was better so."

"Why did you not bring me up in that way, mamma?" said Gwendolen.

But immediately perceiving in the crushed look and rising sob that she had given a deep wound, she tossed down her hat and knelt at her mother's feet, crying—

"Mamma, mamma! I was only speaking in fun. I meant nothing."

"How could I, Gwendolen," said poor Mrs Davilow, unable to hear the retraction, and sobbing violently while she made the effort to speak. "Your will was always too strong for me—if everything else had been different."

This disjointed logic was intelligible enough to the daughter. "Dear mamma, I don't find fault with you—I love you," said Gwendolen, really compunctious. "How can you help what I am? Besides, I am very charming. Come, now." Here Gwendolen with her handkerchief gently rubbed away her mother's tears. "Really—I am contented with myself. I like myself better than I should have liked my aunt and you. How dreadfully dull you must have been."

Although George Eliot sometimes suggests that Gwendolen rides roughshod over the people around her, she shows here how terribly sensitive Mrs. Davilow is to even the slightest suggestion of criticism, how readily Gwendolen feels compunction, and how hard she works at trying to placate her mamma. Her "tender cajolery," we are told, "served to quiet the mother, as it had often done before after like collisions." If this scene is any indication, it did not take much on Gwendolen's part to produce such collisions, given her mother's feelings of guilt and inadequacy as a parent and her histrionic tendencies. It is noteworthy that Gwendolen seeks to soothe her mother by assuring her that she is contented with herself, for Mrs. Davilow interprets any self-dissatisfaction on Gwendolen's part as a failure on hers.

Because of Mrs. Davilow's touchiness, the relationship between mother and daughter is filled with fear on both sides. Their collisions are rarely "repeated at the same point; for in the memory of both they left an association of dread with the particular topics which had occasioned them: Gwendolen dreaded the unpleasant sense of compunction towards her mother, which was the nearest approach to self-condemnation and self-distrust that she had known; and Mrs Davilow's timid maternal conscience dreaded whatever had brought on the slightest hint of reproach" (ch. 9). Gwendolen lives with a mother who not only is depressed but is extremely defensive, easily upset, and given to hysterical sobbing.

Here and elsewhere, the rhetoric presents Gwendolen as insufficiently self-distrustful and self-condemning—a deficiency that is soon to be remedied; but the mimetic portrait of her shows a person who must be extremely wary in her relations with an oversensitive parent about whom she cares deeply and whom she must frequently cajole. Indeed, perhaps partly as a result of her mother's skill in inducing guilt, Gwendolen is prone to remorse—not self-condemnation as

intense as she will later experience, but sufficient to curb her spontaneity and make her cautious in her dealings with others. Having always been petted, she finds it "difficult to think her own pleasure less
important than others [make] it" (ch. 3), and this leads her to behave
in ways that arouse her remorse and that she subsequently regrets.

One instance of this is her refusal to fetch her mother's medicine,
an act followed by pangs of compunction. Another is the strangling of
her sister's canary when its singing interrupts her own. George Eliot
sometimes depicts Gwendolen as demonic or ruthless; but we are told
that she has never, "even as a child," been "thoughtlessly cruel." Indeed, she has delighted in rescuing "drowning insects and watching
their recovery." Having acted in "contradiction [to] her habitual tendencies," she is haunted by her "murder" of the canary, buys her sister
a white mouse in restitution, and, now that she is older, turns "some
of her native force . . . into a self-control by which she guard[s] herself
from penitential humiliation." The rhetorical emphasis in this passage
is on Gwendolen's preference for making "her penances easy," but the
mimesis shows us a young woman in conflict. She tries very hard to
rein in the self-indulgent behavior fostered by the royal treatment she
has received in order to avoid the feelings of guilt to which she is prone.

ENTER GRANDCOURT

The main action in Gwendolen's story begins when Grandcourt arrives at Diplow. In a passage reminiscent of the opening of *Pride and
Prejudice*, George Eliot observes that some of her readers "will doubt-
less regard it as incredible that people should construct matrimonial
prospects on the mere report that a bachelor of good fortune and
possibilities was coming within reach" (ch. 9). Among those construct-
ing such prospects are Gwendolen's mother and uncle and aunt, all of
whom, Gwendolen jokes at the archery meeting, intend Grandcourt to
fall in love with her. Mr. Gascoigne has been working to put Gwendolen
on display since she moved into the neighborhood; and despite her
own unhappy experience, Mrs. Davilow can think of her daughter's
"welfare in no other shape than marriage." The marriage must be to
a man of fortune, which poor Rex is not; for no one can imagine
Gwendolen being satisfied in mean circumstances. Mrs. Davilow tells
herself that "it would not signify her being in love, if she would only
accept the right person." Indeed, no one, including Gwendolen, expects her to marry for love.

Gwendolen is not without interest in the prospects Grandcourt
represents, but she is quite guarded at first. Before she meets

Grandcourt, she takes the satirical attitude that leads to her mother's violent sobbing because she knows that her friends think of him as a desirable match, and she has a need to resist. But she is not indifferent to the impression she will make on this sought-after bachelor. Her fantasies are not of marriage but of winning admiration, receiving an offer, and thus triumphing over Catherine Arrowpoint, who, as an heiress, would presumably be Grandcourt's choice. She wants Grandcourt to want her, whether she wants him or not, but she maintains an ironic detachment to protect herself: "Whatever might come, she, Gwendolen, was not going to be disappointed: the affair was a joke whichever way it turned, for she had never committed herself even by a silent confidence in anything Mr. Grandcourt would do" (ch. 11).

Nonetheless, Gwendolen is disposed to be receptive to Grandcourt. Marriage is the only form her ambition can take, and a grand marriage is the only kind she can consider. She is annoyed by her family's expectations, but she cannot help being influenced by them, especially those of her mother. As we have seen, to fulfill her mother's needs, she must find herself likeable, be happy, and triumph where her mother has failed—in marriage and in relations with men. Her success will redeem her mother's life. Rex is in love with her, but he is not eligible, and no eligible young man of the neighborhood has made her an offer as yet.

As Grandcourt's attentions become unmistakable and she no longer fears disappointment, Gwendolen finds the prospect of marrying him more attractive "than she had believed beforehand that any marriage could be" (ch. 13). She lives for personal preeminence and éclat, and this marriage seems to offer the "dignities" and "luxuries" she "had only imagined and longed for before." She knows she must marry before her youthful bloom fades, and she doesn't see how she can do better than Grandcourt. He is the "most aristocratic looking man" she has ever met (ch. 11) and is "adorably free of absurdities" (ch. 13). The fact that he has been everywhere and seen everything makes his preference for her a great tribute.

Grandcourt's personal reserve and detached style of courting suit Gwendolen very well. There is no attempt at tenderness or importunate love-making to arouse her aversion to emotional closeness and physical contact. His calm, cold manner gives her the illusion that he might be less disagreeable than other men and less likely to interfere with her preferences. This impression is reinforced by his lack of enthusiasm for anything: "The less he had of particular tastes or desires, the more freedom his wife was likely to have in following hers. Gwendolen conceived that after marriage she would most probably be able to manage him thoroughly" (ch. 13). In a terrible miscalculation, she envisions marriage to Grandcourt as "a state of greater freedom" than she has experienced in girlhood.

But despite the attractiveness of the marriage and the pressure she is under to pursue it, Gwendolen keeps evading Grandcourt when he seems to be approaching a proposal and has an "uneasy consciousness of divided impulses" (ch. 13). He suits her purposes, and she intends to accept him, but she has great difficulty fulfilling this intention. She finds herself in the grip of compulsive behavior that she does not understand, and her "subjection to a possible self" whose actions she cannot predict causes her "some astonishment and terror." Since she consciously wants to marry Grandcourt, she welcomes her uncle's warnings against losing her chance and tells him that she means to accept Grandcourt "if possible."

What is going on here? What is the nature of Gwendolen's inner conflict? George Eliot depicts it quite vividly but makes only one comment regarding why the decision is so formidable: "Having come close to accepting Grandcourt, Gwendolen felt this lot of unhoped-for fulness rounding itself too definitely: when we take to wishing a great deal for ourselves, whatever we get turns into mere limitation and exclusion" (ch. 14). According to this explanation, Gwendolen has difficulty accepting Grandcourt because she is so greedy and insatiable that what he has to offer, vast as it is, does not seem enough. Marrying him would mean losing the possibility of other forms of egoistic gratification and triumph. This may be a factor, but I do not think it is the main reason for Gwendolen's hesitation. Here, as elsewhere, George Eliot intuitively grasps and dramatically portrays Gwendolen's behavior better than she explains it.

The mimetic portrait of Gwendolen leads me to believe that her hesitation is principally the product of all the negative feelings she has developed from her observations of woman's lot in general and her mother's matrimonial experience in particular. Her primary fear is of being shackled by domestic fetters and losing her freedom, as happened to her mother when she married Captain Davilow. Despite Gwendolen's effort to convince herself that marriage will be a state of greater freedom than girlhood, she has great difficulty overcoming her anxiety. George Eliot's rhetoric leads us to see Gwendolen as a strong-willed young woman who rules over a domestic empire and gets her own way most of the time, and there is no doubt that she hungers for mastery and power. Her hunger, however, is not simply a product of having been indulged and wanting to be indulged even more; it is partly a result of the frustrations of her lot and her desire to escape them. Marriage seems the only means of escape, but Gwendolen is afraid that it will be even more confining than the life she has led so far.

Like Hedda Gabler, Gwendolen is so intent on getting her way in small things because she is so powerless in large ones (see Paris 1997). Hemmed in by all the restrictions incumbent on her gender and station, she is unable to lead the life of adventure she craves and senses that she is becoming poisonous. She is indulged by her mother but is also burdened by her parent's unhappiness and anxiety. Gwendolen perceives that the life of an unmarried woman who has no power or freedom of movement is bound to be dull, but she has also seen how dull a woman can become when she is subject to the will of a husband. She fears that her fate is to be fettered no matter which way she chooses.

Gwendolen's preoccupation with freedom and doing as she likes reflects an almost phobic reaction to constraint that has grown out of the frustrations of her girlhood. While she is being courted, she must reassure herself that there is no "subjugation of her will," either by Grandcourt or her family (ch. 13). This is one reason she is frightened as well as attracted by "the splendid prospects" Grandcourt means to offer her: "Gwendolen desired every one, that dignified gentleman himself included, to understand that she was going to do just as she liked . . . .If she chose to take this husband, she would have him know that she was not going to renounce her freedom, or according to her favorite formula, 'not going to do as other women did.'" This is highly ironic, of course, in view of what happens after her marriage.

Gwendolen's encounter with Lydia Glasher is so traumatic in part because Mrs. Glasher represents the injustice of women's condition and their fate at the hands of men. She was young and beautiful when Grandcourt first knew her, but her "life has been broken and embittered" by his abandonment (ch. 14). "It is not fair," she proclaims, "that he should be happy and I miserable." Gwendolen reacts out of jealousy, indignation, and pride, and a recognition of Mrs. Glasher's claims. She recoils from Grandcourt with such intensity mainly because her encounter with Lydia Glasher reinforces her fears about her destiny and her profound distrust of men. Without giving her reasons, she tells her mother that she won't marry Grandcourt: "I don't care what comes of it. I don't care if I never marry anyone. There is nothing worth caring for. I believe all men are bad, and I hate them." She flees to the Continent with the von Langens, who had previously invited her to travel with them, and takes to gambling in Leubronn.

The action has now reached the point at which the novel begins. A rereading of the opening chapters in the context of what follows makes George Eliot's initial presentation of Gwendolen appear quite misleading and inadequate. The Gwendolen of the subsequent chapters, which give us her prior history, is not a smug, unconflicted egoist, with a hint of the demonic about her, who takes a naive delight in her fortunate self and cannot believe in sorrow. The scene before the mirror in chapter 2, which does so much to influence our initial impression of Gwendolen, comes to seem not only discordant but implausible. By traveling and gambling, Gwendolen is trying to escape despair, to imagine herself the mistress rather than the victim of fate, and to distract herself with excitements. Having no longer any vision of a possible future in which her dreams will be fulfilled and not caring what comes of her actions, she adopts a reckless attitude. Her cynical pursuit of amusement is an effort to avoid confronting the blankness of her prospects and the emptiness of her life. She responds so intensely to Deronda's measuring gaze in part because he seems to be above her. This intuition injures her pride but also gives her the feeling that he may know something that will help her. The spoiled child, full of grandiose claims, is in a desperate state.

Gwendolen's situation becomes much worse, of course, when her mother loses her fortune. The sense of futility previously induced by her mother's melancholy and their dreary life in exile is now intensified. Men are hateful, and events may turn out badly no matter what she does. She feels that everything has turned against her. What is "the good of living in the midst of hardships, ugliness, and humiliation"? (ch. 21).

Although Gwendolen is daunted, her spirit is not yet subdued. To avoid despair and to cheer her mother, now still more stricken, Gwendolen determines not to relinquish her claims on freedom and happiness. She refuses to resign herself to the will of providence, as her mother advises, and insists that she will not submit to the arrangements her uncle has made for moving to Sawyer's Cottage. She turns to a fantasy she has had before, that of becoming a celebrated actress. Indeed, becoming a great actress would be much better than making a grand match. She now wonders "whether she need take a husband at all—whether she could not achieve substantiality for herself and know gratified ambition *without bondage*" (ch. 23; my emphasis). This is the solution for which Gwendolen has been looking, the means of leading an exciting life and achieving distinction without the enslavement she is so afraid of in marriage.

Her hopes are dashed, however, by Klesmer's discouragement. With the collapse of her dream of winning fame and saving the family by becoming an actress, Gwendolen sinks into depression, which she tries to hide for the sake of her mother. She makes an attempt at resignation. The family must go to Sawyer's Cottage, and she must become a governess: "There is no more to be said. Things cannot be altered, and who cares? It makes no difference to any one else what we do. We must try not to care ourselves" (ch. 23).

Gwendolen tries to dull her pain by adopting the attitude that nothing matters, but it does not work, for the prospect of going to the bishop's daughters is simply unbearable to her. Even as a spoiled child holding sway over a domestic empire, Gwendolen has suffered from a suffocating sense of restriction. She has had a passionate longing for freedom and a fear of further constraint. Now she feels as though she is about to enter an "episcopal penitentiary" and begins "desperately to seek an alternative" (ch. 24). She has "wild thoughts" of running away to be an actress, despite all that Klesmer has said, but is afraid of being with "vulgar people who would treat her with rude familiarity." It seems she has no escape.

Gwendolen is in crisis. The disparity between her expectations and the sad reality of her circumstances fills her with rage and despair. The calm she attempts to maintain for the sake of her mother changes into a "sick motivelessness" that Mrs. Davilow watches with distress. Gwendolen has "a world-nausea upon her" and sees "no reason all through her life why she should wish to live" (ch. 24). Her worst fears are being realized. She has dreaded ending up like her mother, and now it seems that she will be even unhappier. George Eliot pities the creature "to whom distrust in herself and her good fortune has come as a sudden shock, like a rent across the path that she was treading carelessly." This is another jarring authorial observation. Gwendolen has received a shock, to be sure; but, as we have seen, she has hardly been treading carelessly.

It is at this critical moment that Grandcourt's request for a meeting arrives, and with it a new note enters the novel. Gwendolen cannot help feeling triumph at this tribute to her power, but competing with her exultation is a feeling of terror at the thought of wronging Lydia Glasher that is to torment her through the rest of the novel. George Eliot's presentation of Gwendolen's story as one of the chastening and education of an egoist becomes more and more intermittent as another pattern comes to the fore: that of redemption through crime and punishment. Gwendolen the selfish and demanding but not really vicious spoiled child becomes Gwendolen "the crushed penitent" (ch. 58).

6

"The Crushed Penitent": Gwendolen's Transformation

INTRODUCTION

The overall formal and thematic pattern of Gwendolen's story is one of education. Before her engagement to Grandcourt, Gwendolen is presented as an egoist, full of illusions about herself and her place in the world, who is subjected to a series of blows. After the engagement, the education pattern takes a new direction. The process of disillusionment continues, but Gwendolen's story now becomes primarily one of a fortunate fall. The rhetoric assures us that her guilt and remorse, combined with Deronda's tutelage, produce a transformation in Gwendolen that may lead her to become one of the best of women, instead of the narrow, selfish creature she has been.

In *Experiments in Life*, I subscribed to George Eliot's view of Gwendolen's growth and did not register conflicts within the rhetoric, the shifts of emphasis in the novel, or the disparities between rhetoric and mimesis. I now have difficulty integrating all the versions of Gwendolen and her story and seeing her development in a light as positive as George Eliot does. After having been presented predominantly as a spoiled child, Gwendolen becomes a conscience-stricken woman tormented by the feeling that she is wicked. In the second half of the novel, I sometimes feel as though I have entered a different fictional universe. What begins as a rather typical George Eliot story about an egoist who needs to be awakened to other people's feelings and the true order of things becomes at times a Dostoevskian tale of crime, punishment, and redemption, with Daniel acting as Gwendolen's spiritual guide, just as Sonia is Raskolnikov's (see Paris 1991c, 1994b).

Once she contemplates marrying Grandcourt in spite of her knowledge of Mrs. Glasher, Gwendolen experiences intense feelings of terror and guilt. George Eliot offers various explanations of these feelings, but none that I find satisfactory. Why is Gwendolen so terrified at the painting of the dead face and the fleeing figure, why does she feel that marrying Grandcourt is such a wicked act, and why does she have such a dread of retribution? To understand her reactions, we must look not at what George Eliot says about them but at her mimetic portrait of Gwendolen.

George Eliot tells us repeatedly that Gwendolen awakens to a new life and develops a new consciousness as a result of her discontent with herself and the direction it takes under Deronda's influence. It seems unquestionable that Gwendolen undergoes profound changes, but while we are being told that she is experiencing moral growth, we are being shown a woman who is deteriorating psychologically. George Eliot says that Deronda has not spoiled his mission and most critics agree, some even seeing the relation between Daniel and Gwendolen as similar to that between therapist and patient, as I have mentioned. I shall discuss Gwendolin's relationship with Daniel in the next chapter, where I shall make clear why I do not see it as therapeutic. Deronda encourages Gwendolen's excessive self-blame and self-hatred because, like George Eliot, he regards these as correctives. He helps Gwendolen reformulate her defenses, but that is not the same as leading her toward health. She is vastly changed at the end, to be sure, but into what has she been transformed?

GWENDOLEN'S TERROR AND GUILT

Gwendolen's transformation begins when she experiences terror at the thought of marrying Grandcourt. She was afraid of marriage before her encounter with Lydia Glasher, but all her "indistinct grounds of hesitation" are "merged in the final repulsion" that follows. Her impulse to flee comes not only from pride, jealousy, and "the shock of another woman's calamity," but "from her dread of wrong-doing," which is "vague" but "strong" (ch. 27). We are told that Gwendolen does not scruple to anything "consistent with being a lady" but that she shrinks "with mingled pride and terror" from whatever is "called disgraceful, wrong, guilty."

After her mother's loss of fortune, Gwendolen's previous inner conflicts and anxieties recede into the background; she feels that if it were not for Mrs. Glasher, she would unequivocally desire the marriage to Grandcourt as an escape from "helpless subjection to an oppressive lot" (ch. 27). Her conflict is now between her dread of wrongdoing and her desire to save herself and her mother from a seemingly dreadful fate. She agrees to see Grandcourt because she cannot resist the opportunity to renew her sense of power, but she intends to refuse him. Knowing she will be tempted by the prospect of making things easier for her mother, she is determined not to succumb. When Grandcourt offers to provide for her mother, however, his words have "the effect of a draught of wine, which suddenly makes . . . desirable things not so wrong"; and her "repugnance, dread," and "scruples" recede before the prospect of relief from the "pain of hopelessness." She later says that she did not marry Grandcourt solely on her mother's account, and that is true; however, as George Eliot paints the scene, it seems quite possible that Gwendolin would not have accepted Grandcourt's proposal had her desire to rescue her mother been less strong.

After her acceptance of Grandcourt, Gwendolen feels on the verge of embracing in a deliberate way the credo she adopted when she fled in despair to the Continent—that it does not signify what she does, that she has only to amuse herself as best she can. She is frightened by her "lawlessness." The "brilliant position," the "imagined freedom," the "deliverance" from "dull insignificance" for which she has longed have "come to her hunger like food with the taint of sacrilege upon it, which she must snatch with terror" (ch. 28). Alone in her little bed at night, she is overcome by an "onslaught of dread" and calls out for comfort to her mother.

The language of this passage takes us back to the epigraph, which now begins to be applicable to the action of the novel. Gwendolen's hurrying desires lead her to trample on the living rather than the dead, but the epigraph fits her situation in every other respect. She feels the proposed marriage, the spoils she is seizing, to be "a forbidden thing" (ch. 29); she is to be punished by her own soul, by the guilt, the dread, the fear of an avenging power that will breathe pestilence on the joys she has snatched. The epigraph describes a state of terror, and the word *terror*, and its variations, recur frequently from the moment Grandcourt's intention to propose becomes clear. George Eliot's judgment—that marrying Grandcourt is a heinous act that will bring punishment—is shared by Gwendolen, who feels she has done something wicked and is haunted by the fear of retribution.

Why does the thought of marrying Grandcourt induce such guilt and terror in Gwendolen? Let us look more closely at George Eliot's explanations. The first thing she tells us is that Gwendolen has a dread of doing anything inconsistent with ladylike conduct and that she shrinks with pride and terror from anything called disgraceful, wrong, or guilty. The implication is that marrying Grandcourt would violate the mores of her society. But would such a marriage be regarded as disgraceful, even in view of Grandcourt's liaison with Lydia Glasher and the fact that they have had four children together? As part of her portrayal of the unfairness of woman's lot, George Eliot makes it clear that, from a conventional perspective, the burden of blame falls on Mrs. Glasher, and Grandcourt remains a highly eligible match. In a world in which a double standard prevails, he has merely sown his wild oats, whereas she is irrevocably ruined. Would most people blame Gwendolen for marrying a man who has had children out of wedlock, even if she knew about the children beforehand? Probably not. Daniel Deronda is thought to be his "uncle's" illegitimate child, but Lady Mallinger is not blamed for having married Sir Hugo. In the society depicted in this novel, Gwendolen's marrying Grandcourt would not have been inconsistent with the actions of a lady or have been regarded as wrong or reprehensible. Why, then, does Gwendolen feel that the marriage would be a sacrilege? And why does she experience such terror at the thought of it?

George Eliot goes on to observe that "even apart from shame," Gwendolen's "feelings would have made her place any deliberate injury of another in the region of guilt" (ch. 27). Internal sanctions thus exist against the marriage, as well as putative external ones. George Eliot treats her heroine's guilt as appropriate, as a sign of her redeemable nature; it seems to me, however, that Gwendolen has an exaggerated sense of the injury she is doing Mrs. Glasher. Most of the time she seems to accept Mrs. Glasher's version of reality. According to that, if Gwendolen refused Grandcourt, he would marry Mrs. Glasher, thereby ameliorating her suffering, rescuing her children from illegitimacy, and making her eldest son Grandcourt's principal heir. At one point before her marriage, Gwendolen asks herself: "Of what use would it be to her that I should not marry him? He could have married her if he had liked; but he did *not* like" (ch. 28). I think George Eliot means us to see this as a rationalization, an effort to evade responsibility; yet the point is legitimate. Since it seems highly unlikely that Grandcourt would marry Mrs. Glasher under any circumstances, it is not at all clear that Gwendolen has done her a great injury—except in that lady's mind, and in Gwendolen's and George Eliot's perception. It is true that Mrs. Glasher can no longer continue to hope once Grandcourt marries, but her hopes are unfounded, and she is making her demands on the basis of unrealistic expectations.

George Eliot's characterization of Gwendolen's marrying Grandcourt as a wicked act seems insufficiently supported to me. The morality of the situation is not at all as clear as the rhetoric suggests. George Eliot often makes it appear that Gwendolen is just getting what she deserves, and that Mrs. Glasher is the rightful agent of Nemesis. In her initial state of shock, Gwendolen offers not to interfere with Mrs. Glasher's wishes. Does this constitute a solemn promise not to marry Grandcourt, the violation of which makes Gwendolen a wicked woman deserving of horrible punishment? Is such a promise something Mrs. Glasher had a right to ask and Gwendolen a moral obligation to give?

For the most part, Gwendolen does not try to excuse her behavior but holds herself responsible for the consequences of not only her own actions but also those of Grandcourt and Mrs. Glasher, both of whom are far more culpable than she. Mrs. Glasher abandoned her husband and child to run off with Grandcourt, and Grandcourt subsequently abandoned her when he tired of her, although he continued to provide financial support. There is no longer any love between them, but Mrs. Glasher wants to marry for the sake of her children. Even if Grandcourt married her, she would still be a social outcast. She is full of rage toward Grandcourt but, fearful of alienating him, she displaces her anger onto Gwendolen, and strikes out at her in his stead. Gwendolen, who sees things as this bitterly disappointed, vindictive woman wishes her to, blames herself for Mrs. Glasher's fate. The narrator does not provide a more balanced perspective, nor does Gwendolen's mentor, Daniel Deronda.

Gwendolen finds herself in a very uncomfortable position, to be sure. She has good reason to feel queasy about marrying Grandcourt; I think, though, that she has an extreme reaction to her feelings of guilt, which are excessive to begin with. Even though her moral complacency has been shattered by the presentiment that she is wronging Mrs. Glasher, that does not account for the terror she feels "at overstepping the border of wickedness" (ch. 28). The self-righteous girl has become a morally timorous woman with a morbidly sensitive conscience.

In a further effort to account for Gwendolen's terror, George Eliot describes her as being frightened at having approached lawlessness, which comes to her "with the shadowy array of possible calamity behind it" (ch. 28). The author has tried to prepare us for this side of Gwendolen's nature, and hence for her transformation, by providing earlier examples of her fearfulness. When the family is inspecting the house on their first day at Offendene, Isabel opens a panel in the drawing room that discloses a painting of an upturned dead face.

Gwendolen reacts with far greater horror than anyone else, a response that leads Isabel to remark that Gwendolen will never stay in this room by herself (ch. 3). Later, when she is planning charades, Gwendolen observes to her mother that "all the great poetic criminals" were women, and Mrs. Davilow replies, "Well, dear, and you— who are afraid to be alone in the night—I don't think you would be very bold in crime, thank God" (ch. 6). Her mother is right. Gwendolen, feeling that she has done something wicked by agreeing to marry Grandcourt, is overcome by dread in the night, reminding us again of Macbeth, whose sleep is disturbed by guilt and fear. The many echoes of Shakespeare's play in this novel indicate the degree to which George Eliot criminalizes Gwendolen's marriage to Grandcourt, by equating it somehow with Macbeth's murders.

George Eliot highlights Gwendolen's susceptibility to dread principally in the episode of the charades: the panel flies open, once again revealing the picture of the dead face and the fleeing figure, whereupon Gwendolen emits a "piercing cry" and looks "like a statue into which a soul of Fear [has] entered" (ch. 6). The scene is a foreshadowing of Grandcourt's drowning, after which Gwendolen is haunted by his upturned dead face because she feels guilty for not having come to his rescue. This anticipation of future events helps me to understand the author's motivations for introducing the episode but not Gwendolen's behavior within it. George Eliot's rambling commentary does not really make clear why Gwendolen has such a strong reaction to this particular stimulus.

Both the scene and the commentary are part of George Eliot's effort to make Gwendolen's transformation intelligible. As in her treatment of Fred Vincy, she must indicate the potential for growth in a character who is initially presented as extremely egoistic. In the case of Fred, the favorable possibilities are suggested by the comments of other characters, for which it is difficult to see much foundation. In Gwendolen's case, George Eliot's interprets of the heroine's susceptibility to terror as an indication of her nobler potentiality.

George Eliot presents Gwendolen as someone who wishes to be daring in braving moral dangers but is unable to do so. Despite her dismissal of religion, she is subject to fits of spiritual dread and is in fact fettered by moral constraints. Gwendolen does not connect her awe and dread with religion, but through her commentary George Eliot does. She identifies Gwendolen's feelings of helplessness and insignificance when she is alone in a wide scene or studies astronomy at school as religious experiences and implies that they are somehow related to her terror when the panel flies open, although the author never makes the connection clear. She also suggests that these feelings are related to Gwendolen's fear of an avenging power when she contemplates doing something she feels to be wicked. George Eliot attributes this fear to "the infiltrated influences of disregarded religious teaching, as well as the deeper impressions of something awful and inexorable enveloping her" (ch. 28).

From this perspective, Gwendolen's is a story about a vain, shallow, superficially rebellious young woman who has a fountain of awe within her and whose transgression fills her with spiritual dread. Her fits of timidity or terror reveal a hidden side of her nature that gives her a capacity for moral growth. Much of the rhetoric, especially in the first half of the novel, presents Gwendolen as being full of illusions and needing to become more realistic. She must give up her magical thinking and learn the true causal connections of things (see, for example, the epigraphs to chapters 21 and 23). Another strand of rhetoric, however, laments her lack of religious belief and portrays her irrational guilt and fear in a favorable light.

A further component of George Eliot's explanation of Gwendolen's transformation is an insistence on the role of conscience. As we have seen, in the first half of the novel, the author presents Gwendolen as totally fearless about making herself disagreeable when thwarted, and at the same time uncomfortable when her selfishness leads her to do something that hurts her mother or sisters. As long as the transgressions are small ones, she feels compunction rather than guilt and tries to make reparations through caresses and gifts; however, the injury she does Mrs. Glasher is irreparable. Its irrevocable nature, combined with her perception of its magnitude, lead her to suffer torments of conscience and fears of retribution. According to this version of Gwendolen, her conscience has always been there, but it has been slumbering or ignored.

A conscience seems to be something George Eliot ascribes to Gwendolen belatedly, rather than something that belonged to the initial conception of her character. Perhaps for this reason, the author provides a brief discourse on conscience in the epigraph to chapter 35. The gist of the epigraph is that most people have a conscience that prevents them from serenely enjoying the fruits of their wickedness and that Gwendolen is like the majority of her fellows in this respect. George Eliot does not explain Gwendolen's scruples of conscience very well in terms of her individual psychology but tries to account for them, as in this epigraph, by invoking a general human phenomenon. Gwendolen has a conscience, like most everyone else.

CAPTAIN DAVILOW AND MRS. GLASHER

George Eliot may have intuitively grasped and mimetically portrayed facets of her heroine's personality to which her rhetoric is not a reliable guide. The rhetoric presents Gwendolen's fits of timidity or terror as products of a spiritual dread and a fountain of awe that are religious in nature, although Gwendolen does not recognize them as such. In my reading of the mimetic portrait of Gwendolen, these fits seem to be anxiety attacks that have their origin in her psychological vulnerability, rather than in something positive. George Eliot treats them so favorably, I suspect, because they undermine Gwendolen's egoism by making her feel small and weak in a world that is much larger than herself.

In the previous chapter I argued that Gwendolen is a narcissist who is at once self-aggrandizing and profoundly insecure, her insecurity being partly the result of her self-aggrandizement. As a spoiled child, she has an inflated sense of her importance, but she has not earned the deference she receives, and she has no solid sense of worth or center of self. She is dependent on other people to confirm her exalted conception of herself. In the absence of such confirmation, her self-confidence collapses, and she is subject to feelings of weakness and insubstantiality. Without "human ears and eyes about her" (ch. 6), she feels lost in a vast and mysterious universe over which she has no control.

Gwendolen is arrogant, domineering, and grandiose, but she is also full of fears. George Eliot's rhetoric suggests that Gwendolen's anxiety is existential in nature, the kind a sensitive person might feel when confronted by the immensity of the universe and the mysteries of life and death. The mimetic portrait of Gwendolen shows an anxiety that is pathologically intense and allows us to trace this anxiety to the combination of self-idealization and insecurity that has resulted from the specific conditions of her life. Profoundly disconcerted by anything that thwarts her need for dominance or challenges her claims, she goes back and forth between perceiving herself as an extraordinary person who can master her fate and feeling helpless and insignificant. When her idealized image of herself is threatened, her self-doubts and anxieties emerge.

Part of Gwendolen's idealized image of herself is that she is reckless in braving dangers, "both moral and physical" (ch. 6). She displays considerable physical courage, as when riding to the hunt; but she is timid when it comes to violating the mores of her society. She is torn between the yearning to be a free spirit whose life will be different from that of other women and an insatiable need for approval that compels her to do what is expected of a young lady of her position.

This conflict is exacerbated by her family's loss of fortune and Grandcourt's proposal. It is easy to understand the forces propelling Gwendolen toward an acceptance of Grandcourt, especially in view of what awaits her if she refuses; but as George Eliot's struggles to do so suggest, it is difficult to explain the intensity of her terror at the thought of marrying him. She *is* very sensitive to anything that can be construed as disgraceful, wrong, or guilty; but marriage to Grandcourt does not seem to be viewed in that way by her culture. Even if it were, would that be enough to account for the intensity of her guilt and dread?

I suggest that Gwendolen feels marrying Grandcourt to be such a heinous act because she identifies Mrs. Glasher with her mother, the person she has the most powerful taboo against hurting, and in a way with herself, because of her fear that a similar fate awaits her. When she encounters Lydia Glasher at the Whispering Stones, she sees her as another example of what has happened to her mother and may happen to her. She reacts with "a sort of *terror*: it was as if some ghastly vision had come to her in a dream and said, 'I am a woman's life' " (ch. 14; my emphasis). Like Gwendolen's mother, Mrs. Glasher was "exceedingly handsome" in her youth; like the mother, she has been victimized by a man who does not hesitate to make use of his male prerogatives; and like Mrs. Davilow, she has a number of children who must share in her misery. Mrs. Glasher is the image of what Gwendolen dreads becoming.

Gwendolen has always resented Captain Davilow as an intruder into her mother's life and her own. He has deprived them of what was rightfully theirs and forced them into a makeshift existence on the fringes of society. By marrying Grandcourt, Gwendolen may see herself as playing a similar role in relation to Mrs. Glasher and her children—that is, as depriving them of that which should belong to them. Gwendolen is particularly sensitive to the situation of Mrs. Glasher's oldest son, who would become Grandcourt's principal heir should he marry Lydia. Gwendolen has felt deprived of her rightful position by her mother's remarriage, and she seems to feel that by marrying Grandcourt she would be dispossessing this child, doing to him what has been done to her. She would be an instrument of the same sort of injustice from which both she and her mother have suffered, a part of the unfairness she has bitterly resented and hoped to escape.

I think Gwendolen feels that marrying Grandcourt would be committing a terrible wrong not for the reasons George Eliot gives but because she identifies herself with her mother, her mother with Lydia Glasher, and Mrs. Glasher's children with her sisters and herself. She feels she would be doing to Lydia Glasher the kind of injury that has been done to the females in her family. Instead of being the victim while others are at fault, she would be the villain in this scenario, doing irreparable harm to a woman who reminds Gwendolen of her mother and who has already been victimized by the system against which the young woman herself is rebelling.

Gwendolen's disproportionate sense of the grievousness of the wrong she would be doing by marrying Grandcourt may be responsible for the magnitude of her guilt, and the magnitude of her guilt for her dread of an avenging power. She sees marriage to Grandcourt as a sacrilegious act because it is a violation of what she feels she owes to a woman like her mother (at the same time that she is tempted by it because of what it will do *for* her mother), and she feels that she ought to be punished if she does such a thing, just as she has wished others to be punished, specifically Captain Davilow, for making her family miserable.

This brings us back to Gwendolen's reaction to the painting of the dead face and the fleeing figure. The person in Gwendolen's world who has recently died is Captain Davilow; and his death has immense significance; for it liberates her mother, makes possible the move to Offendene, and greatly improves Gwendolen's prospects. As Inêz Sodré has observed, Gwendolen must have had death wishes toward her stepfather (Byatt and Sodré 1995, 87). It is a psychological commonplace that people often experience intense, irrational feelings of guilt when their wish for someone's death is fulfilled, even if they had nothing to do with bringing the death about. The picture of the dead face may be so terrifying to Gwendolen because it taps into her unconscious guilt over wishing Captain Davilow dead, thereby arousing her fear of punishment according to the talion principle; she may see in the fleeing figure an image of herself trying to escape what she has done. The fulfillment of her wish would reinforce Gwendolen's sense of the omnipotence of her will, and that reinforcement would in turn contribute to her sense of responsibility for the death and make her afraid of the power of her anger and her lethal desires—hence her later assertion to Deronda that she has always been wicked (ch. 64). She has been wanting her stepfather and half-sisters out of the way for a long time. We catch a glimpse of her murderous rage when she strangles her sister's canary.

Captain Davilow's death may appear to Gwendolen not only as a fulfillment of her wish to be free of his oppression but also as his punishment for the wrong he has done to her family. This belief would intensify her terror of doing a similar wrong to Mrs. Glasher and would help account for her dread of being punished should she marry

Henleigh Grandcourt. She externalizes her sense of omnipotence, attributing to others, and especially to Mrs. Glasher, the power to do to her what she has done to Captain Davilow. She sympathizes with the plight of Mrs. Glasher and her children; but at the same time, she no doubt wishes them out of the way, as she has done with her mother's second family. This secret wish intensifies her guilt and dread, as well as her susceptibility to Mrs. Glasher's manipulations.

Gwendolen's inner conflicts before her marriage to Grandcourt resemble those of Macbeth before Duncan's murder, in that she is being driven to do something she feels to be dreadfully wrong and whose consequences terrify her. She has a strong resistance to the marriage, but powerful forces are working to override this resistance and compel her to act in a way with which she knows she cannot live. She wants to rescue her mother; she cannot bear the thought of "insignificance and servitude" (ch. 28); and once she accepts Grandcourt, it would be humiliating to jump out of the chariot that now is "going at full speed." She comforts herself by thinking that she cannot "help what other people have done," that "things would not come right" if she should break the engagement, and—in another echo of *Macbeth*—that there would now be "as much ill-doing" in going back as in going forward (ch. 29). On the morning of the wedding, she thrusts down her disturbing thoughts "with a sort of exulting defiance" and experiences a resurgence of "that intoxication of youthful egoism out of which she had been shaken by trouble, humiliation, and a new sense of culpability" (ch. 31).

Gwendolen's effort to repress her misgivings collapses when she receives Lydia Glasher's letter, with its accusations and maledictions. Lydia's malevolent wishes have a profound impact on Gwendolen, perhaps because she is afraid that they will come true, as hers toward Captain Davilow have. She reacts to the letter with a "spasm of terror" and screams "again and again with hysterical violence" when Grandcourt appears (ch. 31).

After this, Gwendolen finds herself haunted, like Macbeth, by the guilt and fear of which she has had a premonition. Her gamble, her bargain, has failed: she is not receiving the rewards for which she has sacrificed her innocence but must suffer the consequences nonetheless. The rest of her story traces the collapse of her illusions, the growth of her murderous rage toward Grandcourt, and her effort to save herself by clinging to Daniel Deronda. George Eliot presents all this as part of an education pattern in which Gwendolen undergoes a positive transformation as a result of her sin and consequent suffering.

POSTMARITAL MISERIES

Gwendolen's relationship with Daniel Deronda is the principal focus of the rhetoric in the second half of her story, but before we can understand that relationship and assess its value, we must appreciate her state of mind and the plight in which she finds herself following her marriage. Before she marries Grandcourt, Gwendolen's situation is one in which all possible choices are abhorrent, given her psychological needs. To escape the consequences of her mother's loss of fortune, she gambles on a course of action about which she has many misgivings, but after her marriage, she finds herself in a far worse position than before. It is a position she cannot bear but one from which no means of escape offers itself that will not be even more intolerable.

As we examine her marital experience, it is important to remember how important the issue of freedom has been to Gwendolen. We have seen that even as a spoiled child who exercised considerable power at home, she suffered from a suffocating sense of restriction and a fear of further constraint. After her mother's misfortune, Gwendolen's anxieties about being subjected to coercion grew even more intense. The prospect of becoming a governess was unbearable to her not only because of the loss of social status it involved, but also because it would subject her to the will of her employer. She would not be able to express her thoughts and feelings or to act as she wished. Her behavior would be constantly monitored. When an alternative appears in the form of Grandcourt's proposal, Gwendolen overcomes her fear of the bondage of marriage by persuading herself that she will be able to manage him. She tries to make it clear that she is not going to renounce her freedom and is going to do as she likes.

George Eliot has created in Grandcourt the worst possible husband for her heroine. Whereas Gwendolen needs to feel free and in control of her life, Grandcourt is one of the most domineering men imaginable. A large part of Gwendolen's appeal for him is that she is a spirited woman who could master most other men but whose will he is sure he can break. Her running away after the encounter with Mrs. Glasher makes her all the more attractive, and her mother's misfortune provides the leverage he needs to obtain her hand in marriage. The fact that Gwendolen knows about Mrs. Glasher adds spice to his conquest, for his past was a formidable obstacle. Grandcourt enjoys the challenge Gwendolen presents, much as he might enjoy mastering an unruly horse—there is a good deal of bit and bridle imagery in the novel.

Grandcourt does not marry for sentiment, any more than does Gwendolen. George Eliot tells us that he prefers "command to love" (ch. 48) and that he is well satisfied with the kind of relationship he has with his wife. His objective is to assert his power over Gwendolen in a way that will let her know that he has complete control and that she has no choice but to submit. He wants to feel that she is his to do with as he likes "and to make her feel it also" (ch. 54). When he forces her to go yachting, he has "an intense satisfaction" in leading her "captive after this fashion." His sense of her inward protest, which he knows she must suppress, adds "to the piquancy of despotism."

Gwendolen's "romantic illusions " in marrying Grandcourt have "turned on her power of using him as she like[s]," but she finds that he is using her as he likes instead (ch. 48). Although she hates her subjection, she is powerless to resist or escape. Grandcourt is a master of manipulation whose use of his masculine power is unchecked by affection for his wife or fear of losing her love. He plays on all her vulnerabilities, including her pride and concern for appearances, to bend her to his will. Gwendolen has rebellious impulses, but defiance seems impossible, and she foresees that she will come to "quail," like his dogs.

Gwendolen's helplessness derives in part from the feelings of guilt and shame that undermine her ability to assert herself. She finds that she cannot speak to Grandcourt on Mrs. Glasher's behalf, as she has intended, to alleviate her sense of culpability, because she does not want him to know that she knew about his mistress and children and has broken her word by marrying him. Her position becomes even more painful when Grandcourt has Lush show her his will, to let her know that he has been aware of her meeting with Mrs. Glasher all along. She feels that this gesture is "meant as a finish to her humiliations and thraldom" (ch. 48).

Gwendolen is ashamed not only of her behavior toward Mrs. Glasher but also of her crassness in having married Grandcourt for money and position, despite her lack of love and her knowledge of his past. After Lush's disclosure, she feels herself "branded in the minds of her husband and his confidant with the meanness that would accept marriage and wealth on any conditions, however dishonourable and humiliating" (ch. 48). She is so branded in her own mind as well. Grandcourt knows that he "won her by the rank and luxuries he had to give her, and he believes that he has fulfilled his side of the contract" (ch. 54). Gwendolen agrees and feels that she has no right to complain. She is unable to protest against Grandcourt's treatment of her, partly because she feels responsible for having put herself in such a horrible position.

Thus, Gwendolen finds herself powerless to alter, or even to remonstrate against, an unbearable state of affairs. She had been afraid of the fetters of marriage, but the bondage she experiences is far worse than that of her mother. She is forced into self-suppression considerably more severe than would have been required of her as a governess and is subjected to a closer supervision. Every action, every word, is monitored by Grandcourt, who forces her to live up to his idea of how his wife should behave. She is compelled to wear the hateful diamonds that came from Mrs. Glasher, is forbidden to visit Mirah again, and is reprimanded for anything Grandcourt finds disagreeable. She now yearns for her family but must keep them at a distance.

If Gwendolen suffered before from a suffocating sense of restriction, we can imagine her desperation when she finds herself trapped, helpless, paralyzed, at the mercy of a man who wants to control her every move and who does not care how he makes her feel, as long as he gets his way. Although she was determined not to be enslaved like other women, she finds herself more enslaved than most. Her enslavement is in part sexual in nature, of course. Some critics have seen an oblique allusion to Gwendolen's sexual oppression when Grandcourt is described as "a dangerous serpent ornamentally coiled in her cabin without invitation" (ch. 54). Whether this is a sexual reference or not, the woman who was so averse to love-making must be tormented by having to submit to Grandcourt's physical demands.

Gwendolen can neither escape Grandcourt's mastery nor find a way to make her situation bearable. She tries to salvage some pride by wearing "the yoke so as not to be pitied," by bearing herself "with dignity, and appear[ing] what is called happy" (ch. 35). Unlike her mother, she will "carry her troubles with spirit, and let none suspect them." She hopes to "find excitements that [will] carry her through life" and help her "get used to her heart-sores." These include gambling, accomplishments, and the chance to make a striking appearance; but she can no longer "feel a keen appetite" for such pleasures, all of which are "clad in her own weariness and disgust."

Just as she sought desperately for an alternative to becoming a governess, Gwendolen tries to think of a way of escaping the misery of living with Grandcourt. She considers insisting on a separation, in which case Mrs. Glasher's eldest son would become Grandcourt's heir, and she would be relieved of some of her guilt. This course of action would bring disgrace to her family, however, and leave her mother destitute. And what sort of life would she have to look forward to? Even if she could attain "that dreary freedom," she would be "solitary, sickened of life": "If the wife of Grandcourt were to run away, she "would be a more pitiable creature than Gwendolen Harleth condemned to teach the Bishop's daughters, and to be inspected by Mrs. Mompert" (ch. 48). But how can she even manage to separate? She can allege nothing against Grandcourt that would carry any weight in judicial ears and can say nothing about her situation that would not be a condemnation of herself. Her uncle would tell her to return to Grandcourt, and her husband could compel her to do so. Even Daniel Deronda would probably tell her that "she ought to bear what she [has] brought on herself." If she is to be miserable in any event, she prefers the misery she can conceal.

Gwendolen is under enormous psychological stress. She feels that Grandcourt delights in torturing her but can think of no way to escape his emotional abuse. Like many a wife in her position, she wishes for the death of her husband. When Grandcourt ignores Mrs. Glasher and her children while he and Gwendolen are riding in Rotten Row, Gwendolen's fears about her own fate should she become a social outcast intensify her hopelessness about ever obtaining relief:

> What possible release could there be for her from this hated vantage-ground, which yet she dared not quit, any more than if fire had been raining outside it? What release but death? Not her own death. . . . it seemed more possible that Grandcourt should die:—and yet not likely. The power of tyranny in him seemed a power of living in the presence of any wish that he should die. The thought that his death was the only deliverance for her was one with the thought that deliverance would never come. . . . No! She foresaw him always living, and her own life dominated by him. . . . The thought of him dying . . . turned as with a dream-change into the terror that she should die with his throttling fingers on her neck avenging that thought. (ch. 48)

We see here a dynamic very similar to the one I proposed to account for Gwendolen's terror at the picture of the dead face. Her wish for Grandcourt's death turns into a fear of retribution, a fear that she will be punished for her evil thoughts. In this case, her dread is not of some larger avenging power but specifically of Grandcourt, whom she imagines doing to her what she would like to do to him. She has been so crushed by this time that she no longer sees her wishes as having any potency. Yet although they will not bring about Grandcourt's demise, she fears they will trigger an avenging action that will destroy her.

Gwendolen entertains not only wishes for Grandcourt's death but active thoughts of killing him. This very important feature of her psychology has been little discussed, perhaps because it is obscured by George Eliot's narrative strategy and the rhetorical emphasis on patterns of growth, transformation, and the fortunate fall. George Eliot does not let us see her heroine's murderous impulses clearly until after Grandcourt drowns, when Gwendolen confesses to Deronda that her fantasies of killing her husband had begun soon after marriage and that during her honeymoon at Ryelands she had concealed a knife in her dressing-case. While visiting the Abbey three weeks after her honeymoon, she fancies that Grandcourt's "white hand," which is touching his whisker, is capable "of clinging round her neck and threatening to throttle her" (ch. 35). It is not Grandcourt, of course, but Gwendolen, who is harboring homicidal impulses, which she externalizes and perceives as belonging to him. Her fear of Grandcourt is a dread of his revenge for what *she* wants to do to *him*.

In chapter 35, Gwendolen is once again described as having a demonic force within her, as she was in the opening chapter. I was mystified by this characterization until I realized that she is already struggling with her desire to murder Grandcourt. When we reread the novel with Gwendolen's later revelations in mind, it becomes clear that this desire is present from early in her marriage and that it grows steadily stronger. She feels humiliated after reading Grandcourt's will but conceals her emotions by showing "a defiant satisfaction in what had been presumed to be disagreeable" (ch. 48). Her husband had no doubt "meant to produce a great effect on her: by-and-by perhaps she would let him see an effect the very opposite of what he intended." What effect does she have in mind? That one of these days she will overthrow his tyranny by killing him? In retrospect, it is clear that, unable to imagine the intensity of his wife's hidden rage, Grandcourt is preparing his own destruction by his cruel treatment of her.

Gwendolen's severest inner conflict in the second half of the novel is between her wish to kill Grandcourt and her fear of her murderous impulses. Her "imaginary annihilation of the detested object" is compared to "the hidden rites of vengeance with which the persecuted have made a dark vent for their rage, and soothed their suffering into dumbness" (ch. 54). These hidden rites do not have a soothing effect on Gwendolen, however; instead, they produce a "struggling terror," a dread of herself that urges her "to flee from the pursuing images wrought by her pent-up impulse." Her mind is full of contrivances for Grandcourt's death, but she fights against them. Already experiencing guilt, self-hatred, and a fear of retribution as a result of "her past wrong-doing," she is terrified by the prospect of committing a far more serious sin and bringing upon herself an even greater punishment. She turns to Daniel Deronda for help with her inner struggle, but he does not fully understand what she is afraid of and cannot be of much assistance.

Gwendolen's murderous desires become even more intense when Grandcourt separates her from Deronda by forcing her to go yachting with him. She is so afraid of committing an impulsive deed that she locks her knife in her dressing-case and throws the key overboard, but then she regrets having done so. When they are forced to dock at Genoa so that the yacht can be repaired, Gwendolen has fantasies of getting a locksmith to open her case. Her encounter with Deronda at the hotel puts such thoughts out of her mind until it becomes clear that Grandcourt will not let her meet with him. She threatens her husband, but he does not comprehend: "And you had better leave me at liberty to speak with any one I like. It would be better for you." "You will allow me to judge of that," is Grandcourt's reply (ch. 54). Her words have "such a clear and tremendous" meaning for Gwendolen that she dreads their effect; but Grandcourt has "the courage and confidence that belong to domination" and is "garrisoned against presentiments and fear." He feels "perfectly satisfied that he [holds] his wife with bit and bridle" and that she will "cease to be restive by the time they [have] been married a year."

The moral pattern of Grandcourt's story requires that his death be the consequence of his egoism, his cruelty, his lack of imagination and empathy. He does not have Gwendolen's sensitive conscience—or, indeed, any conscience at all; but George Eliot wishes to show that he, too, is subject to Nemesis and will be punished for his sins. Partly the result of his arrogance in not listening when the locals warn him about a possible shift in the winds, his drowning is also partly the result of the hatred he has induced in his wife, which leads her to withhold help at the critical moment. He thought he could tyrannize Gwendolen with impunity, but events prove him wrong. As we have seen, there have been ominous foreshadowings of the abused wife's revenge.

If we look at Gwendolen's account of events, we have little doubt that her feelings of guilt in connection with Grandcourt's death are to some degree appropriate. When Grandcourt insists that she go sailing against her will, Gwendolen wishes that she had "forked lightning for a weapon to strike him dead" (ch. 56). While they are on the water, her murderous thoughts gather "a fierce intensity." Her mind is teeming with images of Grandcourt's death, but she can think of no way of killing him. Then the wind shifts, the sail swings about, and Grandcourt is knocked overboard. Apparently, and improbably, this man who loves yachting and sailing cannot swim. Grandcourt surfaces and calls for the rope. Gwendolen wishes him dead and dreads his return, but she picks up the rope, only to see Grandcourt go down again. Then he surfaces once more: "No, there he was again—his face above water—and he cried again—and I held my hand, and my heart said, 'Die!'—and he sank; and I felt 'It is done— I am wicked, I am lost'—and I had the rope in my hand."

We cannot know whether Gwendolen could have saved Grandcourt by throwing the rope immediately, but it seems possible that she might have. It is clear that she did not throw the rope because she wished him dead. Deronda's judgment, which is endorsed by the rhetoric, is that it is "almost certain that her murderous thought had had no outward effect," that Grandcourt's death "was inevitable" (ch. 56). This seems far from certain to me.

We have seen that George Eliot's rhetorical treatment of Gwendolen in the first half of the novel is inconsistent, confusing, and often subverted by the mimesis. These problems persist to the end. George Eliot presents Gwendolen as undergoing a positive transformation, a fortunate fall, while she is increasingly consumed by anxiety, despair, and homicidal rage after her marriage to Grandcourt. She is transformed, to be sure, but is she being regenerated? The rhetoric emphasizes the heinousness of Gwendolen's marrying Grandcourt and the appropriateness of her guilt and dread but makes remarkably little of the much more serious matter of her failure to act when her husband is drowning. George Eliot's claims about Gwendolen's "conversion" escalate after Grandcourt's death, and I shall examine the disparities between these claims and the mimesis in the following chapter.

7

Gwendolen and Daniel:
A Therapeutic Relationship?

CRITICAL DISAGREEMENTS

At the heart of *Daniel Deronda* is the story of the relationship between Gwendolen and Daniel. The novel opens with their initial encounter at Leubronn and closes with their parting when Daniel marries Mirah and prepares to leave for Palestine. It is their relationship that holds the two halves of the novel together and constitutes its thematic center. In terms of plot and rhetoric, the novel is above all about the transformation of Gwendolen as a result of her life experiences and the beneficent influence of Daniel Deronda.

In *Experiments in Life*, I discussed the relationship between Daniel and Gwendolen in Feuerbachian terms, as an example of how individuals can represent the species and be like God to their fellows. "The moral standards and the behavior of a George Eliot character," I wrote, "are often shaped by the values of those he loves and esteems. My fellow man, wrote Feuerbach, is 'my objective conscience; . . . he is my personified feeling of shame'" (225). I still find that the text strongly supports this reading. George Eliot tells us again and again that Gwendolen's moral growth is tied to her acceptance of Deronda as her objective conscience and to her efforts to escape the feelings of shame she experiences when she sees herself through his eyes. "In this way," the author observes, "our brother may be in the stead of God to us, and his opinion which has pierced even to the joints and marrow, may be our virtue in the making" (ch. 64).

As I did in *Experiments in Life*, most critics have agreed with George Eliot's assessment of Gwendolen's growth and Deronda's role in promoting it. Laurence Lerner articulates the predominant view when he describes *Daniel Deronda* as George Eliot's "greatest study in conversion," in the process "by which a limited personality, whose emotional life was constricted by egoism, learns under the influence of a nobler nature to yield to more generous impulses and transcend the bounds of self" (1965, 355).

Lerner expresses another view that has become common when he compares the relationship between Gwendolen and Daniel to that of patient and therapist. This comparison has been made by both literary critics and clinicians. Among critics, Peggy Johnstone sees Gwendolen as having become "a more complete person" (1994, 175), one "cured of her narcissistic disorder" (161), and Gillian Beer says that at the end the heroine is "capable of free-standing life" (1986, 221).

In 1999, I guest edited a special issue of *The American Journal of Psychoanalysis* on the topic of psychoanalytic approaches to George Eliot; and two of the essays, each excellent in its way, were by psychotherapists who thought the interaction between Daniel and Gwendolen to be "prescient of the analytic relationship" (Rotenberg 1999, 262). According to Margot Waddell, *Daniel Deronda* deepens George Eliot's "exploration of the dynamic of mental growth, of the way in which the personality may be 'rescued' by the emotional availability of another and be enabled to develop, despite early deprivation" (1999, 278). Carl Rotenberg feels that at the center of the novel "is a therapeutic relationship in which a person with heightened self-centeredness and guilty homicidal fantasies engages in a healing interaction with an empathic other who helps her to resolve her conflicts, to heal her deeply divided self, and to go on living" (1999, 259). Although Gwendolen is saddened by their separation at the end, "the relationship has left her with inner health and moral strength" (267). The great majority of critics have arrived at a similar conclusion.

There are some dissenters, however. Mary Ellen Doyle observes, for example, that Gwendolen "will be a good woman" but asks, "What else will she be?" (1981, 160). According to Elizabeth Daniels, although "Gwendolen is led by Daniel Deronda to believe that she can find herself among the pieces of her fragmented experience, put herself back together again, and then get on with the business of being a better woman as he would define one," the actual portrayal of Gwendolen at the end suggests that "she may well be emotionally and intellectually, if not morally, crippled for life" (1982, 31). After saying that with Daniel Deronda "as midwife," Gwendolen "achieves the birth of a liveable identity," Gillian Beer acknowledges that "we cannot know whether she is capable of sustaining" her intentions (1986, 223). Rosemarie Bodenheimer identifies the climax of Gwendolen's redemption, "in George Eliot's terms, to be the moment when she is shocked out of her self-obsession by the revelation of Deronda's other life"; but she feels that "the sense of emotional wreckage in the penultimate chapter overshadows the predictable moral message" (1994, 261).

In rereading *Daniel Deronda* from my current perspective, I find myself quarreling with George Eliot's rhetoric and disagreeing with critics, including myself in *Experiments in Life*, who follow the author in celebrating Gwendolen's development and Deronda's success in rescuing her. I am now one of the dissenters. It seems to me that there is a great dissonance between what George Eliot says about Gwendolen's transformation and what she concretely depicts. While we are being told that Gwendolen is undergoing a conversion in which she develops a new consciousness, a new soul, we are being shown a character who is full of rage, despair, and self-hatred, and who finds herself trapped in a situation from which she can find no other escape than the death of her husband. Deronda certainly plays an important role in Gwendolen's psychic life while Grandcourt is alive, but I do not think that he helps her to find effective coping devices or leads her in the direction of psychological health. After Grandcourt's death, Gwendolen becomes even more dependent on Deronda; and, despite her brave words, her prospects after his departure seem very bleak to me.

IS DERONDA'S INFLUENCE TRANSFORMATIVE?

After Leubronn, Gwendolen does not meet Deronda again until Sir Hugo sends him to Diplow to see Grandcourt about giving up his rights to the inheritance of that property in exchange for a sum of money. Between her first and second encounters, Gwendolen has undergone a significant change as a result of her life experiences; and she is now at a much different place in her emotional development than she was at Leubronn. No longer the complacent narcissist she appeared to be in the opening scene, she has received many blows, has been driven to do something she feels to be sinful, and has been tormented by guilt and dread in the watches of the night. These changes have occurred independently of Deronda, ostensibly because her conscience has been awakened by the injury she has done Mrs. Glasher.

Despite George Eliot's emphasis on Deronda's moral influence, I do not think Gwendolen's development would have been significantly different up to this point if he had never appeared on the scene. He does exacerbate her guilt when, asked why he disapproved of her gambling, he tells her that he is revolted by seeing people rejoice when their gain is another's loss. This makes her feel even worse about her behavior toward Mrs. Glasher, but Gwendolen has condemned herself severely before this exchange.

Although Deronda is not responsible for Gwendolen's transformation from narcissist to penitent, as George Eliot's rhetoric insists, he comes to play a major role in her psychic life, as she sees herself more and more from what she imagines to be his perspective. She wonders what he really thinks about her and her proposed marriage and longs to be judged "with unmixed admiration," despite Grandcourt's dismissal of him as a person of no consequence (ch. 29).

Gwendolen's next contact with Deronda occurs when, three weeks after their honeymoon, she and Grandcourt visit Sir Hugo at the Abbey, a property her husband will ultimately inherit. During this episode, George Eliot makes large claims for Deronda's impact on Gwendolen. The author speaks of "the transforming influence of the thoughts we imagine to be going on in another," says that "in some mysterious way he was becoming a part of her conscience," and observes that "it is one of the secrets in that change of mental poise which has been fitly named conversion, that to many among us neither heaven nor earth has any revelation till some personality touches theirs with a peculiar influence, subduing them into receptiveness" (ch. 35). All this seems to suggest that Gwendolen's conversion from complacent egoist to conscience-stricken woman is the result of her contact with Deronda, whereas we have seen that the change has already occurred and that other factors have produced it. George Eliot's statement that Deronda's "influence had entered into the current of that self-suspicion and self-blame which awakens a new consciousness" is more accurate, I think. That current is already present in Gwendolen and the awakening has already occurred, but Deronda certainly reinforces her sense of wrongdoing and discomfort with herself.

We must ask why, already suffering from self-hatred, Gwendolen is so drawn to a man who makes her feel even worse, whose standards, she feels, measure "her into littleness" (ch. 35). Deronda's power over Gwendolen initially derives from the circumstance that he does not feed her pride but threatens it. As she becomes more and more burdened with guilt, the admiration of men she does not respect is no longer of any value to her, for she no longer believes she deserves it. Deronda impresses her "as not . . . her admirer but her superior." His admiration could restore her pride, but it seems beyond her reach. Nonetheless, she adopts him as "an object of reverential belief" and incorporates her image of him into her conscience. Doing so exacerbates her self-hatred, but it also gives her a sense of direction and purpose. She is at sea herself, but someone knows what is good and can tell her how to live. She tries to compensate for the collapse of her grandiose conception of herself, and of her value system, by idealizing Daniel Deronda, whom she hardly knows, and transferring her pride to him. The standards she imagines him to have diminish her, but they also hold out the hope of a new solution.

Gwendolen cannot win from Deronda the unmixed admiration for which she longs; but she realizes, as they speak, that her sinfulness does not preclude winning his interest and approval. Her fulfills her wish that he understand everything without being told by imaginatively reconstructing her story: "He seemed to discern that she was conscious of having done some wrong—inflicted some injury. . . . He dwelt especially on all the slight signs of self-reproach; he was inclined to judge her tenderly, to excuse, to pity" (ch. 36). Thus, when Gwendolen says, "You know you would despise a woman who had done something you thought very wrong," Deronda replies: "That would depend entirely on her own view of what she had done." He goes on to explain that "some would never get their eyes opened if it were not for a violent shock from the consequences of their own deeds" and that those who are suffering from a keen remorse become more worthy of sympathy than they were when they were "comfortably self-satisfied."

These words are precious to Gwendolen. Deronda may have looked down on her before, but as a remorseful sinner whose eyes have been opened by the consequences of her actions, she is an object of interest. Her guilt and suffering, instead of being marks of unworthiness, arouse sympathy and concern and need not make her feel hopeless about herself but can be sources of pride.

Having been shown how to win Deronda's approval, Gwendolen displays her acceptance of his values. She surreptitiously wears the necklace he redeemed as a bracelet because she wishes him to see that she has "submitted her mind to rebuke" (ch. 36). She tells him she has made her gain out of another's loss in a way that is far worse than gambling. She accepts his judgment that she has been selfish and ignorant, her facial expression conveying "the subsidence of self-assertion." She pleads for his advice, asking him what he would do if he were like her, feeling that he was "wrong and miserable, and dreading everything to come?" Indeed, she places the direction of her life in his hands: "You must tell me then what to think and what to do; else why did you not let me go on doing as I liked and not minding?" Because Deronda would not allow her to go on indulging herself and not caring about others, he must tell her how to live. Like George Eliot,

Gwendolen exaggerates Deronda's influence. Looking to Deronda for salvation, she constructs a version of her history that makes him responsible for her.

Deronda responds to the heavy burden Gwendolen places on him by trying to give her advice. Much of it is addressed to his conception of her as a self-absorbed narcissist who has little sense of the world beyond her narrow interests. He tells her to "try to care about something in this vast world besides the gratification of small selfish desires," for "something that is good apart from the accidents of [her] own lot" (ch. 36). When Gwendolen admits to selfishness, he urges her to try to gain "some real knowledge," which will give her "an interest in the world beyond the small drama of personal desires." He says that it is the curse of her life that "all passion is spent in that narrow round, for want of ideas and sympathies to make a larger home for it," and asks if she has any "occupation of mind" that she cares about "with passionate delight." In response to these words, Gwendolen looks "startled and thrilled as by an electric shock." Encouraged by her receptivity, Deronda exhorts her to find refuge from personal trouble in "the higher, the religious life, which holds an enthusiasm for something more than our own appetites and vanities." Shaken out of her "wailings into awe," Gwendolen says "humbly—'I will try. I will think.'"

But in spite Gwendolen's feeling startled, thrilled, and awed, Deronda's advice has little effect. It addresses issues that may have been important before her marriage to Grandcourt but that are no longer at the forefront of her existence. Becoming less selfish, less narrow, less ignorant of the world around her will not alleviate her suffering under Grandcourt's tyranny, her guilt and dread, or her fear of doing something even more sinful. Indeed, George Eliot does not conceal the fact that Deronda's words of wisdom do not have much practical value. Deronda himself has a sense that they are of little use, and Gwendolen is at a loss about how to apply them.

With its invocation of sprouting seeds and rising sap, the epigraph to chapter 44 is part of the rhetoric of rebirth; yet in the chapter itself Gwendolen finds herself unable to make any progress: "He said, I must get more interest in others, and more knowledge, and that I must care about the best things—but how am I to begin?" She assembles a miscellaneous selection of books in her room: "Descartes, Bacon, Locke, Butler, Burke, Guizot—knowing, as a clever young lady of education, that these authors were ornaments of mankind, feeling sure that Deronda had read them, and hoping that by dipping into them all in succession, with her rapid understanding she might get a point of view nearer to his level." Given that she must be constantly on the scene as Mrs. Grandcourt, though, she has astonishingly little time "for these vast mental excursions." The satirical tone of this passage is somewhat surprising in view of George Eliot's usually solemn treatment of Deronda's advice.

In their exchanges at the Abbey, Deronda does address Gwendolen's more immediately pressing problems. Gwendolen tells him that she feels remorse for having injured others and asks him what he would do in a similar case. He replies that he would try to make amends and to avoid injuring anyone again. But Gwendolen tells him that she cannot repair the damage she has done. "That is the bitterest of all," says Deronda, "to wear the yoke of your own wrong-doing. But if you submitted to that, as men submit to maiming or a lifelong incurable disease?—and made the unalterable wrong a reason for more effort toward a good that may do something to counterbalance the evil? One who has committed irremediable errors may be scourged by that consciousness into a higher course than is common" (ch. 36). This is another formulation of the pattern of the fortunate fall. Gwendolen can become better than the average person because of the wrong she has done.

Although we see no evidence that Gwendolen pursues a higher course, Deronda's words are no doubt a comfort in that they hold out the possibility that she may be able to envision herself as a superior being once more. The terms of superiority have been altered, however; for what she must do now is to save other people rather than pursue preeminence and éclat for herself. Deronda's words can also be a source of distress, insofar as Gwendolen is too preoccupied with her own ruined life to give herself to rescuing others, in which case she is failing to live up to his standards.

It is important to note that Deronda's counsel is based on the assumption that Gwendolen has done a great unalterable wrong and that her life is irrevocably spoiled, like that of a person who has been maimed or is suffering from an incurable disease. Those who compare Deronda to a psychotherapist seem to overlook this assumption. He reinforces Gwendolen's dawning awareness that she is selfish and ignorant, but he makes no effort to help her comprehend and come to terms with what she has done in marrying Grandcourt or to take a more balanced view of her responsibility for Mrs. Glasher's fate. Rather, he accepts her own assessment of the heinousness of her behavior. He would not want to soften judgment because he welcomes her self-reproach and remorse.

Deronda is not interested in Gwendolen's psychological well-being—which would require self-understanding, self-acceptance, and self-forgiveness—but wants to use her guilt to motivate her to live for others, to be less egoistic. He believes in the beneficial effects of self-condemnation. Gwendolen is to become a better person not through emotional growth but through continued self-flagellation, efforts at restitution, and the avoidance of any behavior that would increase her self-hatred.

Deronda is more like a clergyman than a therapist—indeed, he describes his activity as "preaching" (ch. 45). He is what Gwendolen puts in place of organized religion. He is trying to help her find a way to rescue herself by developing a sense of meaning and purpose in the face of hopelessness about her own possibilities for happiness. I am not suggesting that Deronda could have offered Gwendolen effective psychological help at that time and place, considering the nature of her problems and the circumstances governing their interactions, but I am amazed that so many commentators have seen his ministrations as precursors of psychotherapy.

Gwendolen is haunted not only by her guilt for having injured Mrs. Glasher (as though she were the principal cause of that woman's plight) but also by a fear of her murderous impulses toward Grandcourt. We must remember that within a few weeks of her marriage, she secreted a knife in her dressing case and began having fantasies of killing her husband. In their conversation in the library of the Abbey, she tells Deronda that when her "blood is fired" she can "do daring things—take any leap" and that she is frightened of herself (ch. 36). Not really knowing what Gwendolen is talking about (any more than does the reader as yet), Deronda feels as if he is "seizing a faint chance of rescuing her from some indefinite danger" and urges her to turn her "fear into a safeguard," to keep her "dread fixed on the idea of increasing that remorse which is so bitter" to her. Gwendolen already dreads the increased fear and self-hatred she knows she would feel if she acted on her impulses, but she is afraid that they are not enough to deter her: "But if feelings rose—there are some feelings— hatred and anger—how can I be good when they keep rising? And if there came a moment when I felt stifled and could bear it no longer?"

At this point Deronda realizes the full extent of his inability to help her: "It was as if he saw her drowning while his limbs were bound" (ch. 36). In response to his suffering, Gwendolen is filled with compunction: "I am grieving you. I am ungrateful. You *can* help me. I will think of everything. I will try." She now feels guilty for having pained Deronda, and she tries to alleviate her guilt by reminding him that he "began it" when he "rebuked" her and proclaiming that it shall be better with her because she has known him. Sparing Deronda pain by showing, or at least saying, that he has helped her becomes one of Gwendolen's inner dictates.

I do not mean to suggest that her relationship with Deronda is of no value to Gwendolen. He cannot solve her problems (could anyone?); but because she can talk to him, she does not feel entirely alone with her troubles. He gives her emotional support and the feeling that there is someone who cares and wants to help. Her idealization of him gives her something in which to believe, and the desire for his approval something for which to strive. When Grandcourt suggests that Mirah is Deronda's mistress, Gwendolen is extremely distraught at having her faith in her mentor shaken and dashes off to see Mirah to have it restored.

Because Deronda is Gwendolen's only resource in an otherwise hopeless situation, she becomes excessively dependent and clings to him "with a beseeching persistent need" (ch. 48). She oscillates between a despair of living up to his standards and a belief that he can save her, can show her the way somehow. When she sees him at a musical evening, she confesses that she has not been "able to do anything better," despite everything he has said, that she doesn't "know how to set about being wise" (ch. 45). Discouraged by this admission, Deronda says that he "might as well have kept from meddling." Alarmed at the sense of futility she herself has induced, Gwendolen assigns him the duty of sustaining her virtue and morale: "If you say you wish you had not meddled—that means, you despair of me and forsake me. And then you will decide for me that I shall not be good. It is you who will decide; because you might have made me different by keeping as near to me as you could, and believing in me."

This is extremely manipulative, of course, as well as a way of disowning responsibility for herself. She is telling Deronda that his exhortations have not enabled her to do any better but that if he loses faith in her, she cannot be good, and it will be his fault. He must not only have faith but must stay as near to her as he can. Gwendolen is making enormous irrational claims upon him. It is no wonder that, given his involvement with Mordecai, he has a foreboding of some painful collision.

After her murderous impulses toward Grandcourt are exacerbated by his maligning of Deronda, his forbidding her to visit Mirah again, his having Lush show her his will, and his snubbing of Mrs. Glasher in Rotten Row, Gwendolen takes the opportunity of an encounter at the Klesmers' to ask Deronda to visit her the following afternoon. When he arrives, she once again expresses contempt for herself and despair about changing for the better. Indeed, she is afraid that she will become worse: "I want not to get worse. I should like to be what you wish. There are people who are good and enjoy great things—I know there are. I am a contemptible creature. I feel as if I should get wicked with hating people" (ch. 48). Deronda's words about the higher, the religious life were meant to inspire Gwendolen, but they have become a measure of her littleness and intensify her self-contempt.

When Gwendolen reiterates her fear of becoming wicked and asks Deronda to tell her what she can do, he has no answer and can only experience once more the anguish of frustrated concern: "The feeling Deronda endured in these moments he afterwards called horrible. Words seemed to have no more rescue in them than if he had been beholding a vessel in peril of wreck." (ch. 48). The thought that is foremost in his mind is to urge Gwendolen to "confess everything to [her] husband," to "leave nothing concealed"; but before he can speak, Grandcourt appears. Gwendolen later tells Deronda that she had asked for this meeting in order to tell him about her murderous impulses toward her husband, in hopes that revelation would act as a deterrent. Under the circumstances, it would hardly have been a good idea for her to confess everything to Grandcourt. Indeed, that Deronda was about to give this advice indicates how very far he was from comprehending her plight.

When Grandcourt takes Gwendolen yachting to get her away from Deronda, her longing for his death is intensified. She is torn between her desire for vengeance and her fear of the dread and self-hatred that would follow on the attainment of that desire, just as guilt, remorse, and anxiety followed on her earlier evildoing. Moreover, George Eliot tells us, "she had learned to see all her acts through the impression they would make on Deronda: whatever relief might come to her, she could not sever it from the judgment of her that would be created in his mind" (ch. 54).

I am frankly stunned by this passage. Is George Eliot really saying that a major factor in Gwendolen's not murdering Grandcourt is her knowledge that Deronda would not approve—that otherwise she might have done it, even though she has been experiencing anguish over a far less serious transgression? This seems to me to be another extravagant, and unsuccessful, effort to cast Deronda in the role of Gwendolen's savior, an effort that so far has been consistently subverted by the mimetic portrayal of her heroine.

Gwendolen's only hope, George Eliot tells us, resides in "the possible remedies that lay in [Deronda's] mind, nay the remedy that lay in her feeling for him" (ch. 54). As we have seen, Deronda has no remedies for Gwendolen's murderous rage; she clings to him for a rescue he cannot provide. And I do not know what George Eliot has in mind when she speaks of the remedy that lies in Gwendolen's feelings for Deronda, since those feelings, whatever they are, do not prevent her from continuing to lust for her husband's death. When she meets Deronda in Genoa, she feels that the knowledge he is there will "save her from acting out the evil within. And yet quick, quick, came images, plans of evil that would come again and seize her in the night, like furies preparing the deed that they would straightway avenge." Neither her feeling for Deronda nor her fear of his disapproval nor her dread of an avenging power prevents Gwendolen from becoming complicit in Grandcourt's drowning when she fails to throw him a rope.

GWENDOLEN AND GRANDCOURT'S DEATH

Up to this point, repeated claims have been made for Gwendolen's conversion; but they seem problematic when we examine George Eliot's psychological portrait of her heroine. Deronda is presented as having a transformative influence. He has provided emotional support, but Gwendolen is too trapped in an unbearable situation to be able to follow his advice. She cannot take refuge from personal troubles and become a better person by leading the higher life, or even resist doing more wrong, in an effort to avoid further remorse. George Eliot in fact portrays in brilliant detail Gwendolen's increasing desperation as she finds herself unable to imagine any escape from her difficulties other than Grandcourt's death.

By killing off Grandcourt, George Eliot gets rid of problems that neither Gwendolen nor Deronda can solve and opens the possibility that she can profit from his counsel, that her fall can turn out to be a fortunate one. An escalation now occurs in the claims for Gwendolen's transformation and Deronda's beneficent influence. When evaluating these claims, we should keep in mind that they are made not only by the narrator, who is not always reliable, but also by the principal characters, and especially by Gwendolen, who is in a highly disturbed state. What Gwendolen says about Deronda's effect on her is part of the rhetoric, just as praise of Dorothea by other characters is part of the rhetoric in *Middlemarch*. What Gwendolen says seems intended to carry authority, but it is motivated by her powerful psychological needs and often appears to be exaggerated.

Following Grandcourt's death, Gwendolen unburdens herself to Deronda, but doing so makes her fearful of alienating him, and she goes to great lengths to hold on to his support. She prefaces her confession by assuring him that she has benefited from his efforts to help her and pleads with him not to forsake her when she tells him everything: "Am I worse than I was when you found me and wanted to make me better? All the wrong I have done was in me then—and more—and more—if you had not come and been patient with me. And now, will you forsake me?" George Eliot lets Gwendolen's statements stand unchallenged, but is she truly no worse now than she was at Leubronn? Was all the wrong she has done in her then? If so, there was hardly a hint of this in the first half of the novel. In her eagerness to repudiate her earlier egoism, she is inclined to magnify her transgressions. Would she have done even more wrong if Deronda had not intervened and been patient with her? What additional wrong would that have been? Gwendolen's claims for the positive influence of Deronda's intercessions make psychological sense in light of her desire to win his continued support by assuring him that he has had a transforming effect on her life; but I do not believe these claims to be credible. Gwendolen's guilt and self-abhorrence when she confesses to Deronda are in part an effort to placate him by showing she has learned the lessons he has taught. They make her into an object of pity rather than of reproach.

Gwendolen seeks to bind Deronda to her by venerating him and humbling herself. He is not only the God of judgment, in whose eyes she knows she is guilty, but also the merciful and suffering Christ. Perceiving Deronda's "anguish of passionate pity," Gwendolen is pierced by compunction, "as she [was] by his face of sorrow at the Abbey" (ch. 56). Her "need of getting nearer to that compassion" turns "into an impulse to humble herself more." She is almost "ready to throw herself on her knees before him." She tells Deronda that he represents the good for which she has been longing but from which her sins have cut her off: "Getting wicked was misery—being shut out for ever from knowing what you—what better lives were."

The relationship between Gwendolen and Deronda is clearly meant to exemplify George Eliot's Religion of Humanity. Gwendolen is the worshiper and penitent who confesses her sins and humbles herself before the divine justice and mercy, as embodied in a fellow human being. Deronda is the representative of the species, which, according to Feuerbach, is the highest humans can know and is therefore divine to them. Gwendolen believes that through her sins she has separated herself from the good. Her adulation is intoxicating to Deronda, who is not averse to casting himself in a godlike role.

Not only does Deronda not forsake Gwendolen, but he grants her a kind of absolution. When he sees her next, he tells her that she bears no responsibility for Grandcourt's drowning. She says that if she had "not had that murderous will" and "had thrown the rope on the instant," it might "have hindered death" (ch. 57). I find it hard to argue with this, but Deronda assures her that Grandcourt "must have been seized with cramp" and that her "momentary murderous will cannot . . . have altered events"—as though a man with a cramp could not have been saved by a rope. Gwendolen continues to feel herself guilty in relation to Grandcourt; but in the novel as a whole, her failure to come to his rescue is largely dismissed, whereas her earlier selfish acts and her "crime" against Mrs. Glasher continue to be magnified. Her desire to kill her husband—which may have contributed to his death—is assimilated into the pattern of the fortunate fall. Sooner or later, says Deronda, our evil will "works its way outside us—it may be in the vitiation that breeds evil acts, but also it may be in the self-abhorrence that stings us into better striving." We are asked to view Gwendolen's evil will as of the second sort.

I think George Eliot wants us to see Gwendolen as self-abhorring, full of remorse, and hence morally redeemed, but also as free of responsibility for Grandcourt's death. If her failure to throw the rope were taken seriously, it would be difficult to regard her as having been converted by Deronda and possessing the potential to become a morally superior person. After exaggerating Gwendolen's wickedness through most of the novel, both author and hero now dismiss her account of her husband's drowning and downplay her possible contribution to his death.

DERONDA NOT GWENDOLEN'S THERAPIST

For the remainder of Gwendolen's story, the principal issues are whether she is capable of regeneration and the degree to which her regeneration is dependent on Deronda. When Gwendolen expresses her fear that she is beyond redemption and that Daniel cannot bear to look at her because she is so wicked, Deronda affirms his belief that she can become "worthy to lead a life that may be a blessing" (ch. 57). He preaches salvation through duty. "We must find our duties in what comes to us." She "will discern new duties," he tells her, when she is once more among her friends. Gwendolen says that she will "bear any penance," "lead any life" he prescribes, but he must not forsake her: "You must be near. If you had been near me—if I could have said everything to you, I should have been different." This very dubious statement is part of Gwendolen's effort to cling to Deronda. She would not have been so evil if they had not been separated, and she can only become worthy if she has his presence and support.

When Deronda parts from her after the meeting I have been describing, Gwendolen sinks "on her knees in hysterical crying. The distance between them was too great. She was a banished soul—beholding a possible life which she had sinned herself away from" (ch.

57). Servants entering the room find her "crushed on the floor." Some critics feel that Gwendolen is in love with Deronda and that the life from which she feels cut off is that of being his wife. This could be the case. One way for Gwendolen to have Deronda always near her would be for him to marry her, and she may well feel that she has sinned herself away from that possibility. But the larger possibility from which she feels cut off by her sins is the ability to escape self-hatred and rebuild an idealized image of herself. We are told that the previous year's experience "turned the brilliant, self-confident Gwendolen Harleth of the archery meeting into the crushed penitent impelled to confess her unworthiness where it would have been her happiness to be held worthy" (ch. 58). The only way she can restore her pride is to become worthy in the eyes of Deronda, but she fears that the distance between them is too great for this to happen.

In an effort to gain Deronda's approval, Gwendolen strives to be "very wise" and "good" (ch. 64), but she no longer has any trust in herself and seeks constant guidance from him. She feels "strong enough to do anything that would give her a higher place in Deronda's mind," if only she were sure what that was. She asks him to tell her what to do about Grandcourt's will, in which she has been left a modest bequest. Because of her guilt, she wants to take nothing for herself; but Deronda advises her to accept the bequest because doing so will "cause others less pain." She can be guided in the use of her money by her remorse and her desire to lead a beneficent life. She tells him that she wants "to be kind" to all the members of her family who "can be happier" than she. "Is that the best I can do?" she asks. "I think so," Deronda replies. "It is a duty than cannot be doubtful. . . . Other duties will spring from it."

Gwendolen feels that she has ruined her life through her sins and wishes she could do more by way of penance and reparation. Deronda urges her to think of what has happened "not as a spoiling of [her] life, but as a preparation for it" (Ch. 65). Then, in a frequently quoted speech, he tells her that she can be "among the best of women":

> See! You have been saved from the worst evils that might have come from your marriage, which you feel was wrong. You have had a vision of injurious, selfish action—a vision of possible degradation; think that a severe angel, seeing you along the road of error, grasped you by the wrist, and showed you the horror of the life you must avoid. And it has come to you in your springtime. Think of it as a preparation. You can, you will, be among the best of women, such as make others glad that they were born.

These words are "like the touch of a miraculous hand to Gwendolen." She has (once again) arrived at "the beginning of a new existence," thanks to Daniel Deronda: "So pregnant is the divine hope of moral recovery with the energy that fulfils it. So potent in us is the infused action of another soul, before which we bow in complete love. But the new existence seemed inseparable from Deronda: the hope seemed to make his presence permanent."

Several questions arise for me from the passages I have quoted. What should we make of Deronda's speech, which does not quite fit the facts of Gwendolen's experience? What is the nature of the new existence at which Gwendolen has arrived? Is this new existence inseparable from Deronda?

Deronda tells Gwendolen that she has been saved from the worst evils that might have come from her wrongful marriage. What are those evils? Foremost seems to be her dispossession of Mrs. Glasher (which is treated as a fact, rather than as an unlikely eventuality). Gwendolen has had "a vision of injurious, selfish action"; Deronda asks her to imagine that "a severe angel" has prevented her from continuing along the road of error by showing her the horror of the life she must avoid. I find this hard to follow. Gwendolen is saved from wronging Mrs. Glasher and her children neither by becoming aware of her selfishness nor by heeding the admonitions of a severe angel (taken by many critics to be Deronda himself), but by the death of Grandcourt and the provisions of his will. Grandcourt's death and Gwendolen's complicity in it might be seen as another evil that has resulted from her wrongful marriage, but it is not an evil from which she has been saved. Perhaps Deronda means that she has been saved from the evil of killing Grandcourt with her own hands by virtue of his accident, but that seems unlikely. I am not sure what he means.

If we do not read the passage closely, we may guess that what Deronda means is that the guilt and remorse Gwendolen feels on account of her selfish behavior will cause her to turn away from pursuing her own pleasure without regard to the price others must pay, and to turn toward doing her duty instead. Her guilt and remorse may lead her in that direction; but as we have seen, her efforts to change are futile as long as Grandcourt is alive. Both George Eliot and Deronda tend to obscure Gwendolen's role in Grandcourt's death and the role of that death in creating the opportunity for her to lead a new life. She can leave the road of error only once she has allowed Grandcourt to drown.

Deronda's words are like the touch of a miraculous hand to Gwendolen because they hold out the possibility that instead of feeling wicked and worthless, she can be among the best of women. She begins to see the way in which she can escape her self-abhorrence and rebuild her sense of herself as a superior person. She must forever relinquish her narcissistic claims, but she can become instead an exemplary person who lives for duty, like Daniel Deronda. If she does her duty to those nearest to her, other duties will follow. Once she begins to act with a "penitential, loving purpose," she will discover "newly-opening needs—continually coming to carry [her] on from day to day," and she will find her "life growing like a plant" (ch. 65). The new needs will not be hers but those of people who have a better chance of happiness than she. Her life can have great meaning in the absence of personal fulfillment if she looks at it "as a debt," as a means of redeeming herself by living for others.

Given their situations and personalities, it is quite understandable that Deronda would preach living for duty as the solution to Gwendolen's problems and that she would respond so positively to his message. Deronda has said similar things before, but that was while Grandcourt was alive, and Gwendolen could not follow his counsel. Now that she does not have to cope with Grandcourt's psychological abuse and her own murderous rage, the solution Deronda offers seems like a real possibility. It provides her with a defense against self-hatred and despair and holds out the prospect that she may gain his approval and rise above other women. Under the circumstances, perhaps the best Gwendolen can do is to resign herself to personal unhappiness, regard her life as a debt, and alleviate her guilt and restore her pride by becoming one of those women who makes *others* glad they were born. This is certainly a better solution than hopelessness and self-loathing, but I would not call it therapeutic.

The problem Deronda is addressing is that Gwendolen feels she is bad, and the help he offers is to tell her that it is not too late to become good. He is concerned with the unfolding of her moral potentialities but not with her development into a fully functioning, self-regulating human being. These are not his values, of course, nor are they George Eliot's; but I should hope they would be the values of a psychotherapist. Deronda does not help Gwendolen toward either knowledge of herself (except of her ignorance and selfishness) or a broader comprehension of her history and her role in what has happened. He endorses her exaggerated feelings of guilt in relation to Mrs. Glasher, and he ignores her possible contribution to the death of her husband—although she continues to be haunted by it and must deal with it if she is to find peace. He encourages a new search for glory by preaching an unselfish and penitential devotion to duty that will make her one of the best of women. The lofty goals he sets may be beyond her reach and therefore another source of self-hatred and despair.

Deronda does not encourage the kind of self-awareness, self-forgiveness, and self-acceptance that, in my understanding, are essential to emotional growth. He does not want to do anything that will diminish Gwendolen's self-reproach; she blames herself too much, often for the wrong reasons, and takes responsibility for the consequences of other people's bad behavior. Deronda does not help her to see herself as the product of her past and to recognize the contribution that others, including her mother, have made to her difficulties. He sees her failings almost entirely as moral deficiencies rather than as problems arising from the conditions under which she grew up. Her problems result in moral deficiencies, to be sure; but I am not sure that self-reproach is the best way to deal with them.

Given his own problems, the times, and their very limited contact with each other, Deronda could not have been Gwendolen's therapist—and he was not. Gwendolen has escaped Grandcourt's tyranny, but in her new existence she is subject to the pressure of Deronda's conception of how she ought to feel and behave. She is driven to be unselfish and dutiful by her fear of self-abhorrence and her desperate need for his approval.

From George Eliot's point of view, Deronda has not spoiled his mission because he has helped Gwendolen change from a bad person into a good one. Her new life is defined almost entirely in moral terms, quite independently of her psychological state, which causes her to move from crisis to crisis rather than toward self- knowledge, inner peace, and emotional maturity.

It seems to me that *Daniel Deronda* is at once George Eliot's most complex psychological novel and, with the possible exception of *Silas Marner*, her most simplistic moral tale. The novel opens with the question of whether good or evil is dominant in Gwendolen, and it can be read as the story of a struggle between these forces in both Gwendolen's psyche and the world of the book as a whole. There is no sophisticated exploration of ethical issues here, of the nature of good and evil. These simple terms are used with disturbing frequency and are assumed to have a self-evident meaning by which characters can be unambiguously judged. Mirah, Mordecai, and their mother are good. Lapidoth is evil, as are gamblers in general. Daniel Deronda and the Meyrick women are good; Grandcourt, Mrs. Glasher, and Lush are bad. Selfishness is evil; self-sacrifice is good. Although Alcharisi generates some sympathy, her behavior is selfish, and her intentions for Daniel are negated by larger forces. Hans is a combination of good and bad qualities, but Gwendolen is the principal character in whom good and evil are mixed. She is predominantly bad to begin with but becomes good as a result of her sin, which awakens her dormant conscience. As her values shift from self-indulgence to self-abnegation, under the stings of her conscience and the guidance of Daniel Deronda, she is on her way to becoming a morally superior person.

GWENDOLEN'S NEW EXISTENCE

Gwendolen feels her new existence to be inseparable from Deronda's, yet is separated from him at the end, and we cannot help wondering how much of her new existence will survive his departure. Gwendolen believes that she can do whatever Deronda prescribes, whatever will win his esteem; but she has no resources of her own, no inner strength, no autonomy. The future to which she turns "with a willing step" is "one where she would be continually assimilating herself to some type that he would hold before her" (ch. 69). She derives her sense of direction entirely from Deronda, and she needs him to tell her how to go about trying to become what he feels she should be. Her reliance on Deronda has "become to her imagination like the firmness of the earth, the only condition of her walking."

Even with Deronda's assistance, Gwendolen's entrance into her new existence is tenuous at best. Living with her family at Offendene, she experiences some of the peaceful melancholy that comes from self-renunciation; but she is still in deep trouble, still full of guilt, self-hatred, and despair. Deronda visits with the object of announcing his plans to marry Mirah and travel to Palestine, but in their first interview he shrinks from inflicting a wound when she is so dependent on him. In their second interview he finds her deeply depressed and hysterical—she is much like her mother in her hysterical sobbing. In their third interview, she expresses regret for having been so full of grief and despair and tells him that she is trying to keep up her hope and be cheerful so as not to cause him pain. She is trying to suppress her real feelings out of a fear of being selfish and of driving him away. Even before she learns of Deronda's plans, Gwendolen is not doing well.

The news that Deronda is leaving is a devastating blow, but George Eliot treats his departure as another stage of Gwendolen's education. Despite all her chastening experiences, Gwendolen is still an egoist. She still has the "impression which had accompanied her from childhood, that whatever surrounded her was somehow specially for her" (ch. 69). She has no sense of Deronda's separate life, imagines herself to be more important to him than she is, and assumes that he will always be present for her. Gwendolen still needs to be made aware of her insignificance, of the narrowness of her life and the pettiness of her concerns.

Through Deronda she is brought into contact with "the larger destinies of mankind" (ch. 69). George Eliot surrounds Deronda's announcement with bombastic rhetoric, the effect of which is to turn his mission into "something spiritual and vaguely tremendous," while Gwendolen feels reduced "to a mere speck." From George Eliot's point of view, such a humbling experience is salutary. It represents an important step in the heroine's journey toward moral maturity.

Gwendolen does not complain about being abandoned at a time of desperate need, for to do so would be selfish. Still seeing her misery as all her own fault, she says that she deserves to be forsaken because she has "been a cruel woman" (ch. 69). Deronda feels guilty to see her "the victim of his happiness"; and moved once again by his anguish, Gwendolen manages to say, "brokenly," that she will be the better for having known him. She needs to hold on to her idealization of Deronda and her belief that his influence will save her. She says that he has been good to her, that she has deserved nothing, and that she does not want to add to the evil she has done by damaging him: "Don't let me be harm to *you*." Not wanting to disappoint Deronda, she makes an "intense effort" to maintain a "difficult rectitude," but "her frame totter[s]" under the weight of the burden. She keeps her composure until Deronda leaves but "burst[s] out hysterically" when she is alone with her mother. Through the day and half the night she falls "continually into fits of shrieking," in the midst of which she cries out that she means to live. Her proclaiming her intention to live suggests a fear that she will literally perish without Deronda.

At the beginning of this chapter, I cited Carl Rotenberg's view that the interaction between Daniel and Gwendolen is "prescient of the analytic relationship" and that although Gwendolen is saddened by their separation at the end, "the relationship has left her with inner health and moral strength" (1999, 262, 267). Rotenberg reaffirmed his position in a response to a version of this chapter that was published as an article (Paris 2002). In the course of doing so, however, he provided an account of the effect of Deronda's departure on Gwendolen that supports my sense of her desolate state:

> he breaks off peremptorily the intense transference relationship to Gwendolen, announces to her his intention to marry someone else, and says that he is leaving Gwendolen, probably never to see her again. It is as if a psychoanalyst in midtreatment were to announce without warning to a regressed and highly dependent patient that at the end of the session, treatment would be terminated and that the patient would most likely never see the analyst again. Is there any wonder

that Gwendolen crumbles, cries, becomes ill, and regresses
into hysterical weeping? (2002, 131)

Rotenberg acknowledges that this casts doubt on George Eliot's "rhetorical argument" that Gwendolen has achieved "significant psychological and moral change."

Gwendolen will survive Deronda's departure, but what sort of life
will she have? What will she do with her guilt, self-hatred, and despair, which were barely under control even with Deronda's ministrations? She will try to be a good daughter, of course. When she wakes
from her night of hysterical shrieking, she is solicitous of her mother:
"Ah, poor mamma! You have been sitting up with me. Don't be unhappy. I shall live. I shall be better." I think we are supposed to see
how much less selfish Gwendolen has become, but we should remember that she has always been extremely sensitive to her mother's
unhappiness. I can imagine the two women living out their lives
hovering about each other, with Mrs. Davilow worrying about
Gwendolen and Gwendolen putting on a brave face to spare her mother
pain. Not much progress there.

Those who see Gwendolen as "saved" tend to rely heavily on the
letter Deronda receives from her on his wedding day:

> Do not think of me sorrowfully on your wedding-day. I have
> remembered your words—that I may live to be one of the best
> of women, who make others glad that they were born. I do
> not yet see how that can be, but you know better than I. If it
> ever comes true, it will be because you helped me. I only
> thought of myself, and I made you grieve. It hurts me now to
> think of your grief. You must not grieve any more for me. It
> is better—it shall be better with me because I have known
> you. (ch. 70)

Gwendolen is saying what she wants to believe, what she feels she
ought to say, and what Deronda wants to hear. At first glance, the
letter sounds very positive; but it does not inspire confidence that
Gwendolen can live up to Deronda's ideals, as she must do if she is
not to go on berating herself. I am not sure whether her faith that she
can be one of the best of women if Deronda says so will be a source
more of hope or of despair. The anticipated transformation imposes
lofty demands on a woman who does not know how to meet them,
who has been left without a guide, and who is completely unable to
cope with life on her own.

The letter itself is a sign of Gwendolen's effort to be what Deronda wants. It is full of gratitude, unselfishness, and self-reproach. Deronda has fostered her dependency and then withdrawn, with hardly a transition; but Gwendolen is apologizing for having made him grieve. Her blaming herself rather than Deronda disarms our criticism of him, and her reassuring words enable George Eliot to achieve a positive ending, with Deronda's happiness untainted by the burden of having to worry about Gwendolen. I worry about her, however, and do not believe the rhetoric of conversion, rebirth, and the fortunate fall. Gwendolen has changed, of course, and is now a crushed penitent; still, I do not regard being crushed as a good thing.

It is to George Eliot's credit that she does not sacrifice the realistic depiction of her heroine to the demands of form and theme. Much of the critical controversy about the end of the novel derives, I think, from the dissonance between the mimetic portrait, which is accurate, and the rhetorical claims, which are not. Most critics focus on either one or the other; I have tried to attend to both. Barry Qualls says that "the reader who cannot feel Gwendolen's leaving the world of despair behind has missed her strong terrible vision. Her final repetition of 'it shall be better with me because I have known you' is cathartic. We must share it if we have paid attention to George Eliot's guiding voice" (1986, 220). Indeed we must, if we believe what that voice has been telling us. But we cannot share it if we have paid attention to the character George Eliot has actually created rather than to the one who exists in the rhetoric. If we have done that, we are more likely to agree with such observations as that of Elizabeth Daniels: "Not free of the guilt of her past, weak from the chaos of her inner turmoil, with no sustaining dream of the future, [Gwendolen] was apparently left in a state of collapse—a pitiable bundle of conflicts" (1982, 35). This seems right to me.

8

Deronda the Deliverer

AN IMAGINED HUMAN BEING

Whereas Gwendolen's side of the story has been widely celebrated as one of George Eliot's greatest achievements, it is difficult to find anyone who will offer praise for Deronda's portion of the novel. The notes struck by Henry James in *"Daniel Deronda*: A Conversation" have reverberated through much of the subsequent criticism. The Jewish portion suffers from "poor illusion" and is wearisome (Leavis 1948, 254). Daniel, Mirah, and Mordecai are "hardly more than shadows" beside Gwendolen and Grandcourt. In Deronda, George Eliot intended to create a "faultless human being" (256); instead, without realizing it, she fashioned a "dreadful prig" who has "no blood in his body."

F. R. Leavis, who reprinted James's "Conversation" as an appendix to *The Great Tradition*, contrasts the "magnificent" achievement of Gwendolen's half of the story with "the astonishing badness of the bad half" (1948, 80). "There is significant agreement," Leavis observes in a later introduction to the novel, "that the hero is not a man," that he cannot "be credited with any reality, let alone the convincingness necessary to a major *dramatis persona*" (1961, xvi). We are to take Deronda as "the beau ideal of masculinity"; but "insofar as he is anything, [he] is a prig" (xviii). Like James, Leavis is struck by George Eliot's seeming unawareness of the discrepancy between Deronda and the Zionist story "and the wonderfully vital art of which there is such a wealth" in the rest of the novel (xvii).

Judgments of this kind have been uttered repeatedly. Harold Bloom describes Deronda as "nine-tenths a prig and one-tenth a passionate

179

idealist" (1986, 5). Gwendolen "vaults off the page," but Deronda "lacks personality, or else possesses so much character that he sinks with it, into a veritable bathos in a few places." A. S. Byatt finds Deronda to be "insubstantial" (1995, 98); he is not "a created human being in the way Gwendolen is" but sometimes "just a stick." Ignês Sodré feels that George Eliot "falls for the idealisation" of Daniel "because of her own wish to do something heroic, of her wanting to save the Jewish people" (Byatt and Sodré 1995, 99). Margot Waddell argues that the weakness of the novel "lies in the (inevitable) failure to make moral abstractions incarnate" (1999, 280). The unconvincingness of the Daniel, Mirah, and Mordecai portions of the story "is rooted in the . . . static presentation of ideal types, the origins for which remain mysterious and inexplicable. It is as if, in these characters, George Eliot is describing an 'ego ideal' without reference to the myriad of other aspects of internal and external life" (279). Overall, Deronda's characterization "amounts to a kind of agglomeration of admirable qualities" (278).

Not everyone regards Deronda as a collection of admirable qualities. Indeed, as we have seen, many find him to be a prig. Mary Ellen Doyle writes that "like *Adam Bede* and *Felix Holt*, this novel has a sermonizing male hero whose deficiencies are not adequately interpreted, together with a religious enthusiast [Mordecai] dehumanized [even more than Dinah Morris and Rufus Lyon] by perfect virtue and incredible speech patterns (1981, 159). According to Doyle, Deronda has many flaws; but they are obscured by George Eliot's sympathetic treatment of him. We find "no intimations of his errors or character defects" (163); for instance, "his lack of direction, though noted, seems always due to his circumstances, not to his character" (160).

Because Deronda is usually regarded as one of George Eliot's failures, he has received little close attention. The best discussion of him I have found is in Barbara Hardy's introduction to a Penguin edition of the novel. Hardy observes that although Daniel, Mirah, and Mordecai are idealized, Deronda is "fairly complex in psychological presentation" (1967, 18). She describes some of his problems and conflicts and a number of features of his character, which is shown "in the process of growing. Like Goethe's Wilhelm Meister, he serves an apprenticeship, and searches for relationships and a vocation." George Eliot is trying to create a character who is "complicated, moving, [and] changing" (19); Hardy claims that Deronda can be discussed in ways that make him sound interesting. Nevertheless, most readers find him to be "wooden and static and unreal" (18).

Hardy argues that we object not so much to Deronda's nobility as to his lack of personality: "The question of personality in literature is not an easy one, but I think it depends on an impression of vital responsiveness in characters who change according to the company they keep. Even Pecksniff varies from situation to situation, and is created through a multitude of viewpoints. Not so Daniel Deronda." Deronda is only seen from "the author's admiring point of view. When he is criticized it is only for very noble faults, like excessive sympathy and altruism" (20). He is never "subjected to irony or even mild satire," and "this exemption is a sign of lifelessness." We might want to call Adam Bede or Dorothea Brooke prigs, "but so does the author. If you could smile at Deronda, and be ironical about him, it would be in defiance of the author."

I am not going to argue that the half of the novel concerning Deronda, which includes the excessively quaint and good Meyricks, is as successful as the part concerning Gwendolen. I, too, find it frequently defective. Even so, as I observed at the outset, I believe that Gwendolen's story has more flaws and Deronda's story greater psychological richness than critics, including myself in *Experiments in Life*, have recognized.

Deronda must be distinguished from Mordecai, Mirah, and the Meyricks. He is surrounded by the same cloying rhetoric, but he is not the purely idealized, illustrative character he has often been taken to be. He is presented in enough realistic detail that we can understand him independently of the author's admiring point of view. When we see him as an imagined human being, he escapes George Eliot's rhetoric and subverts her thematic intentions. With Daniel Deronda, as with other characters George Eliot glorifies, we must defy the author if we are to recover her psychological intuitions and do justice to her mimetic achievement.

That Deronda is not subjected to irony or satire makes him seem lifeless only if we fail to distinguish between rhetoric and mimesis. Allowing George Eliot's admiring view of Deronda to take the place of the character she has actually created obscures the fact that he is leading a life of quiet desperation and is as much in need of rescue as those whom he "saves." Leavis observes that whereas Deronda tells Gwendolen that she needs to find refuge from trouble in the higher, the religious life, he himself is "a paragon of virtue, generosity, intelligence and disinterestedness" who "has no 'troubles' he needs a refuge from" (1948, 84). I do not believe this to be true.

In my discussion of Gwendolen, I have suggested that Deronda offers her solutions he has developed for himself and that these solutions are not as efficacious or desirable as the author would have us believe. It is difficult to see Deronda's "troubles" because he is presented as such a wonderful person, and it is difficult to see the inadequacies of his solutions because George Eliot makes them work, for him if not for Gwendolen. The universe of the novel is ordered in such a way as to honor Deronda's defenses, thereby obscuring their problematic nature.

DANIEL'S PECULIAR POSITION

With regard to the troubles from which Deronda needs to take refuge, it seems to me that George Eliot is at pains to spell out the difficulties emanating from his uncertainty about his birth. Once he begins to suspect, at the age of thirteen, that he may be Sir Hugo's illegitimate son, his faith in Sir Hugo is shaken, he believes that he and his mother have been wronged, he struggles with resentment, he feels cut off from normal relations with his fellows, and he develops a "premature reserve" (ch. 16). As he grows to manhood, the same uncertainty about his birth makes it hard for him to decide on a vocation. I think that critics have trouble registering and believing in Deronda's difficulties, and hence his reality, because George Eliot presents them, except for their effect on his sense of direction, not as damaging him but as turning him into a paragon of virtue, generosity, and disinterestedness.

Deronda's suspicion that Sir Hugo is his father is depicted as a profoundly disillusioning experience. Life had been "delightful" to the boy, "with an uncle who was always indulgent and cheerful—a fine man in the bright noon of life, whom Daniel thought absolutely perfect"; but now care has arrived "with an enigmatic veiled face," bearing "dimly-conjectured, dreaded revelations" (ch. 16). The narrator observes that the first discovery of a flaw in his hero "is hardly a less revolutionary shock to a passionate child than the threatened downfall of habitual beliefs which makes the world seem to totter for us in maturer life." Daniel's entire sense of himself, of his relation to Sir Hugo, and of his place in the world has been called into question. The man in whom he has trusted completely now takes "the aspect of a father who held secrets about him," secrets about which he can "never inquire."

As a result of his questionable position, Daniel loses his spontaneity. He becomes reserved not only with Sir Hugo but with everyone in his life. He feels that others probably know things about him they do not mention and that he does not want to hear. Brooding on his situation leads him to become introspective, remote, and secretive. If his father has done wrong, it is "a cutting thought that such knowledge might be in other minds," and he does not want it spoken of to him (ch. 16). Suffering keenly from the belief that some dark secret surrounds his birth, he avoids relationships that would involve an exchange of confidences. When a school friend talks about his home and parents and expects him to do the same, Daniel shrinks "into a reserve, and this experience remain[s] a check on his naturally strong bent toward the formation of intimate friendships." He is described as having an "ardently affectionate nature," but his sensitivities and suspicions deprive him of the warmth he craves both from Sir Hugo and from companions his own age.

Somewhat like Lydgate, Deronda tries to satisfy his emotional needs by being of use to others in one-sided relationships. Friends like Hans confide in him but show no reciprocal interest in his life. This both frustrates him and satisfies his desire to be close to others without revealing himself. It mitigates but does not dispel his feeling of isolation.

Deronda feels indignation, resentment, and a sense of grievance toward Sir Hugo, both on his own behalf and on behalf of his mother, whom he imagines to have been victimized. Because he has loved Sir Hugo, who has been unfailingly kind, he experiences a conflict between gratitude and affection on the one hand and resentment on the other. His contradictory feelings are evenly balanced: his love for Sir Hugo tempers his resentment and prevents him from displaying it, but he cannot relinquish it or feel the same as he did before. Sir Hugo is unaware of his ward's inner struggles, partly because of an insensitivity to the difficulties of Deronda's position that is so great as to challenge credibility, and partly because Daniel disguises so much of what he is feeling. On Daniel's side, his relationship with the most important person in his life is marked by repressed resentment, distrust, and concealment.

Afraid to make enquiries about his birth, Deronda becomes convinced that he is Sir Hugo's natural son and that there is "a tinge of dishonour about his lot" (ch. 16). He feels disadvantaged, set apart, marked out as illegitimate. Sir Hugo's marriage strengthens "the silent consciousness of a grief within, which might be compared in some ways with Byron's susceptibility about his deformed foot." Since Deronda believes he is Sir Hugo's son, the children of the marriage will occupy a position that might otherwise belong to him, intensifying his sense of exclusion. His not having a definite place in his family and his society contributes greatly to his alienation, his detachment, and his inability to choose a vocation.

Thus, Deronda has many troubles from which he needs a refuge. George Eliot presents these troubles as part of a process of education that takes place in his teenage years and makes him into a morally superior person. He illustrates par excellence the pattern of moral development I described in *Experiments in Life*. His own sorrows enable him to imagine the suffering of others, and his vision of their inner states arouses his sympathy. His troubles ennoble rather than damage him because of an "inborn lovingness" that is "strong enough to keep itself level with resentment" (ch. 16). He thinks he is a bastard; but he is "the reverse of that type painted for us in Faulconbridge and Edmund of Gloster, whose coarse ambition for personal success is inflamed by a defiance of accidental disadvantages" (ch. 37).

Deronda's inborn lovingness transforms his suffering into a source of moral growth and prevents him from becoming another Byron: "The sense of an entailed disadvantage—the deformed foot doubtfully hidden by the shoe, makes a restlessly active spiritual yeast, and easily turns a self-centered, unloving nature into an Ishmaelite. But in the rarer sort, who presently see their own frustrated claim as one among a myriad, the inexorable sorrow takes the form of fellowship and makes the imagination tender" (ch. 16). Deronda is of the rarer sort. He has "a subdued fervour of sympathy, an activity of imagination on behalf of others," that result in "acts of considerateness" which strike "his companions as moral eccentricity" (ch. 16). Someone in Deronda's position might have felt Sir Hugo's marriage "as a new ground of resentment," but he does not blame Lady Mallinger for dispossessing him, and his "silent grievances" make him tolerant rather than bitter because they are directed toward a man whom he loves.

Feeling himself to suffer from an entailed disadvantage, Deronda is drawn to victims and underdogs and tries to take care of those least able to take care of themselves. His "sense of injury breeds—not the will to inflict injuries . . . , but a hatred of all injury" (ch. 16). Thinking about his wrongs leads him to develop "a meditative interest in learning how human miseries are wrought" that is "as precocious in him as another sort of genius in the poet who writes a Queen Mab at nineteen." He is a moral genius who displays an "exquisite goodness which can never be written or even spoken—only divined by each of us, according to the inward instruction of our own privacy."

I believe it is this version of Deronda that readers find wooden, boring, and unreal. We are told he is suffering acutely, but he seems to transcend his pain with such ease and profit that we have trouble believing in it. He seems too good to be true-to-life. George Eliot's admiring point of view obscures the imagined human being she has actually created, and we must distinguish her mimetic portrait of Deronda from it to appreciate his complexity. Critics have sensed a disparity between rhetoric and mimesis when they have observed that Deronda has deficiencies which are not adequately interpreted and that George Eliot meant to depict an ideal human being but has created a prig without realizing it. The position in which Deronda finds himself does damage him psychologically. Except for his lack of direction, however, the damage takes a form to which neither George Eliot nor the critics have given sufficient weight.

In comparing Deronda to Edmund of Gloucester and Byron, George Eliot accounts for the difference in his reaction to accidental disadvantages by reference to his given nature, which is not self-centered like theirs, but innately loving. Like Mirah, he is inherently good; moreover, his goodness, like hers, is not threatened but enhanced by adverse circumstances. Although there may be a temperamental component in Deronda's response to his situation, George Eliot's explanation does not seem adequate. I believe that if we look closely at her mimetic portrait of Deronda, we can understand his response more fully. His "goodness" is at least partly defensive in nature, and it is this defensiveness that many readers have found annoying.

I believe that Deronda's anger toward Sir Hugo and his efforts to cope with that anger have exercised a major influence on the formation of his personality. In my most recent reading of the novel, I have been surprised to discover how frequent and persistent are the references to his bitterness. They are present from the beginning to near the end of his story, often in the form of an assertion that his "lifelong affection for Sir Hugo" is "stronger than all his resentment" (ch. 41). The epigraph to chapter 49, in which Sir Hugo tells Daniel that his mother has sent for him, begins: "Ever in his soul / That larger justice which makes gratitude / Triumphed above resentment. 'Tis the mark / Of regal natures." After Sir Hugo delivers Alcharisi's message, Daniel asks if his father is also living, doing so "with a tremulous reverence in his voice—dreading to convey indirectly the reproach that affection [has] for years been stifling."

Learning that Sir Hugo is not his father and has not wronged his mother does not greatly change Daniel's attitude toward him. He feels that Sir Hugo's "ignorant kindness" has had "the effect of cruelty," but the hero's "affectionate gratitude" makes him "wish to find grounds of excuse rather than blame, for it is . . . possible to be rigid in principle and tender in blame" (ch. 59). Instead of feeling that he has been mistaken about Sir Hugo and that much in his earlier resentment was unjustified, he seems to be holding on to the position that Sir Hugo has wronged him and that he, Daniel, is nobly rising above his sense of injury.

From the age of thirteen, Daniel has been struggling against his resentment, stifling the reproaches he harbors. George Eliot attributes this struggle to his inborn lovingness, but her description of him as having an "ardent clinging nature" (ch. 16) helps us better, I think, to understand why he handles his resentment as he does. The kindly Sir

Hugo is Daniel's sole source of love and security, the only person to whom he can attach himself. Apart from Sir Hugo, the boy is quite alone in the world. He has no other family and no definite place in society. Before his suspicions are aroused, Daniel has every reason to love and be grateful to Sir Hugo. Once he becomes convinced that his guardian is really his father, he feels humiliated and victimized. His resentment threatens his security, however, and he is terribly afraid of expressing it. He defends himself against his anxiety by stifling his reproaches and being submissive. He no longer believes in Sir Hugo's absolute rightness and indeed often feels critical, but his "early inwrought affection" makes him "gratefully deferential to wishes with which he [has] little agreement" (ch. 37). He experiences "a fear of being ungrateful" and falsifies his behavior to avoid losing the love to which he clings. He behaves in a deferential manner, while inwardly seething with indignation.

Deronda does not displace his anger toward Sir Hugo onto others, overtly at least, but he develops a general fear of being bitter and aggressive. When he finally meets his mother, he is shaken by an anger toward her that "no reflection [can] come soon enough to check," because it seems that she has "borne him unwillingly," has "willingly made herself a stranger to him," and is "now making herself known unwillingly" (ch. 51). He has good reason for resentment; but terrified by his anger, he experiences "a horror . . . lest he should say something too hard" to the woman who has abandoned him. He cannot allow himself to continue to feel hostility and becomes solicitous and sympathetic instead. In his dealings with others, he lacks normal self-interest and aggressiveness. Other people think that something is missing in him, that he would be first-rate if he had more ambition, and that he is morally eccentric. From George Eliot's perspective, his lack of personal ambition, his stifling of anger, and his fervor of sympathy are signs of moral grandeur, of course.

Although Deronda submits to what he imagines to be wrongs at the hands of Sir Hugo, he intervenes energetically on behalf of others whom he perceives to be mistreated. At school, he is averse to the "ugly forms of boyish energy," but he does not try to escape from nasty scenes. Rather, he is "inclined to sit through them and take care of the fellow least able to take care of himself," even though he is somewhat "compromised by this apparent comradeship" (ch. 16). Daniel identifies with those he perceives to be weak or victimized by injustice. He sees their lot as similar to his own and stands up for them in a way that he cannot do for himself. His self-pity translates into sympathy for them and a readiness to enter into their suffering. He cannot direct his anger toward Sir Hugo, but he can become the champion of people who are disadvantaged, and thereby release some of his indignation in a way that is both virtuous and safe.

I think that Deronda has a powerful need to be noble, in order to compensate for what he believes to be the stigma of his illegitimacy. George Eliot tells us that his "early wakened susceptibility" was "charged at first with ready indignation and resistant pride" (ch. 16), before it was transformed into heightened sympathy and conscientiousness. The resistant pride remains but usually manifests itself in ways that are difficult to detect. It is quite evident, however, in the following description of his feelings toward Grandcourt:

> No reasoning as to the foundations of custom could do away with the early-rooted feeling that his birth had been attended with injury for which his father was to blame; and seeing that but for this injury Grandcourt's prospect might have been his, he was proudly resolute not to behave in any way that might be interpreted into irritation on that score. He saw a very easy descent into mean unreasoning rancour and triumph in others' frustrations; and being determined not to go down that ugly pit, he turned his back on it, clinging to the kindlier affections within him as a possession. Pride certainly helped him well—the pride of not recognising a disadvantage for one's self which vulgar minds are disposed to exaggerate . . . : he would not have a man like Grandcourt suppose himself envied by him. (ch. 25)

As he has with Sir Hugo, Deronda disguises his true attitude toward Grandcourt. He *is* irritated that Grandcourt is to inherit what should rightfully be his, but it would add to his humiliation for Grandcourt to know that and to think that he envies him. To display his irritation would be to acknowledge a sense of inferiority to a man he despises and whom he cannot bear to have look down on him.

The passage quoted is about more than Grandcourt. It is about how Deronda restores his pride by responding nobly to an unjust fate that could easily generate vindictiveness and rancor, as it does in Edmund of Gloucester, who also reasons on the foundations of custom. Deronda is grateful, reverential, and affectionate to the man who has deeply injured him, and perhaps his mother as well. " 'Tis the mark / Of regal natures." Inwardly, he has a patronizing attitude toward Sir Hugo: You have wronged me and are morally obtuse, but I excuse you and will give you filial affection and respect. Instead of triumphing in others' frustrations, he champions the boys who are picked on at school. In so doing, he makes himself superior to those who are persecuting them. He is suffering from an entailed disadvantage, but he is a better person than those of honorable birth.

I think that readers find Deronda to be a prig because he has a judgmental attitude and an air of moral superiority, both of which are on display in the opening scene at Leubronn. He wears a disturbing expression, "which threatens to affect opinion—as if one's standards were somehow wrong" (ch. 29). Feeling himself to be in a dishonorable position, he looks down on others from the height of his rectitude, putting them on the defensive as a way of defending himself. George Eliot says that Deronda is rigid in principle and tender in blame. It is the rigidity that his expression conveys. When Gwendolen tells Sir Hugo that she is afraid of Daniel, Sir Hugo replies: "Gad! I'm rather afraid of him myself when he doesn't approve." Deronda himself appears conscious of the figure he cuts, when he hopes that discovering his origin will give him a calling and enable him "to escape standing as a critic outside the activities of men, stiffened into the ridiculous attitude of self-assigned superiority" (ch. 37).

In this passage, George Eliot seems more aware of Deronda's priggishness than critics have thought her to be. Perhaps she is indulgent toward it because Deronda is in some ways a version of herself. I am reminded of Henry James's observation that George Eliot's "compensatory earnestness," her "refined conscience, her exalted sense of responsibility, were colored by her peculiar position" (Carroll 1971, 495). Exactly the same thing can be said of Deronda.

Deronda's peculiar position induces him to adopt a variety of pride-restoring devices. His rigidity of principle establishes him as having moral standards that are higher than other people's, and his tenderness in blame is the mark of a regal nature in which love triumphs over resentment. To compensate for his sense of being tainted, he develops an idealized image of himself as a giving, caring, unselfish person who sacrifices himself for others and puts their interests above his own. His resentment toward Sir Hugo is so threatening not only because he fears the loss of love but also because giving vent to it would violate his inner dictates, deprive him of his sense of rectitude, and make him hate himself.

We can see his inner dynamics at play when he becomes terrified at feeling anger toward his mother. He forces himself to enter into her experience and see things from her perspective, much as Dorothea forces herself to transcend her anger with Will by thinking of those she has set out to rescue. He is helped, George Eliot tells us, by "his habitual shame at the acceptance of events as if they were his only" (ch. 51). This is a remarkable statement in view of the trouble Deronda has in responding to events in terms of his own needs. That he habitually feels shame gives some idea of the impossibly high standard of unselfishness he has set for himself and the threat of self-condemnation that drives him to try to live up to that standard. Deronda works hard, often in quite conscious ways, at being exquisitely good. This effort finds a reflection in his advice to Gwendolen.

In spite of the defenses that compensate for his peculiar position by giving him a sense of moral superiority, Deronda cannot escape the "anguish of exceptional sensitiveness into which many a carelessly-begotten child of men is born" (ch. 37). He feels that he is doomed to unhappiness. He tells his mother of his love for Mirah but observes that he has no assurance that she reciprocates it: "I have always felt that I should prepare myself to renounce, not cherish that prospect. But I suppose I might also feel so of happiness in general. Whether it may come or not, one should try to prepare one's self to do without it" (ch. 53). "Do you feel in that way?" says his mother. "Poor boy!"

Deronda is such a paragon of virtue, generosity, and disinterestedness that characters in the novel—like some critics—do not see him as having needs and frustrations of his own. Mirah tells him of Hans's observation that Daniel thinks so much about others that he hardly wants anything for himself: "He told us a wonderful story of Bouddha giving himself to the famished tigress to save her and her little ones from starving. And he said you were like Bouddha. That is what we all imagine of you" (ch. 37). " 'Pray don't imagine that,' said Deronda, who had lately been finding such suppositions rather exasperating. 'Even if it were true that I thought so much of others, it would not follow that I had no wants for myself. When Bouddha let the tigress eat him he might have been very hungry himself." Like Buddha in this story, Deronda sacrifices himself for others, but he is very hungry and does have wants of his own.

One of the reasons Deronda thinks so much of others is precisely that he is so hungry, so frustrated and unfulfilled. I shall discuss separately his inability to settle on a vocation, but it is important to observe here that this inability gives him a sense of aimlessness, of seeing no point to his life. He needs for other people to need him; he wants to give them what they desire, to be what they wish him to be. He sacrifices himself to help Hans pass his exams, in part because Daniel doesn't find his own studies meaningful and cares little about his own success. When he returns from completing his education on the Continent, he hunts, he boats, he plays cricket; he reads law in a desultory way; he is at Sir Hugo's beck and call. He welcomes opportunities to serve and save others because they fill his empty existence and give him a sense of doing something significant with his life. He needs to live for others because he is unable to live for himself.

Deronda comes to the rescue not only of Hans but also of Mirah, Mordecai, and Gwendolen. Before he learns he is Jewish, he is in a delicate position with Mordecai; for Mordecai requires something of Daniel that he cannot possibly provide if he is Sir Hugo's son, as he believes himself to be. He tries to walk a fine line between being sympathetic and not encouraging illusions. He tells Mordecai, "It is my wish to meet and satisfy your wishes wherever that is possible to me" (ch. 40). Why is this his wish? George Eliot says that "it accorded with his habitual disposition that he should meet rather than resist any claim on him in the shape of another's need." I suggest that this characterological trait is in part the result of a compensatory need to give meaning to his life by fulfilling the wishes of other people. He suffers greatly if he cannot do so—for example, when he must disappoint Gwendolen at the end.

SEARCH FOR A VOCATION

Although George Eliot does not seem to recognize many of the ways in which Deronda's peculiar position has damaged him, she is quite conscious that it has resulted in his aimlessness and detachment. At the center of his story is his search for a vocation, and the chief obstacle is his uncertainty about his birth. George Eliot depicts the psychological consequences of his uncertainty, but she sees his problem as situational, and she solves it by manipulating the action in such a way that the world of the novel exactly conforms to his emotional needs. His "virtues" contribute to the happy outcome by leading him to rescue Mirah, to search for her family, and to feel a sympathetic bond with Mordecai. Without these preparatory events, his discovery of his Jewish identity would not have the meaning for him that it does.

George Eliot observes that Deronda's "demerits" are "on the side of reflective hesitation," a trait she attributes largely to "his position" (ch. 16). He has no immediate need to earn an income or to fit himself for a profession, and his uncertainty about his parentage gives him "an excuse for lingering longer than others in a state of social neutrality." Other men, he feels, have "a more definite place and duties." The combination of his uncertainty about his birth, his wide-ranging sympathy, and his reflectiveness paralyzes him, except when it comes to helping other people. Sir Hugo sees him as "hampered with ideas" (ch. 17) and urges him not to carry being "unselfish and generous" too far: "You must know where to find yourself" (ch. 16). But this is precisely what Deronda does not know. He is so accustomed to looking at things from other people's perspective that he has no standpoint of his own. As he drifts down the Thames, carried by the tide, he wonders "how far it might be possible habitually to shift his centre till his own personality would be no less outside him than the landscape" (ch. 17). Passivity, drifting, and the lack of a center are recurring motifs in his story.

Deronda's problems are the opposite of those of George Eliot's egoists, who see the world as an "udder to feed their supreme selves." Whereas egoists are passionately caught up in the pursuit of their goals, Deronda is so aware of conflicting claims and complexities that he has trouble seeing why he should "draw strongly at any thread in the hopelessly-entangled scheme of things" (ch. 17), and even his altruism is blunted. His "too reflective and diffusive sympathy [is] in danger of paralysing in him that indignation against wrong and that selectiveness of fellowship which are the conditions of moral force" (ch. 32). George Eliot is aware of Deronda's malaise, of his "meditative numbness," but critics have not taken it seriously.

Like Dorothea, Deronda longs to make a difference for the better; but, also like her, he does not know how to do it—except through his incidental rescues. He is not hindered by the restrictions Dorothea experiences because she is a woman but rather by the lack of a hereditary place and duties. He has been brought up as an English gentleman but never quite feels like one. Sir Hugo's suggestion that his protégé may become a great singer seems to indicate that he is not a member of the class to which the baronet belongs. Daniel has difficulty identifying with that class or sharing its interests and attitudes. When he announces that he would like to leave Cambridge and study on the Continent, Sir Hugo asks: "So you don't want to be an Englishman to the backbone after all?" "I want to be an Englishman," Deronda replies, "but I want to understand other points of view."

His cosmopolitanism is part of the problem. It gives him a broader perspective, but it works against "that selectiveness of fellowship" which is one of the "conditions of moral force." Deronda's cosmopolitanism contributes to what George Eliot describes as his ennui. He knows he must choose sides if he is to be effective, but in the absence of hereditary duties and strong identification with a group, he feels no compelling reason to embrace one course rather than another. He wants to have such a reason and has fantasies about finding one.

As we shall see, George Eliot's understanding of Deronda's difficulties is influenced by theories about race that emerge later in the novel; but her initial treatment of his lack of direction is compatible with a psychological view of his character. Other forces are at work, however, than those to which she calls our attention. Before leaving for Cambridge, Deronda asks his guardian, "What do you intend me to be, sir?" Sir Hugo replies: "Whatever your inclination leads you to, my boy" (ch. 16). But Deronda has no strong inclination toward any calling, and in the absence of an emotional leaning, he is unable to choose. Both he and George Eliot see his mental paralysis as the result of his uncertainty about his place in the world. Deronda is detached not only from his society, however, but also from himself. He has difficulty deciding what he wants to do with his life because the defenses he has adopted have distanced him from many of his feelings.

I have already suggested that a major cause of Deronda's lack of vitality and inner direction is his repression of his resentment toward Sir Hugo. Afraid that expressing anger will make him hate himself and will jeopardize his relationship with his guardian, he overcompensates by being grateful, reverential, and serviceable. He works hard at diffusing his pent-up aggression by cultivating vision and sympathy, by seeing things from other people's perspective and making allowances for them. He strives to become selfless in part because he is afraid of himself, and in the process he suppresses so much of his spontaneous expansiveness, ambition, and interest that he does not know what he wants and nothing strongly appeals to him. In addition, his failure to choose a vocation may be a way of acting out his resentment. Sir Hugo says he can be whatever he likes but is openly disappointed that Daniel does not follow him into politics. Deronda's aimlessness may be a way of frustrating Sir Hugo and showing what he has done to him. It is also a way of romanticizing his plight and holding onto his victimization. To get on with his life would mean relinquishing his position as a man who is doomed to inexorable sorrow.

If Deronda is to find a vocation, it must have certain characteristics. It must not violate his taboos against personal ambition and aggressiveness—hence, the practice of law is not a real possibility. Like Dorothea, he does not want to have wishes that are merely for himself, while, at the same time, he aspires to do something of world-historical importance. He is another searcher for glory. "Since I began to read and know," he tells Mordecai at the end, "I have always longed for some ideal task, in which I might feel myself the heart and brain of a multitude—some social captainship, which would come to me as a duty, and not be striven for as a personal prize" (ch. 63).

It is essential to Deronda that his vocation come to him as a responsibility rather than as a personal preference. Instead of chafing under hereditary obligations, as some men do, he laments that his uncertainty about his birth has robbed him of "sharp duty" and hopes that learning the truth will provide him with bonds that will save him "from having to make an arbitrary selection where he [feels] no preponderance of desire" (ch. 37). Whereas his mother experiences a conflict between her duties as a Jewish woman and her aspiration to be a singer, Deronda has no aspiration to give direction to his life. He is oppressed by his freedom to follow his inclinations and wants to be told what he should do. He returns to England after meeting his mother "with what was better than freedom—with a duteous bond which his experience had been preparing him to accept" (ch. 63).

Deronda is saved from freedom and finds exactly the sort of vocation he has longed for through his encounter with Mordecai and his discovery of his Jewish identity. This part of the novel has a wish-fulfillment quality that contrasts sharply with the insistence on confronting reality that is dominant in Gwendolen's story. While Gwendolen's egoistic dreams are crushed, Deronda's altruism is rewarded. His story has a mythic, heroic character, as he himself feels. To him, his "finding of Mirah [is] as heart-stirring as anything that befell Orestes or Rinaldo" (ch. 19). He is self-dramatizing in both frustration and fulfillment. His saga is placed in the context of "the world-wide legends of youthful heroes going to seek the hidden tokens of their birth and its inheritance of tasks" (ch. 41). It is not only Deronda's wishes that are fulfilled but, despite his mother, also those of his grandfather, who wanted a grandson with "a true Jewish heart. Every Jew should rear his family as if he hoped that a Deliverer might spring from it" (ch. 51). Daniel Deronda is to be a Deliverer!

The wish-fulfillment quality of the Deronda plot is strongest in the relationship between Deronda and Mordecai, which brings seemingly impossible, ideal consummation to both men. Mordecai longs for a "deliverer" who is to "rescue [his] spiritual travail from oblivion, and give it an abiding place in the best heritage of his people" (ch. 38). This deliverer "must be a Jew, intellectually cultured, morally fervid," and free of "sordid need." His "face and frame must be beautiful and strong," and he must be "used to all the refinements of social life." Above all, he must be receptive to Mordecai's vision and "behold a glory where I behold it" (ch. 40). Deronda fits Mordecai's requirements perfectly, except that apparently he is not a Jew. Gifted with a kind of second sight, however, Mordecai is convinced that Daniel is. In the face of a seemingly insuperable obstacle, Mordecai is certain that at last the disciple for whom he has been waiting has arrived. Mordecai rescues Deronda no less than Deronda rescues him, for he provides Daniel with a vocation that is exactly suited to his psychological needs. Even before he knows he is a Jew, Deronda hopes that he may "receive from Mordecai's mind the complete ideal shape of that personal duty and citizenship" for which he has longed (ch. 41). Each man delivers the other from a seemingly wasted life and makes his dreams of glory come true.

Deronda finds what Dorothea was looking for, a great man engaged in a great work through whom he can lead a life of world-historical importance. He will carry on Mordecai's work after his death, as Casaubon had wanted Dorothea to carry on his. In this case, the work is worth doing. Deronda is presented not as great in himself, though he is exquisitely good, but as someone who, like Dorothea, wants to lead a grand life without knowing how. He is a perfect disciple. In this novel, the epic treatment is given to Mordecai and to his vision of a Jewish state. Not only George Eliot but also Deronda glorifies Mordecai. He has "as reverential an interest in Mordecai and Mirah as he could have had in the offspring of Agamemnon; but he was caring for destinies still moving in the dim streets of our earthly life, not yet lifted among the constellations" (ch. 43). George Eliot strives mightily to give her characters heroic stature and to suggest that the time for world-shaping deeds has not yet passed. The grand life can be lived here and now—although not, in this case, in England. The sense of Mordecai's greatness is conveyed largely through Deronda, who idealizes Mordecai to satisfy his own needs. Although aspects of Mordecai's vision have turned out to be prescient, few readers, myself included, have been as impressed with Mordecai as are the author and her hero.

I earlier made reference to theories about race that enter into George Eliot's understanding of Deronda as the novel progresses. From a thematic perspective, what at first appear to be characterological problems created by Deronda's uncertainty about his birth turn out to be a result of his separation from his people and his racial heritage. I have discussed this fully in *Experiments in Life* (chs. 3 and 10) and shall give only a brief account here in order to complete the picture of George Eliot's thematic treatment of her hero.

Like Herbert Spencer, George Henry Lewes, and Darwin in *The Descent of Man*, George Eliot believed in the inheritance of acquired moral characteristics. Since she thought these characteristics were transmitted along racial lines, she believed in national character and racial identity. People are so responsive to their culture because they have an inborn predisposition to be so. The culture is transmitted not only through external influences but also biologically. We do not inherit specific beliefs, values, and behaviors but a receptivity to the cultural embodiments of racial experience, which resides, so to speak, in our bones. If we are raised in a culture that is compatible with our biological inheritance, its traditions, values, and aspirations will have an emotional impact that has nothing to do with rational considerations. For George Eliot, moral life is based largely on sentiment, which is a product of the interaction between culture and an inborn nature that has evolved along with it.

In *The Spanish Gypsy* and *Daniel Deronda*, George Eliot portrays characters who have been removed from the culture of their birth and raised in an alien society. The gypsy-born Fedalma can never be a Spanish lady; and Deronda can never be English to the backbone, because he is not, in fact, an Englishman. He is not inwardly attuned to the values of the culture in which he has been raised and can never feel himself to be an organic part of it. Not bound by sentiment, duty, or "selectiveness of fellowship," he is a paralyzed intellectual, a rootless cosmopolitan, whose "yearning disembodied spirit" is "gliding farther and farther from that life of practically energetic sentiment" which he regards as "the only life worth living" (ch. 32). From this perspective, Deronda's paralysis is the product not of the psychological factors that George Eliot has portrayed and I have been analyzing, but of his deracination. His indecision and meditative numbness are not personal demerits, but rather the result of his separation from the culture whose sentiments he is biologically programmed to share and toward which he can feel a meaningful sense of belonging. Deronda accuses "himself, as he would have accused another, of being weakly self-conscious and wanting in resolve" (ch. 37); but he is being unfair to himself, because he does not yet understand his true situation.

His story is, in part, about arriving at this understanding, but the process is very gradual. He is attracted to other Jews, Mirah and Mordecai, in ways that are mysterious to himself. It is difficult to explain his allowing himself to fall in love with Mirah without the premise of an unconscious knowledge of their suitability for each other, for he knows that Mirah could never marry outside her religion, and he is very protective of her well-being. And why does Mirah allow herself to fall in love with Deronda? Her remaining unsullied in the midst of a sordid environment seems to be attributed to her fidelity to the values of her people as transmitted by her mother. Mordecai's intuition that in Deronda he has found his disciple and Deronda's responsiveness to Mordecai's vision are the most striking instances of the unconscious operation of racial identity.

Once Deronda learns of his Jewish identity, everything falls into place for him; and he experiences the most complete fulfillment, perhaps, of any George Eliot character, as he finds both love and an epic life. He also finds an explanation of his prior lack of direction and his responsiveness to Mordecai. "It is you," he tells Mordecai, who have given shape to what, I believe, was an inherited yearning—the effect of brooding, passionate thoughts in many ancestors. . . . Suppose the stolen offspring of some mountain tribe brought up in a city of the plain . . .—the ancestral life would lie within them as a dim longing for unknown objects and sensations, and the spell-bound habit of their inherited frames would be like a cunningly-wrought musical instrument never played on, but quivering throughout in uneasy mysterious moanings of its intricate structure, that, under the right touch, gives music. Something like that, I think, has been my experience. (ch. 63)

Deronda now understands why he has been such a yearning, disembodied spirit; but he is one no longer. With the discovery that he is a Jew comes "a release of all the energy which had long been spent in self-checking and suppression," and he stops being indecisive: "It was as if he had found an added soul in finding his ancestry—his judgment no longer wandering in mazes of impartial sympathy, but choosing, with that noble partiality which is man's best strength, the closer fellowship that makes sympathy practical."

George Eliot not only manipulates the plot to fulfill Deronda's wishes; she also explains his problems in such a way that they are not deficiencies at all but, like Dorothea's, signs of his frustrated noble nature. When his spiritual grandeur is, unlike Dorothea's, suitably matched with the greatness of opportunity, he becomes less real, less vital, less interesting. As Rosemarie Bodenheimer observes, he "sails out of psychological space and into the mythic-historical beyond" (1994, 265).

DERONDA'S AMBIVALENCE

Deronda's relationship with Gwendolen occupies a central position in Gwendolen's life, and also in the novel, which opens and closes with it. The main action of Deronda's own story, however, could have gone on without Gwendolen. Although F. R. Leavis initially proposed separating out the "good" part of the novel and calling it *Gwendolen Harleth*, he subsequently realized that Gwendolen's tale cannot be told without Deronda. One could, however, create a novel called *Daniel Deronda* in which Gwendolen did not appear; indeed, something like this was done in contemporary translations aimed at Jewish readers. The main role of Gwendolen in the Deronda plot is to create a painful conflict for Deronda between his wish to help Gwendolen, who is so dependent on him, and his desire to fulfill his "mythic-historical" destiny.

The smaller concerns must give way to the larger ones, of course, and that necessity hardly benefits Gwendolen. His relationship with Gwendolen is also presented as an education of sorts for Deronda, presumably concerning the limits of altruism, of what we can do for other people.

Although it does not figure in the resolution of his problems, Deronda's relationship with Gwendolen is nonetheless a rich and interesting part of his story, creating inner tensions and revealing much about his character. When we look at the relationship from Deronda's side of it, we can understand more fully how the advice he gives is related to his own experience and what he gets out of his often painful involvement with Gwendolen. Some things are puzzling, however. How are we to explain Deronda's behavior at Leubronn, especially his returning Gwendolen's necklace? And what is the exact nature of his feelings toward her? Is he or is he not enamored of her? If he is, what is the basis of the attraction, given the vast differences between them and his sense of her deficiencies?

As we have seen, Gwendolen's initial encounter with Deronda takes on immense significance for her as the novel proceeds. It fosters her discontentment with herself and leads to Deronda's moral sway over her. Deronda's behavior at Leubronn is much glorified, by both Deronda himself and George Eliot. Deronda sees himself as having hindered Gwendolen "from stepping where there was danger" (ch. 48) and begun a rescue "in that monitory redemption of the necklace" (ch. 65). In her commentary, George Eliot goes much further. By becoming her "outer conscience," Deronda brings to Gwendolen "that judgment of the Invisible and Universal which self-flattery and the world's tolerance would easily melt and disperse." The author continues: "In this way our brother may be in the stead of God to us, and his opinion . . . may be our virtue in the making. That mission of Deronda to Gwendolen [began] with what she . . . felt to be his judgment of her at the gaming-table" (ch. 64).

A close reading of the opening chapters makes these views of Deronda's behavior difficult to sustain. The novel begins with Deronda asking himself if Gwendolen is beautiful or not and whether "the good or the evil genius" is dominant in her glance. He concludes that it is probably the evil, "else why was the effect that of unrest rather than of undisturbed charm? Why was the wish to look again felt as coercion and not as a longing in which the whole being consents?" This passage is usually discussed for what it says about Gwendolen, but it may tell us more about Deronda. He is clearly attracted to Gwendolen and wants to keep looking at her, but he is uncomfortable about it. He attributes his unrest to an evil genius dominant in

Gwendolen, but we learn as the novel progresses that his affections are engaged elsewhere and that his attraction to Gwendolen conflicts with his feeling for Mirah. Under these circumstances, it is difficult to imagine his whole being consenting in his longing to look at Gwendolen, but he experiences his discomfort as a product of evil in her rather than of unruly emotions in himself.

The "inward debate" Gwendolen raises in Deronda gives "his eyes a growing expression of scrutiny" (rather than of unmixed admiration). It is this expression that threatens Gwendolen's pride and, according to George Eliot, initiates a process that will eventually lead to her regeneration (ch. 65). Gwendolen has "the darting sense" that Deronda is "looking down on her as an inferior," that he feels "himself in a region outside and above her" and is examining her "as a specimen of a lower order" (ch. 1). Gwendolen's perceptions of how Deronda is looking at her may be in part a manifestation of her own insecurity; from what we come to know of Deronda, however, it seems that, even if perhaps exaggerated, they are essentially correct.

As we have seen, Deronda develops a judgmental attitude and an air of moral superiority as a way of compensating for his sense of the dishonor of his position. He puts others on the defensive to prevent them from looking down on him. One of his characteristic attributes becomes a look, a facial expression, a measuring gaze that makes people feel that their standards are somehow wrong. His gaze has this effect on Gwendolen: he takes hold on her mind "as one who had an unknown standard by which he judge[s] her" (ch. 35). He is conscious enough of his attitude of "self-assigned superiority" to be uneasy about it. When he goes to the Hand and Banner with Mordecai, he offers his cigar case, which he carries, even though he does not smoke, because he likes "to indulge others," in an effort not to seem "straight-laced" (ch. 42). Rigid in principle, Deronda *is* straitlaced, and he makes others uncomfortable with his judgmental manner.

One of the things Deronda is straitlaced about is gambling, and there is no doubt that he looks at Gwendolen and others at the table with disapproval. When she later asks him why he thought it was wrong for her to gamble, he replies that "there is something revolting to [him] in raking a heap of money together, and internally chuckling over it, when others are feeling the loss of it.... There are enough inevitable turns of fortune which force us to see that our gain is another's loss" (ch. 29). This attitude toward gambling, which is endorsed by George Eliot, becomes a recurring motif in the novel, but it seems a not entirely rational product of Deronda's personal experience. The gamblers who are suffering the loss of money others have won have not been treated unfairly; they staked their money voluntarily and were themselves out to win. Deronda thinks that he has been victimized by fortune and that others have gained by his loss. He identifies with losers, whom he sees as having been dispossessed, and envisions winners as gloating, much as Grandcourt, he imagines, relishes the idea of inheriting what should have been his. When Gwendolen turns from the table after losing everything she has previously won, she sees a "smile of irony" in his eyes (ch. 1) that she interprets as scorn for her gambling and satisfaction at her loss.

I find Deronda's returning Gwendolen's necklace more difficult to understand than the way he looks at her while she is playing roulette. He sees her enter the shop in which she sells the necklace to provide herself with a new stake. After she leaves, he buys the necklace and sends it to her with an anonymous note expressing the hope that she "will not again risk the loss of it" (ch. 2). Her selling the necklace is especially significant because it contains turquoises that had belonged to her father, but Deronda does not know this. His object, apparently, is to discourage her from gambling by shaming her, and he succeeds, because she leaves Leubronn immediately in order to avoid seeing him again.

On receiving the note, Gwendolen reddens "with the vexation of wounded pride" (ch. 2). She guesses Deronda has sent it and feels that he has "taken an unpardonable liberty," entangled her in "helpless humiliation," and assumed "the air of a supercilious mentor." Deronda's behavior *is* humiliating, and Gwendolen has good reason to be vexed. It is hard to imagine a gentleman in that society behaving in such a way to a lady he does not know. When Gwendolen later reminds him that he hindered her from gambling, she blushes; and Deronda blushes also, "conscious that in the little affair of the necklace he had taken a questionable freedom" (ch. 29). Indeed, he had. His action is similar to Felix Holt's denunciation of Esther Lyon's petty vanities, which has such a transforming effect. Felix's behavior is less shocking than Daniel's, however, since he is not a gentleman, he is notoriously confrontational, he knows Esther, and he would like her to become a woman he can love.

Daniel later interprets his act as hindering Gwendolen from stepping into danger, but all that would have happened had he not intervened is that she would have lost the money she received for the necklace and returned home without it. George Eliot presents Deronda's encounter with Gwendolen in Leubronn as the beginning of a mission in which he leads her toward regeneration, but did Deronda have such lofty objectives? If so, was it not terribly presumptuous of him to assume such a role?

What could have induced Deronda to behave in such an officious way? We know that he needs to have people need him; but does he also have a compulsion to intrude himself into their lives, to pass judgment, to play mentor? A possible explanation for his behavior is that he feels such a powerful attraction to Gwendolen that he uses the necklace to become involved with her, to get her attention, to feel himself a factor in her life. To justify his action, he may perceive her as an object of rescue, which is what she eventually becomes, despite her seeming self-possession.

The exact nature of Deronda's feeling toward Gwendolen is difficult to specify. George Eliot tells us late in the novel that it is "poor Gwendolen's lot" that "her dependence on Deronda tend[s] to rouse in him the enthusiasm of self-martyring pity rather than of personal love" (ch. 63). Nonetheless, there are indications that Deronda has an amorous attraction to Gwendolen. When Grandcourt arrives in Leubronn in search of her and Sir Hugo asks Deronda whether he has seen his "gambling beauty" lately, Daniel's replies are strangely cold and abrupt (ch. 15), suggesting an emotional tension where Gwendolen is concerned. Upon his expression of the hope, "in a tone of disgust," that a marriage between Gwendolen and Grandcourt will not come off, Sir Hugo says, "What! are you a little touched with the sublime lash?" and asks if he is "inclined to run after her." Deronda protests that he "should rather be inclined to run away from her." It passes through his mind "that under other circumstances he should have given way to the interest this girl had raised in him, and tried to know more of her. But his history had given him a stronger bias in another direction. He felt himself in no sense free."

I conclude from this that Deronda's feelings toward Gwendolen are strongly ambivalent, that he is both attracted and repelled, and that he might be inclined to pursue her if he felt free. He does not feel free because of his attachment to Mirah, a woman he has no hope of marrying, and his involvement with Mordecai, whose dreams for him he feels he can never fulfill. He has put himself in a strange position.

In the course of the novel, we find scattered indications of Deronda's amorous attraction to Gwendolen, even as he becomes more and more burdened by her woes and her dependency on him. He suffers from his inability to help her, but he "like[s] being near her— how could it be otherwise? She was something more than a problem: she was a lovely woman, for the turn of whose mind and fate he had a care" (ch. 48). After Grandcourt's death, he feels that had "this happened little more than a year ago, he would hardly have asked himself whether he loved her: the imperious determining impulse which would have moved him would have been to save her from sorrow, to shelter her life for evermore from the dangers of loneliness," and to complete the rescue begun in Leubronn (ch. 65). The impulse to marry Gwendolen without asking himself whether he loves her seems compulsively self-disregarding, but perhaps he would not have asked himself this question because he does love her—or feels that he would have, had he met her before meeting Mirah.

Despite George Eliot's statement that what Deronda feels for Gwendolen is self-martyring pity, her fullest account of his emotions suggests that they are more in the nature of personal love:

> In the wonderful mixtures of our nature there is a feeling distinct from . . . exclusive passionate love . . . , which yet is not the same with friendship, nor with a merely benevolent regard, whether admiring or compassionate: a man . . . hardly represents to himself this shade of feeling toward a woman more nearly than in the words, 'I should have loved her, if—:' the 'if' covering some prior growth in the inclinations, or else some circumstances which have made an inward prohibitory law as a stay against the emotions ready to quiver out of balance. The 'if' in Deronda's case carried reasons of both kinds; yet he had never throughout his relations with Gwendolen been free from the nervous consciousness that there was something to guard against not only on her account but on his own—some precipitancy in the manifestation of impulsive feeling—some ruinous inroad of what is but momentary on the permanent chosen treasure of the heart—some spoiling of her trust. . . . How could his feeling for Gwendolen ever be exactly like his feeling for other women, even when there was one by whose side he desired to stand apart from them? (ch. 50)

According to this passage, Deronda would have loved Gwendolen had there not been a prior inclination toward another or an inward prohibition. We are told that both reasons apply in this case, but do they? George Eliot seems to be conflating Deronda's relationships with Gwendolen and with Mirah. He has a prior inclination toward Mirah that stands between him and Gwendolen but an inner prohibition only in relation to Mirah. Before he learns that he is a Jew, he is afraid that a revelation of his feelings will spoil their relationship, because Mirah could never marry outside her religion. Indeed, we might expect that this consideration would keep his feelings for Mirah in that borderline region between friendship and love which George Eliot describes. It is one of the puzzles of his character that he allows himself to fall in love with Mirah and feels himself committed to her, in spite of the obstacles between them—unless this is to be explained by an unconscious knowledge of their racial affinity.

In both relationships, Deronda is afraid of his emotions' getting out of control, and he is again faced with the need for self-suppression that has been a constant feature of his life. In the case of Gwendolen, the emotions that are ready to "quiver out of balance" seem to be strongly erotic. He must guard against the manifestation of impulsive feelings that are momentary in nature and that will spoil Gwendolen's trust and be destructive of his love for Mirah. He seems to be struggling against sexual desire, the expression of which would damage not only his relationships with the women but also his image of himself as a man of superior rectitude. When George Eliot says that Deronda has not spoiled his mission, one of the things to which she seems to be referring is his sexual self-restraint: "Not one word of flattery, of indulgence, of dependence on her favour, could be fastened on by her in all their intercourse, to weaken his restraining power over her (in this way Deronda's effort over himself was repaid)" (ch. 54). Isn't this about Deronda's not allowing himself to approach Gwendolen as a lover? Had he so approached her, he could never have been "a terrible-browed angel" from whom she could not hope "to win an ignorant regard."

How can we integrate the evidence of Deronda's attraction to Gwendolen with the rest of his character? The erotic component can be accounted for by her physical attractiveness, but there seems to be more going on than that. George Eliot says that he enjoys being with Gwendolen because she is a lovely woman "for whose turn of mind and fate he had a care" (ch. 48). After he comes to know her and tries to help, he would take an interest in her fate, but why in her turn of mind? It appears that notwithstanding his constant critique of her narrow, selfish, petty nature, something about her appeals to him, and this from the very beginning. Although he treats her with supercilliousness and irony, Gwendolen finds it "difficult to believe that he [does] not admire her spirit as well as her person" (ch. 1), and she may be right. His conclusion that the evil genius is dominant in her glance seems to spark his interest rather than to discourage it.

I believe that Deronda's ambivalence toward Gwendolen reflects his inner conflicts. He is constantly battling against his own aggressive impulses, striving to rise above them and to be understanding, forgiving, and helpful. To compensate for his sense of being tainted by his birth, he aims for moral perfection. He feels discouraged about his own life and strives for meaning and purpose by living for others. All of this makes him the paragon of virtue, generosity, and disinterestedness so many critics find bloodless and unconvincing. Whereas the good and dutiful Mirah embodies Deronda's ideal, Gwendolen represents what he has repressed in himself: egoism, the energetic pursuit of personal desires, and confidence in the ability to master fate. The moralistic side of Deronda disapproves of Gwendolen's gambling and her exultation in her triumphs, and he identifies himself with the losers he sees as her victims. Yet he is attracted by her "dynamic quality" (ch. 1) as she acts on impulses he cannot allow in himself. He experiences his desire to study her as a coercion, and he is uncomfortable with it not only because of Mirah but also because of his intimation that what fascinates him about Gwendolen is her evil genius.

Deronda wants to keep looking at Gwendolen because she stirs the suppressed side of his own nature, but he also needs to convey his disapproval, to reaffirm his values. I believe that Gwendolen is right in thinking that he admires her spirit, but the admiration is not something he can consciously acknowledge. While he admires her spirit, he also wishes to see it broken—hence his smile when she loses her winnings, and his humiliating behavior. He feels threatened by Gwendolen and by his intense interest in her, and he needs to do something that will subdue her and ease his own anxiety. Perhaps it is this which drives him to take the extraordinary liberty of returning the necklace with an admonitory note. Deronda is both attracted to Gwendolen and repelled by her because she displays the expansiveness he has stifled. The mission that both he and George Eliot glorify is essentially to make Gwendolen more like himself.

THE FAILED RELATIONSHIP WITH GWENDOLEN

After Gwendolen marries Grandcourt, she becomes the sort of troubled person Deronda likes to help. She submits her mind to rebuke and adopts him as her mentor, the role he assumed in Leubronn. As long as he can control his sexual impulses, this allows him to be involved with the woman to whom he is attracted in an innocent—indeed, a noble—way. Becoming another of his worshipers, Gwendolen casts him in the role of her deliverer, the part he likes to play. He draws on his own experiences to enter into hers, and he offers her the solutions he has worked out for himself. It is frustrating to him, of course, that his counsel is so ineffectual.

When Deronda learns of Mrs. Glasher and her children, he begins to reconstruct what has happened and to see that Gwendolen is suffering from the consciousness of having done something wrong: "His own acute experience made him alive to the form of injury which might affect the unavowed children and their mother" (ch. 36). Because he identifies himself with the children, and Mrs. Glasher with his mother, he cannot try "to nullify" Gwendolen's remorse. Perhaps he thinks she is feeling what Sir Hugo ought to feel. Instead of helping her to see the situation more clearly, he reinforces her sense of guilt. Gwendolen's self-castigation arouses his pity and interest, but he makes no effort to relieve her excessive self-hatred.

What Deronda says to Gwendolen often gives us deeper insight into his character and experience. George Eliot repeatedly calls attention to the personal note in his utterances but in ways that seemed enigmatic to me until I understood his inner conflicts. When they meet at the Abbey, Deronda tells Gwendolen that some people can do wrong without remorse but that he does not believe she is one of them. His "unconscious fervour" gathers as he goes on because he is "uttering thoughts which he had used for himself in moments of painful meditation" (ch. 36). Presumably, the meditations were on his feelings of resentment, his resulting vindictive impulses, and the guilt and remorse he would suffer if he acted out his fantasies. When Gwendolen asks him how she can do better, he urges her to pay attention to other people's troubles, to care for "something that is good apart from the accidents of [her] own lot." This is Deronda's way of dealing with the accidents of his lot, with his sense of leading a crippled existence.

During their interview in the library, Deronda tells Gwendolen that those who have done irremediable wrongs can be chastised into taking a higher course than the common one. She quickly points out that he has not injured anyone but has been wronged himself. Deronda explains his own higher course as a result of "remorse before commission" (ch. 36). Our keen feeling for ourselves can give us a feeling for others and an awareness of what they will suffer if we injure them. Again I have the sense of someone who keeps working hard to turn his pain into sympathy and to refrain from striking out. He has been scourged into a higher course not by wrongs he has committed but by his fear of what he might do as a result of having been injured. He keeps imagining what he would feel if his efforts at repression failed. His own struggles with resentment and rage enable him to empathize with Gwendolen when she says that she is full of hatred and anger and is frightened at herself, even though he has no clear idea of what she is angry about or what she is afraid she will do. He urges her to turn her "fear into a safeguard" (this is what he has done with his) and to keep her "dread fixed on the idea of increasing that remorse which is so bitter" to her.

The excessively guilt-ridden Gwendolen is being counseled by a man whose conscience is even more hyperactive than hers. When she feels like a criminal after Grandcourt's death (appropriately in this case; it seems to me), Deronda empathizes with her urge toward "some scourging of the self that disobeyed [her] better will" (ch. 65). He tells her, "I have known something of that myself." This surprising remark suggests that he has felt a need for self-punishment in spite of having stifled his resentment and behaved so virtuously. If that is the case, it is no wonder he is so hard on Gwendolen, except in the matter of Grandcourt's death, and that he wants to do nothing to discourage her self-reproach. He seems to castigate himself for his temptations to disobey his better will as a way of preserving his innocence.

During their conversation in the library, Deronda's remonstrance with Gwendolen over the narrowness of her life also has personal overtones. What is "the good of trying to know more," she asks, "unless life were worth more" (ch. 36). This query draws an impassioned response: "What sort of earth or heaven would hold any spiritual wealth in it for souls pauperized by inaction? If one firmament has no stimulus for our attention and awe, I don't see how four would have it. We should stamp every possible world with the flatness of our own inanity." He then urges Gwendolen to take refuge in "the higher, the religious life, which holds an enthusiasm for something more than our own appetites and vanities." George Eliot observes that the "half-indignant remonstrance that vibrated in Deronda's voice came, as often happens, from the habit of inward argument with himself rather than severity toward Gwendolen."

Deronda is talking not only about Gwendolen but also about *his* being pauperized by inaction, his feeling that life is not worth more, and his having a sense of the inanity of his existence. This passage suggests the degree of his lassitude and emptiness. Despite what Leavis says, Daniel too needs a refuge from his troubles in the higher life. He has given himself the same counsel he gives Gwendolen, evidently without success. He has not yet found the higher life, but it is waiting for him. Following his advice, Gwendolen also seeks the higher life, but nothing is waiting for her. I can't help feeling that her search will be in vain, as his was until George Eliot provided him with a vocation.

After Grandcourt's death, Deronda presses on Gwendolen his solution of living for duty, which is what sustained him before he found his calling. Being kind to her family is "a duty that cannot be doubtful," and "other duties will spring from it" (ch. 65). He assures her that this admittedly dreary view of things will offer "unexpected satisfactions" as "newly opening needs" will carry her from day to day. As I have already observed, these needs will be not hers but those of other people. Her life will grow "like a plant"; however, the growth will be an unfolding not of her potential as a person but of her opportunities to live for others. This has been the pattern of Deronda's life. In his case, moving from duty to duty has eventually led him to Mordecai and the discovery of his heroic mission, and also to fulfillment in love with Mirah. The solution has worked for him, but will it work for Gwendolen?

Deronda finds Gwendolen's growing dependency on him to be a source of satisfaction, frustration, and conflict. The more she needs him, the greater his importance in her life and the greater his opportunity to do something worthwhile, to make a difference for the better. He does his utmost to help her and he keeps assuring her that she can become one of the best of women, an extremely doubtful proposition. He may feel that his guilt and remorse before any commission of ill have made him one of the best of men and be projecting his experience onto Gwendolen.

I think that Deronda's desire to believe in his success leads him to dismiss Gwendolen's complicity in Grandcourt's death. He needed to blame her for marrying Grandcourt because of his identification of Mrs. Glasher with his mother and of her children with himself, but he has no such motive for condemning her role in Grandcourt's death—a death which may indeed have not been unwelcome. Rather, he has a strong motive for exonerating her, because acknowledging her guilt would mean that he has not been instrumental in her rebirth, that he has failed in the past and has no chance of future success. George Eliot presents Deronda's behavior as beneficial, and it appears to provide Gwendolen with some immediate relief; nevertheless, failing to help Gwendolen deal with her part in Grandcourt's drowning and setting goals beyond her reach must ultimately be destructive.

Deronda frequently feels frustrated in his efforts to help Gwendolen. When she confesses she has been unable to follow his advice, he says that he has done little good by his preaching and might as well have kept from meddling. In his meeting with Gwendolen before Grandcourt takes her yachting, he feels powerless to rescue her when she asks how she can avoid becoming more wicked: "How could he grasp the long-growing process of this young creature's wretchedness?—how arrest and change it with a sentence?" (ch. 48). He later describes this as a horrible experience.

Deronda is attempting an impossible task, given the severity of Gwendolen's problems, the conditions under which they meet, the limitations imposed by his culture, and his own lack of objectivity and self-understanding. As I have said, I do not think he is a proto-psychotherapist. Before Grandcourt's death, he sees Gwendolen infrequently, converses with her little, and does not really know her very well. She does not disclose the exact nature of her inner struggles, and he is so much in the dark about her murderous impulses that he advises her to confess everything to her husband, to "leave nothing concealed" (ch. 48). He preaches more than he listens, with the aim that she should adopt the same defenses he has employed. These do not work for Gwendolen because she is a different person with her own history, character structure, and psychological needs. Daniel is able to empathize with some of her feelings by drawing on his own experiences, but his identification often limits or distorts his understanding of her inner life. His involvement with her, moreover, is far from disinterested. He does have genuine concern for her, but he is also motivated by erotic attraction, a desire to see her tamed, and a need to give meaning to his life by acting as her deliverer. I discern some countertransference issues here, to say the least.

Even before he knows he is Jewish, Deronda has the foreboding of a collision between Gwendolen's claims on him and Mordecai's. This is his major source of conflict in the second half of the novel. While talking to Gwendolen at the musical evening, he has "a vision of himself besought with outstretched arms and cries, while [being] caught by the waves and compelled to mount the vessel bound for a far-off coast" (ch. 45). He is caught not between love and duty or duty and desire but between two forms of duty, two sets of calls on his nobility. He experiences an unresolvable opposition between his desire to help Gwendolen, indeed to sacrifice himself for her, and his perceived obligations to Mirah and Mordecai.

His departure for the East is a wrenching experience for Deronda as well as for Gwendolen. It cannot be called selfish, because it is undertaken in the name of duty and the future of his people; but it promises to fulfill his personal dreams, and thus makes Gwendolen "the victim of his happiness" (ch. 69). Deronda undergoes intolerable anguish and accuses himself of cruelty. His anguish derives in part from his compassion for Gwendolen and in part from the frustration of his wish to meet the needs of all who depend on him. He finds himself in a situation in which he is bound to disappoint someone no matter what he does, and this makes him extremely uncomfortable.

I am not suggesting that Deronda cares more for his own frustration than he does for Gwendolen's pain. He has trouble bringing himself to tell her of his plans because he knows she will suffer greatly. Even so, he does not seem truly aware of the impact of his precipitous departure and of the precarious emotional state in which he will be leaving Gwendolen. His departure *is* cruel, especially in its abruptness; one wonders if he could not have disengaged more gradually, weaning her from her dependency, at least to some degree.

The usually sensitive Deronda seems insensitive here, as does George Eliot. Perhaps neither could afford to register the devastating effect of the abandonment on Gwendolen, an abandonment that confirms her sense of unworthiness and guilt, fulfills her fears that she will be forsaken, and undermines whatever progress she may have made. The palliative Deronda offers is that he will write. When he asks if she will reply, there is a pause before Gwendolen says, "in a whisper, 'I will try' " (ch. 69). "I shall be more with you than I used to be," Deronda continues. "If we had been much together before, we should have felt our differences more, and seemed to get farther apart. Now we can perhaps never see each other again. But our minds may get nearer." This seems awfully feeble to me. It is followed, as soon as he leaves the house, by Gwendolen's fits of hysterical shrieking, which last through the day and half the night.

I have already discussed Gwendolen's motives for writing such a reassuring letter to Deronda on his wedding day and the reasons that George Eliot's rhetoric endorses its upbeat tone—the whole pattern of the fortunate fall and the claims for Deronda as Gwendolen's deliverer would otherwise be compromised. Deronda, of course, is quite ready to be reassured. Gwendolen's letter is "more precious than gold or gems" to him (ch. 70). The last obstacle to his happiness has been removed.

What is most remarkable to me about *Daniel Deronda* is that George Eliot provides such a brilliant picture of the failed relationship between Daniel and Gwendolen, while persuading most readers to see it as a great success. Both she and Deronda are in denial about what has occurred. The novel becomes far more fascinating if we pay attention to what has really happened, if we believe not what George Eliot says but what she shows.

Conclusion

In 1876, George Eliot wrote to Joseph Frank Payne that her novels were "simply a set of experiments in life—an endeavor to see what our thought and emotion may be capable of—what stores of motive, actual or hinted as possible, give promise of a better after which we may strive—what gains from past revelations and discipline we must strive to keep hold of as something more sure than shifting theory" (Haight 1954, vol. 6, 216). Because theories keep changing, she has become, she says, "more and more timid—with less daring to adopt any formula which does not get itself clothed for me in some human figure and individual experience, and perhaps that is a sign that if I help others to see at all it must be through that medium of art" (216–17).

In *Experiments in Life*, I adopted George Eliot's view of her novels as instruments of knowledge that enabled her to discover something more certain than shifting theory and to envision "a better after which we may strive." I saw them as offering a Religion of Humanity that provides meaning and values in a universe without God. As the preceding chapters have made clear, I no longer find in George Eliot the eminent sanity, the wholesome understanding, the awareness of the possibilities of life, the subtle analysis of the moral imagination that critics such as Henry James, Virginia Woolf, F. R. Leavis, and Harold Bloom have attributed to her—and that I felt she displayed when I was writing my dissertation.

I now see George Eliot's novels not as validating her beliefs but as calling them into question. Her experiments are often rigged to produce favorable outcomes for characters whose solutions she wishes to show as succeeding. Casaubon dies before Dorothea says yes to her own doom, characters and events conspire to make Fred a fit husband for Mary, and Daniel Deronda is saved from an aimless existence by finding an epic life ready-made. Most important, the human figures George Eliot imagines become creations inside a creation, who, full of the spirit of mutiny, often engage in treason against the main scheme of the book and "kick it to pieces," as Gwendolen does with her fits of hysterical shrieking. When viewed as imagined human beings, Dorothea, Lydgate, Mary, Fred, Gwendolen, and Daniel do not illustrate what they are supposed to.

In the preface to *Experiments in Life*, I write that the time has come in George Eliot criticism "when she no longer needs to be defended as an important artist, when she can be studied as an acknowledged master." It may seem that I am now denying her that status, but this is not the case. It is true that when I first became critical of the values she was affirming and aware of the flaws in her novels, she sank in my estimation, but that was because I was still looking to literature for answers to the question of Ecclesiastes and still demanding of novels the kind of organic unity they almost never achieve.

What I have come to see in subsequent years is that literature reflects the defensive strategies of the author and that it is inappropriate to judge it by the soundness of its view of life or its values. We will be attracted to those authors who celebrate solutions close to our own, as I was to George Eliot, but that has nothing to do with literary merit. Telling us what we should do under heaven all the days of our life is not the hallmark of great literature, even when the author attempts to do so or thinks that it is.

The masterpieces of realistic fiction are almost never organically unified, for reasons that E. M. Forster has explained very well. The great mimetic characters are creations inside a creation who subvert the larger structures of which they are a part. As I have tried to show in *A Psychological Approach to Fiction* and *Imagined Human Beings*, the tensions between rhetoric and mimesis can be exacerbated or reduced by an author's choice of narrative technique. Whereas dramatized narration from multiple perspectives, as in *Lord Jim* and *Wuthering Heights*, virtually eliminates these tensions, intrusive omniscient narration, such as George Eliot's, intensifies them. Despite Harold Bloom's claims, George Eliot's interventions are artistic defects. Even so, the virtues of her novels far outweigh their flaws.

Middlemarch and *Daniel Deronda* are heavily rhetorical, as we have seen; yet in the final analysis, they are not moralized fables, the last word of a philosophy endeavoring to teach by example, as Henry James contends. Or perhaps they are—if we emphasize the word "endeavoring"—and are saved by the fact that the examples subvert the teaching. The rhetoric affirms that it is good to be like Dorothea Brooke or Mary Garth or Daniel Deronda; the mimesis shows that it is not. Despite rhetorical claims to the contrary, the mimesis shows that Deronda is not a good counselor and that Gwendolen is not saved. If George Eliot's novels were really moralized fables, these characters would have died and destroyed the novels by intestinal decay. They are not kept too sternly in check, however, but are given enough freedom to live their own lives and escape their illustrative roles. This creates the kinds of problems I have discussed, which are nonetheless far less serious than those created when characters are kept under too tight a rein.

I have argued, in effect, that George Eliot's success in creating mimetic characters doomed her experiments in life to failure. She thought that clothing her ideas in human figures and individual experience would confirm them, but it subverted them instead. The failure of her experiments is inseparable from her greatest triumph, however, for the characters she created have remained alive, and will continue to, I believe, amid the procession of shifting theories, including hers and mine. I quarrel with George Eliot's interpretations and judgments, which, as I see it, often obscure and falsify the characters she has depicted. In trying to make her characters stand clear of her rhetoric, I have substituted interpretations and judgments of my own. Like George Eliot's, these belong to the realm of shifting theory. They reflect my time and place, my culturally shaped mode of thought, my psychological needs and dispositions. Others will quarrel with me, as I have with George Eliot, but the characters are timeless and will continue to tantalize. They will outlive my view of them, but I hope to contribute to their enduring vitality by making them "pop out," by encouraging readers to see them as imagined human beings rather than simply as embodiments of George Eliot's themes.

I have said that George Eliot's mimetic gifts doomed her experiments in life to failure, but have her experiments really failed? They did not enable her to discover a "better after which we may strive," but they did arrive at something more sure than shifting theory—namely, mimetic truth, which is truth *to* rather than truth *about* experience. George Eliot was right when she said that if she were to help others see at all it must be through the medium of art. Perhaps she herself distrusted her formulas.

The mimetic truths in George Eliot's novels are often opposed to what she thinks she has discovered or confirmed. She preaches living for others but shows us how desperate a strategy this is and how destructive to the self. Yet therein lies much of her greatness. Although the rhetoric of her novels is driven by her personal needs and defenses, she is able to transcend these in the mimesis and to make her novels, in Iris Murdoch's words, "a house fit for free characters to live in" (1959, 271). These liberated characters yield the most valuable results of George Eliot's experiments. In them we find revelations about the human psyche and human relationships that are deeper and more enduring than anything George Eliot consciously knew or could formulate in her commentary.

Iris Murdoch praises the masters of realistic fiction for their tolerance, their respect for reality, their "real apprehension" of other people "as having a right to exist and to have a separate mode of being" (1959, 257). The individuals portrayed in their novels "are free, independent of their author, and not merely puppets in the exteriorization of some closely locked psychological conflict of his own." It is to George Eliot's great credit that in the face of her own needs, preconceptions, and vested interests, she could so often allow her characters to be themselves, to lead their own lives. She is not alone in this. As Murdoch's comments suggest, and as I have tried to show elsewhere, this independence occurs again and again in the great realistic novels. I believe that the very process of imagining human beings, of supplying their thoughts, feelings, and behaviors, their histories and motives, is an instrument of discovery, a form of knowledge. Although she misread the results, in her mimetic portrayals of characters and relationships George Eliot's experiments in life succeed.

References

Bedient, Calvin. 1972. *Architects of the Self: George Eliot, D. H. Lawrence, and E. M. Forster*. Berkeley: University of California Press.

Beer, Gillian. 1986. *George Eliot*. Bloomington: Indiana University Press.

Bloom, Harold. 1986. "Introduction." In *Modern Critical Views: George Eliot*. Ed. Harold Bloom. New York: Chelsea House.

———. 1994. *The Western Canon*. New York: Harcourt Brace.

Bodenheimer, Rosemarie. 1994. *The Real Life of Marian Evans: George Eliot, Her Letters and Fiction*. Ithaca: Cornell University Press.

Booth, Wayne. 1961. *The Rhetoric of Fiction*. Chicago: University of Chicago Press.

Byatt, A. S., and Ignês Sodré. 1995. *Imagining Characters*. London: Chatto & Windus.

Carroll, David. 1971. *George Eliot: The Critical Heritage*. New York: Barnes & Noble.

Daniels, Elizabeth. 1982. "A Meredithian Glance at Gwendolen Harleth." In *George Eliot: A Centenary Tribute*. Ed. G. S. Haight and R. T. VanArsdel. Totowa, N.J.: Barnes & Noble.

Doyle, Mary Ellen. 1981. *The Sympathetic Response: George Eliot's Fictional Rhetoric*. Rutherford, N.J.: Fairleigh Dickinson University Press.

Eliot, George. 1856. "Belles Lettres." *Westminster Review* 66: 566–82.

———. *Adam Bede*. 1948 [1859]. Ed. G. S. Haight. New York: Rinehart.

———. *Middlemarch*. 1956 [1872]. Ed. G. S. Haight. Boston: Houghton Mifflin.

———. *Daniel Deronda*. 1995 [1876]. Ed. Terence Cave. London: Penguin Books.

Forster, E. M. 1927. *Aspects of the Novel*. London: Edward Arnold.

Frye, Northrop. 1963. "Myth, Fiction, and Displacement." In *Fables of Identity*. New York: Harcourt, Brace, & World.

Haight, Gordon S. 1954–78. *The George Eliot Letters*, 9 vols. New Haven, Conn.: Yale University Press.

———. 1965. *A Century of George Eliot Criticism*. Boston: Houghton Mifflin.

Hardy, Barbara. 1967. "Introduction." *Daniel Deronda*. Harmondsworth, Eng.: Penguin Books.

Horney, Karen. 1945. *Our Inner Conflicts*. New York: Norton.

———. 1950. *Neurosis and Human Growth: The Struggle toward Self-Realization*. New York: Norton.

James, Henry. 1953. "George Eliot's *Middlemarch*." *Nineteenth-Century Fiction* 8: 161–70.

Johnstone, Peggy. 1994. *The Transformation of Rage: Mourning and Creativity in George Eliot's Fiction*. New York: New York University Press.

Karl, Frederick R. 1995. *George Eliot: Voice of a Century*. New York: Norton.

Leavis, F. R. 1948. *The Great Tradition*. London: Chatto & Windus.

———. 1961. "Introduction." *Daniel Deronda*. New York: Harper & Brothers.

Lerner, Laurence. 1965. "The Education of Gwendolen Harleth." *Critical Quarterly* 7: 355–64.

Maslow, Abraham. 1970. *Motivation and Personality*. 2d ed. New York: Harper & Row.

Paris, Bernard J. 1956. "Towards a Revaluation of George Eliot's *The Mill on the Floss*." *Nineteenth Century Fiction* 11: 18–31.

———. 1965. *Experiments in Life: George Eliot's Quest for Values*. Detroit: Wayne State University Press.

———. 1969. "The Inner Conflicts of Maggie Tulliver: A Horneyan Analysis." *Centennial Review* 13: 166–99.

———. 1974. *A Psychological Approach to Fiction: Studies in Thackeray, Stendhal, George Eliot, Dostoevsky, and Conrad*. Bloomington: Indiana University Press.

———. 1976. "Experiences of Thomas Hardy." In *The Victorian Experience*. Ed. Richard A. Levine. Athens: Ohio University Press.

———. 1978. *Character and Conflict in Jane Austen's Novels: A Psychological Approach*. Detroit: Wayne State University Press.

———. 1986a. "Horney, Maslow, and the Third Force." In *Third Force Psychology and the Study of Literature*. Ed. B. J. Paris. Rutherford, N.J.: Fairleigh Dickinson University Press.

———. 1986b. "Third Force Psychology and the Study of Literature, Biography, Criticism, and Culture." In *Third Force Psychology and the Study of*

Literature. Ed. B. J. Paris. Rutherford, N.J. : Fairleigh Dickinson University Press.

―――. 1991a. *Bargains with Fate: Psychological Crises and Conflicts in Shakespeare and His Plays.* New York: Plenum.

―――. 1991b. *Character as a Subversive Force in Shakespeare: The History and Roman Plays.* Rutherford, N.J.: Fairleigh Dickinson University Press.

―――. 1991c. "A Horneyan Approach to Literature." *American Journal of Psychoanalysis* 51: 319–37.

―――. 1994a. *Karen Horney: A Psychoanalyst's Search for Self-Understanding.* New Haven, Conn.: Yale University Press.

―――. 1994b. "Pulkheria Alexandrovna and Raskolnikov, My Mother and Me." In *Self-Analysis in Literary Criticism.* Ed. Daniel Rancour-Laferriere. New York: New York University Press.

―――. 1997. *Imagined Human Beings: A Psychological Approach to Character and Conflict in Literature.* New York: New York University Press.

―――. 1999. "*Middlemarch* Revisited: Changing Responses to George Eliot." *American Journal of Psychoanalysis* 59: 237–55.

―――. 2002. "Daniel Deronda and Gwendolen Harleth: A Therapeutic Relationship?" *Journal of the American Academy of Psychoanalysis*, 30: 99–122.

Price, Martin. 1983. *Forms of Life: Character and Moral Imagination in the Novel.* New Haven, Conn.: Yale University Press.

Qualls, Barry V. 1986. "Speaking through Parable: 'Daniel Deronda.' " In *Modern Critical Views of George Eliot.* Ed. Harold Bloom. New York: Chelsea House.

Rotenberg, Carl. 1999. "George Eliot—Proto-Psychoanalyst." *American Journal of Psychoanalysis* 59: 257–70.

―――. "Commentary on 'Daniel Deronda and Gwendolen Harleth: A Therapeutic Relationship?' by Bernard J. Paris." *Journal of the American Academy of Psychoanalysis*, 30: 123–32.

Waddell, Margot. 1999. "On Ideas of 'the Good' and 'the Ideal' in George Eliot's Novels and Post-Kleinian Psychoanalytic Thought." *American Journal of Psychoanalysis* 59: 271–86.

Index